A Commentary on the
BOOK OF
REVELATION

A Commentary on the
BOOK OF
REVELATION

DR. JOHN THOMAS WYLIE

ARPress
ILLUMINATING IDEAS
EMPOWERING VOICES

ARPress
45 Dan Road Suite 36
Canton MA 02021

Hotline: 1(888) 821-0229
Fax: 1(508) 545-7580

Ordering Information:
Quantity Sales. Special discounts are available on quantity purchases by corporations, associations, and others. For details, contact the publisher at the address above.

Printed in the United States of America.

ISBN-13 Paperback   979-8-89356-377-1
               eBook   978-8-89356-376-4

Library of Congress Control Number: 2024903069

CONTENTS

PREFACE

Disclosure, the last book of the New Testament, which depicts the battle in the middle of good and insidious and the triumph of Christ and his Church. It is now and then called "the Apocalypse" from its first work in the Gk. Unique; it is the head of every single Apocalyptic book. The New Testament contains Apocalyptic* sections (e.g., mark 13, 2 Thess. 2), however Revelation, similar to Daniel in the Old Testament, is offered completely to this kind of composing.

W.S. Thompson once expressed: "The Revelation, the day John composed it, was all that it is today. It uncovered indistinguishably the same standards as it does today. Nothing has been included through verifiable occasions and episodes which help us to comprehend it. Nothing has been lost. On the off chance that we were constrained to hope to disrespect history for records of persons and occasions which would help us to comprehend the Revelation, then befoul history would be the premise for our comprehension, and not the Revelation.

The Scriptures are the best and best hotspot for a clarification of the Revelation. There is not really any image, counsel, or rule expressed in the Revelation that has not been very much introduced in every one of the past ages. The basic role of this production is to advance studies in the book of Revelation.

Reverend Dr. John Thomas Wylie

CREATION

The creator is called John (Rev. 1:4,9), however from the accessible proof it is difficult to figure out who this John was. "Divine" in the A.V. inscription implies scholar. The book bears the stamp of a solitary writer to its arrangement, in its awe-inspiring portrayals, and in its elevated flights of creative energy. From inner proof come the accompanying realities about the writer:

(1) He called himself a "worker" of Jesus Christ and a "sibling and friend in tribulation" of his peruses, who were Asiatic Christians (Rev.1:1, 4, 9).

(2) He was familiar with the history and present issues of the seven temples of Asia (2,3).

(3) He called himself a prophet, however there is no clue that he had official status in the seven houses of worship (1:3, 19:10, 22:7, 9).

(4) Though the likelihood that he was an Apostle can't be precluded, he never asserted Apostolic power or associate with the noteworthy Jesus. His references to the Apostles have a "review tinge" (18:20, 21:14).

(5) The creator got his dreams while he was a detainee on the island of Patmos, where foes of Rome were banished and compelled to quarry stone. Topic and phonetic contemplations make it sensibly clear that the creator of the Fourth Gospel was not the creator of Revelation. The personality of the last remains an open question (Harper's Bible Dictionary, 1961).

THE DATE OF COMPOSITION

There have been two distinctive real feelings concerning the time this book was composed. Some have put it as right on time as the rule of Nero, in the seventh decade of the primary century. In any case, for some reason it appears this is too soon. The consistent decision of the early church was that the Apostle John was ousted to the Isle of Patmos by the ruler Domitian (A.D. 81 to 96), a few essayists setting the outcast in the fourteenth year of his rule, A.D. 95 (The Wycliff Bible Commentary, 1962).

The Apocalypse unmistakably uncovers that it was composed in a period of incredible mistreatment. The abuse under Nero was pretty much limited to Rome, however that under Domitian came to different parts of the Roman Empire. Domitian expelled men to different spots of outcast, yet Nero did not. Moreover, the seven houses of worship in Asia here demonstrate an experienced advancement, which could scarcely have existed as right on time as A.D. 65. Also, we have no confirmation whatever that the Apostle practiced any power over the temples of Asia before the obliteration of Jerusalem The Wycliff Bible Commentary, 1962).

EVENT AND PURPOSE

The requirement of sovereign love int the last part of the rule of Domitian, A.D. 81-96, debilitated the Christians of Asia Minor with a perilous emergency. The writer trusted that general mistreatment was going to break upon the Church (2:10, 6:10); and he composed this book. Disclosure to his kindred Christians on the grounds that he was persuaded that Jesus Christ had given him a message for them in this season of unpleasant criticalness (1:1). The message was one of support for the dedicated and cautioning to the self-satisfied. The creator's motivation was totally commonsense; he had no expectation of being dark. His first century pursuers comprehended his message since they were versed in Apocalyptic thought and had the way to its imagery. Here and there the creator is intentionally secretive keeping in mind the end goal to maintain a strategic distance from peril from the Church's adversaries. In any case, his essential longing to be obviously comprehended is appeared by his regular clarifications of his significance (1:20, 4:5, 5:6, 7:17, and so forth). Be that as it may, the way to the intending to prophetically calamitous imagery was soon lost; and lamentably a hefty portion of the endeavors to locate the lost key have been embraced by those with more eagerness than information. To endeavor to comprehend Revelation one must attempt to find the creator's viewpoint and his message for his own time (The Harper's Bible Dictionary, 1961).

THE MESSAGE

The creator trusted that God was going to intercede in human undertakings: this was an essential origination of the prophetically catastrophic thought about the early Church. A fiasco or last occasion would soon happen which would convey the current world request to an end and introduce the new age. The disaster included powerful fear and the entry of Antichrist. John composed to set up his kindred Christians for these dread, which he accepted were at that point starting, and to guarantee them that the result would be the triumph of Christ and his Church. His message, similar to that of all Apocalyptists, was worried with the future; yet it was not a message of fate, but rather a call to valor and confidence (The Harper's Bible Dictionary, 1961).

Disclosure is loaded with dreams and images, a lot of whose significance can be seen just by concentrating on John's utilization of Scriptural and Non-Scruptural Apocalypses. He was all the more, nonetheless, than a proofreader of more established materials, for he had himself gained happy encounters.

These endeavored to report: "What thou seest, write in a Book" (1:11). It was in looking for words to pass on his dreams that, maybe unknowingly, he made utilization of the images and traditions of Apocalyptic books natural to himself and his perusers. He agonized over Old Testament predictions until be trusted he saw their message for his own particular day. Subordinate through Revelation might be on Jewish Apocalypses for a number of its points of interest. It is fundamentally Christian in its message of God's last triumph through Christ.

SUBSTANCE

After preparatory letters to the seven houses of worship of Asia Minor, Revelation reports a progression of dreams portraying the occasions of the most recent days and a definitive triumph of Christ.

These dreams don't take after an entirely ordered plan, yet are total in their impact. John found in God's grasp a fixed book containing the last hardships. Christ starts to break the seals, and as every seal is broken a disaster happens. After the seventh seal is broken, seven heavenly attendants show up with trumpets; and the blowing of every trumpet is the start of another misfortune. Chaps. 12-14 describe in mysterious dialect the happening to Antichrist. Next takes after another arrangement of troubles symbolized by the pouring out of seven dishes of anger. At last comes the end; Antichrist and Satan are crushed, and man are gotten before God judgment. The last two sections picture the opening of the new age when God's kin will enter brilliant Jerusalem (The Harper's Bible Dictionary, 1961).

Antichrist is thought about as Nero resurrecting to make war on God's kin. He is not named, but rather the number 666 connected to him speaks to the whole of the numerical estimation of the letters in "Nero Caesar" (13:18). Babylon symbolizes Rome. John appended awesome significance to numbers, particularly the number seven, which was the image of celestial flawlessness (The Harper's Bible Dictionary, 1961).

ESTEEM

The predictions of Revelation stayed unfulfilled. Domitian was not succeeded by Antichrist, but rather by the five goo heads. Rome did not fall, but rather kept on decision for a considerable length of time. The apocalypse did not come, nor did Christ come back to judge men. The powerful fear John anticipated neglected to show up. These prophetic disappointments have prompted a few analysts to search for the satisfaction of John's predictions in their own particular times or in a far off future. Any thought of such a future satisfaction was unmistakably not in John's brain when he composed of the "things which should without further ado happen" (1:1) and pronounced that "the time is close by" (22:10). The estimation of Revelation then, can't be found in its predictions of comings occasions, however in its extraordinary feelings. John is sure that the world is God's creation, and that men can't overstep His ethical laws without punishment. The force epitomized in the Roman Empire John saw as basically underhanded, and he realized that the Church which contradicted the Empire was little, feeble, scattered, and spoiled by experience. In any case he had wonderful certainty that in the contention between these two triumphs would be won by the Church, since Christ by his passing and Resurrection had effectively won the triumph for himself and his Church (The Harper's Bible Dictionary, 1961). Drawn out study is required for the comprehension of Revelation.

CHAPTER 1

A Spiritual Journey
Into The Future

1:1 The Revelation of Jesus Christ, which God gave unto him, to shew unto his hirelings things which should in the blink of an eye happen; and he sent and connoted [it] by his holy messenger unto his worker John:

We begin Revelation part one with not a "philosophical" outing, but rather a profound excursion into the future as we start the investigation of the Book of Revelation composed by John the Apostle while detained on the Island of Patmos. John didn't get a dry, dead, religious clarification of future occasions. He got an effective, dynamic, extraordinary prophetic disclosure. He got a disclosure of Christ in all His Glory, he saw into the throne room of Heaven, and he got an extraordinary divulging of God's end time arrangement. It was awesome to the point that John really tumbled down as if he were dead:

The Greek word, Apokalupsis, intends to "uncover" or "disclose" what is covered up. The expression "meant" does not imply this is a book of mysterious signs, yet that God meant by the phenomenal vicinity of the declaring holy messenger that the message was from Him.

This Revelation is an uncovering of the puzzles of Jesus Christ. God the Father gives this message to Jesus, Jesus offers it to His own heavenly attendant, the holy messenger gives the message to John, and John composes this message to all professors in the Lord Jesus Christ. This message is given to John to empower the Christians. These Christians ought not be gotten unconscious. These things must happen on the grounds that it is the will of the Father.

"Meant" implies made known by image and figure. Some may say signs which uncover God's truth.

Holy messengers are serving spirits. This specific heavenly attendant was Jesus' very own blessed messenger who brought this message. "Jesus Christ" implies the Savior, the Anointed One.

1:2 Who exposed record of the expression of God, and of the confirmation of Jesus Christ, and for goodness' sake that he saw.

To "exposed record" shows that John really saw these things. John declares in his books that he is an onlooker affirming of all he saw and listened.

There are actually many more than seven Spirits. This seven is a symbolic number meaning all. "Spirits" is capitalized so this is the Holy Spirit in all His workings. When it speaks of these Spirits ever before the throne, we see Teacher, Guide, Helper, Provider, just a few of the works of the Holy Spirit. John explains in this who Jesus is.

1:5 And from Jesus Christ, [who is] the faithful witness, [and] the first begotten of the dead, and the prince of the kings of the earth.

Unto him that loved us, and washed us from our sins in his own blood,

Jesus Christ is the faithful witness in that He has finished His work of revealing the Father (John 17), the first begotten of the dead in that He is the firstfruits of the first resurrection (Rev. 20:6).

We see in verse 4 and 5 the Father, Son, and Holy Spirit. As we said Jesus' witness is faithful, because He is the Truth. Jesus was the very first person ever resurrected. There was someone who went to heaven before, Enoch, when he was carried away into heaven mysteriously disappearing from the earth because he pleased God. Then there was Elijah, who was carried to heaven in a whirlwind accompanied by the chariot of fire. Neither of these, however, were resurrected. They were never buried.

Lazarus rose as did several others the bible mentions, but only to die again. Christ rose to die no more as will all believers in Christ.

We read in Matthew 27: verses 52 and 53 "And the graves were opened; and many bodies of the saints which slept arose," "And came out of the graves after His resurrection, and went into the holy city, and appeared unto many."

Notice here that these saints' bodies were resurrected after Jesus' resurrection. You see Jesus' body was the first body to rise from the grave.

Notice, too, that we are spoken of as rulers in verse 5 of Revelation. During the 1000 year reign of Jesus Christ here upon the earth, we Christians will rule with Him. We will not be His equal, however. This tells us that He will be ruler above us.

The love that is spoken of here, that He has for us, is "agape love". This is love beyond our comprehension. So much love that He willingly suffered the pain and humiliation of the cross for us. I love the song that says "when He was on the cross, I was on His mind" How true this is. He died for us individually.

More noteworthy adoration hath no man than this, that a man set out his life for his companions." John 15:13

It is this valuable blood that washes down us from all indecency. We tackle His righteousness. This affection that Jesus has for us is not in the previous strained, but rather is still pretty much as intense today. His affection is ceaseless.

1:6 And hath made us rulers and clerics unto God and his Father; to him [be] greatness and territory for ever and ever. So be it.

The most imperative articulation in V-6 is that Jesus is called God. The announcement "God and his Father" leaves most likely Jesus was, is, and dependably will be God. Notice that it is nothing we do that makes us rulers and priests. Jesus made us rulers and ministers.

We will sit on thrones in paradise with Jesus. There is no more prominent magnificence due anybody than Jesus who really did all the work.

We see that Jesus is incomparable in domain in Philippians 2:9 - 11 "Wherefore God additionally hath very magnified him, and given him a name which is over each name:" "That at the name of Jesus each knee ought to bow, of [things] in paradise, and [things] in earth, and [things] under the earth;" "And [that] each tongue ought to admit that Jesus Christ [is] Lord, to the radiance of God the Father."

Every Christian shares in Jesus' priesthood. He is the High Priest until the end of time. So be it. Everlastingly never closes.

In the genuine church, nobody is called "minister" (particular) with the exception of Christ. Devotees are a piece of an "illustrious Priesthood" in Christ (1 Peter 2: v.9; Rev. 5:10). The wonderfulness and domain (power) of Christ are underscored all through the book. (Romans 5: v.8; 1 John 3: v.16). Washed us: Believers have been recovered from their wrongdoings through the blood and passing of Christ. Made us lords and clerics:

1:7 Behold, he cometh with mists; and each eye should see him, and they [also] which pierced him: and all kindreds of the earth might wail on account of him. Indeed, even in this way, Amen.

This truth is the immense trust and desire of every genuine adherent today and it is the topic of Revelation. The passing and restoration of Christ and the guarantee of His second coming are the establishment of our trust. They were an incredible wellspring of quality to the Early Church and are considerably all the more so to us today as we move into the last days of time before Christ's arrival. This verse uncovers how Jesus will return. He will come in the same way in which He climbed into Heaven.

The fascinating thing here is Jesus is coming in the mists generally as the blessed messengers said He would in Acts. In part one of Acts, Jesus was made up for lost time to paradise in the mists and the followers were told by the holy messengers, that Jesus would return the same way. Acts 1: verses 9 - 11 "And when he had talked these things, while they observed, he was taken up; and a cloud got him out of their sight." "Keeping in mind they looked undauntedly toward paradise as he went up, view, two men remained by them in white attire;" "Which likewise said, Ye men of Galilee, why stand ye looking up into paradise? This same Jesus which is taken up from you into paradise, should so come in like way as ye have seen him go into paradise."

A few individuals trust Jesus' arrival will be mystery, I do not. How could each eye see Him, on the off chance that He returned secretly? Don't you realize that there will be some lamenting individuals, when they understand who Jesus truly is? Wouldn't you prefer not to be the person who spit on Him, or the person who drove the nails in His grasp, or even the Scribes and Pharisees? Any individual who rejected Him will have misery past clarification. The melancholy will be great to the point that they will be groaning and grinding their teeth.

Here John demonstrated in V-7, regardless of the fact that this is along these lines, let it be. The loathsome thing much more terrible than the primary torturous killing for our transgressions is the horrendous times when we, knowing not, Him once more. We should stroll in our salvation. We should not enter over into sin after we have been liberated from sin by His valuable blood.

1:8 I am Alpha and Omega, the starting and the completion, saith the Lord, which is, and which was, and which is to come, the Almighty.

The principal expressions of Jesus to John by and by recognize him with the "I AM' of Scripture, for He calls Himself the "Alpha and Omega." These are the first and last letters of the Greek letter set. The title means, in the dialect of correspondence, the culmination with which God uncovered Himself to humankind through Christ. This is nothing not exactly an official confirmation by Jesus of His own divinity. No common human would ever say of himself, "I am the first and last.

We see here that God the Father, God the Word, and God the Holy Spirit are every one of the three eternal. They each have no starting and no end. Their Spirit is one. Their epitomes are three.

"God-like" shows the force of the Godhead as being boundless and supreme, inescapable, omniscient. There is no other force. This word shows control past human creative energy. Jesus is equivalent to the Father and the Holy Spirit. Each of the three are the Spirit of God. They have separate identities. This is Jesus talking when He says "I am Alpha and Omega, the starting and the completion". It is red in my Bible demonstrating Jesus' own particular talked words.

1:9 I John, who likewise am your sibling, and partner in tribulation, and in the kingdom and tolerance of Jesus Christ, was in the isle that is called Patmos, for the expression of God, and for the confirmation of Jesus Christ.

John relates to the anguish devotees to Rev. 1 v.9 by alluding to himself as their "sibling, and buddy in tribulation," then he depicts the spot where he got the Revelation, banished and alone on the Isle of Patmos. Wouldn't you be able to simply imagine John remaining there on the Lord's Day, alone, spurned, cool, and fatigued? The sound of the crying wind echoes through the Rocky Mountains. The waves crash upon the left rough shoreline.

As John is talking here, he is not a divine being but rather a man, as we may be. Genuinely he is an anointed worker of Jesus. He clarifies that devotees to Jesus, then and now, will have tribulation. Tribulation is to make adherents solid. Additionally to see, if under distressing circumstances, despite everything we accept. This new message the congregation is conveying that Christians don't have issues is in mistake. In the Old and New Testament, men and ladies of God have needed to stand middle tribulations and trials. Indeed, even Jesus was attempted forty days and evenings. Issues go to all. The distinction is standing out you handle the issues.

John was not attempting to awe anybody of how profound he was. He was separated from everyone else on the isle of Patmos. The powers had sent John to this isle to prevent him from announcing Jesus. Yet, we see that God had plans for this stay, also. God's motivation in John being on the isle was to get the Word of God, and for the confirmation of Jesus. The foe arranged insidiousness for John's stay here, however God transformed something awful into something superb for untouched.

John was brimming with tolerance, not his own, but rather the persistence of Jesus. John knew the main issue about the kingdom, also. This was not a period of hopelessness; he observed this an awesome time to be with Jesus without any intrusions.

Romans 5: v.3 "And [so], as well as we radiance in tribulations likewise: realizing that tribulation worketh persistence;"

Acts 14: "Affirming the souls of the followers, [and] admonishing them to proceed in the confidence, and that we should through much tribulation go into the kingdom of God."

This isle of Patmos was a unique spot for what we would call solidified offenders.

It was in a state of banishment that Jacob met God at Bethel. God helps us in our most noteworthy need. Moses was in a state of banishment when he saw the blazing shrub.

Elijah heard the still calm voice of God while he was running for wellbeing. Daniel was additionally estranged abroad when he saw the Ancient of Days.

Some of the time God must get only us before He can uncover Himself to us.

1:10 I was in the Spirit on the Lord's day, and heard behind me an incredible voice, starting a trumpet,

We note here that John was in the Spirit. Spirit is promoted. This shows John was completely devoured by the Holy Spirit. This incredible voice is a magnificent sound. There is no doubt whose voice this is. When the Lord returns and blows the silver trumpet to recover His kin from the earth, it will really be His voice, which is similar to a trumpet. God's voice unnerved the offspring of Israel on their way to the Promised Land. They thought it thundered the voice was so extraordinary.

1:11 Saying, I am Alpha and Omega, the first and the last: and, What thou seest, write in a book, and send [it] unto the seven holy places which are in Asia; unto Ephesus, and unto Smyrna, and unto Pergamos, and unto Thyatira, and unto Sardis, and unto Philadelphia, and unto Laodicea.

Be that as it may, as John starts to love God, something extraordinary happens. All of a sudden, he hears a voice behind him as boisterous and clear as a trumpet proclaiming, "I am Alpha and Omega, the first and the last!" Alpha and Omega is the first and last letters of the Greek letters in order. Christ was depicting Himself similar to the everlasting, complete, disclosure of God and He was charging John to compose what he would find in a book to be protected for the Church. At the point when John swung to see the wellspring of the relentless voice making this revelation, Jesus Christ, in all His energy and brilliance was disclosed before his eyes. John saw into the domain of the Spirit and he was so overcome at Christ's great vicinity that he was dreadful and fell at His feet just as he were dead!

Everything that was said here is in red, this implies it is all said by Jesus Himself. Here Jesus is stating to John to record all that he sees, and place it in a book, and send it to the holy places. I truly trust that it was to these seven physical holy places, as well as to all the houses of worship which are every one of the devotees to Jesus Christ. As we see the issues in these places of worship, we can without much of a stretch relate it to issues that we find in our holy places today. We can likewise take a gander at the things that God is satisfied with in these temples, and we will comprehend what He discovers satisfying in our congregation.

These places of worship were not physically exceptionally a long way from where John was on the island so he was acquainted with them. There were around sixty known places of worship at the time this was composed, so we should note that these were decided for their eccentricities of worship.

John did not pick these, Jesus did. The reason in sending these messages to the places of worship is so they can see their blunder and change. Take one more note this is from Jesus the everlasting one, the start to finish.

This message, John is to record, is the thingrthermore listens. Once in a while it is troublesome for us to perceive what he is depicting. You need to recollect that John is portraying things he has never seen. Things that would not be in presence until a large number of years after his time. You can envision how he would portray a helicopter or a plane. This vision is fundamentally the same to the anecdotes. This, as the stories, must be profoundly recognized.

1:12 And I swung to see the voice that spoke with me. What's more, being turned, I saw seven brilliant candles;

You comprehend that we can't see a voice. This is stating, I swung to see where this voice was originating from.

This is not one candle with seven woodwinds, but instead seven separate stands. John needs us to see, not the happenings, but rather the one that makes it happen. This uncovering is not of verifiable occasions but rather uncovering Jesus to us. One thing we see by the seven separate candles is that there is sufficiently light for each of these chapels. They can have their own light. The gold in these stands demonstrates the vicinity of God, in light of the fact that the otherworldly importance of gold is virtue of God. These chapels' light or learning is not common knowledge. This information and light originates from God.

1:13 And amidst the seven candles [one] like unto the Son of man, dressed with an article of clothing down to the foot, and girt about the paps with a brilliant support.

Where a few are assembled for the sake of the Lord there He is amidst them. This piece of clothing down to the foot is a holy robe, a robe of authority. This "Child of man" is Jesus who is amidst the church. This brilliant support is stating this is God.

Christ was wearing the robe of the High Priest. John states He was "dressed with a piece of clothing down to the foot, and girt about the paps with a brilliant support." In the Old Testament, the devout clerics wore full length robes with a support made of fine material, weaved with embroidery, secured around their waist. In this vision, Christ had on the robe of a consecrated minister, yet the support He wore around His mid-section was made of gold, which means the respect of an imperative office and implies His office as our Great High Priest "However this man, since he continueth ever, hath an unchangeable ministry. Wherefore he is capable additionally to spare them to the furthest that come unto God by him, seeing he ever liveth to make intervention for them." (Hebrews 7 verses 24 to 25).

The three presents that were conveyed to Jesus at His introduction to the world remembered Him for who He was. The gold remembered Him as God, the frankincense remembered Him as the ideal Lamb penance, and the myrrh remembered Him as the man of the hour of the lady of Christ. John sees Jesus in a body with a robe. Jesus, our High Priest, speaks to us before

His Father. He is not a natural devout minister but rather a great Priest. He shows up before God to favor the Christians, to argue our case maybe.

His appearance in the holy places would be as the Son of man. In different words in a body as man. The motivation behind the esteemed minister was to take the conciliatory blood into the Holy of Holies; and that is exactly what Jesus did, when He conveyed His own valuable blood to the Father to cancel our transgression. Not to cover them up, but rather to get rid of them.

1:14 His head and [his] hairs [were] white like fleece, as white as snow; and his eyes [were] as a fire of flame;

Christ's hair was white like fleece (Rev. 1 v.14). Christ's white hair is typical of His title, the Alpha and Omega, the first and the last. Christ is interminable, from everlasting to everlasting. At the point when the prophet Daniel had a comparative vision, he additionally portrayed Him as having hair "such as immaculate fleece, "garment" white as snow, "and eyes "as a fire of flame." (Dan 7 v.9)

Christ's eyes were as a fire of flame (Rev.1 v.14). This depiction is likewise found in Revelation 19 v.11-12 where Christ is imagined as a judge and Conqueror over the Antichrist and the countries of the earth who have assembled for the Battle of Armageddon. His eyes of flame symbolize immaculate insight.

John was at the transfiguration of Jesus and had seen a look at what He would be similar to then. We are looking here through John's eyes as he portrays what he sees. This white hair can mean a few unique things. One is that white hair runs with Daniel's depiction of the Ancient of Days.

My own particular knowledge into this whiteness is a direct result of the colossal Light. Jesus is the wellspring of all light. We realize that in paradise there is no requirement for the sun and moon, on account of the vicinity of the Light which is Jesus.

This much light can make anything look white. I am certain this hair is white, however. This white is bright to the point that no sanitizer on earth could make it so bright. The light just makes it look brighter.

Jesus was seen of John as Son of man, yet now John is considering Him to be the second individual of the Godhead. This time everlasting of Jesus (now known as King of Kings and Lord of Lords) is appearing in all His grandness. We have seen God all through the Bible connected with flame. We read that God is a devouring flame. We saw Him in the smoldering shrub, the searing finger of God that blazed the Ten Commandments in the stone, and we are informed that Jesus sanctifies through water with flame. This flame of the Holy Ghost washes down us inside by wearing out the old self clearing a path for the new.

Eyes demonstrate insight. Jesus' look is so loaded with shrewdness and flame that it investigates our heart and cleanses out the transgression with fire. This look (with these piercing, blazing eyes) will come into a Holy Ghost filled church and will smolder so brilliantly this look will cleanse the congregation. The individuals who can't remain to be cleansed will clear out. The congregation that is left, paying little heed to how little, will be lined up with the will of God.

1:15 And his feet like unto fine metal, as though they smoldered in a heater, and his voice as the sound of numerous waters.

Christ's feet were "similar to unto fine metal". Metal, a solid, decontaminated metal which comes about because of extreme warmth, indicates the virtue and force with which Christ will bring judgment upon the wicked of the earth.

This metal shows the colossal quality and immovability of Jesus. Metal likewise implies judgment and Jesus is the Judge. Jesus here is remaining amidst the places of worship. Judgment starts at the place of God. Jesus has overcome Satan and the demons. We know the Word says that Satan, his evil spirits, and all who reject Jesus have been judged; and they genuinely will spend an unending length of time in damnation (heater).

The Bible says Satan is under Jesus' feet. Here this is Jesus, upright, not vanquished, conquering the villain and his heavenly attendants. Christ's voice was "as the sound of numerous waters." The voice John first heard in his vision was depicted as "an incredible voice, as the sound of a trumpet," boisterous and clear. In this verse, John depicts Christ's voice as "the sound of numerous waters" which is like the portrayal given by the prophet in Ezekiel 43 v.2. His voice is compelling and capable, excellent however alarming.

1:16 And he had in his right hand seven stars: and out of his mouth went a sharp two-edged sword: and his face [was] as the sun shineth in his quality.

Out of Christ's mouth continued "a two-edged sword". (Rev. 1 v.16) This sword speaks to the force and power of Christ's words by which the world will be judged (Rev. 19 v.15) and those adjusted to Satan and the Antichrist will be crushed.

Christ's face was "as the sun shineth in his quality". The effective light encompassing Christ was blinding to the point that John contrasted it with the intense beams of the sun in its entire being. In 2 Thessalonians 2 v.8, Paul lets us know that Christ will wreck the Antichrist with the brilliance of His coming. Later on in the Book of Revelation (part 22), John lets us know that in the New Jerusalem there will be no need of the sun, for the Lord God will be our light.

The right hand needs to do with the endowments of God. The right-hand gift was dependably the special blessing. These seven stars are honored over plentifully of God since they are in the right hand of Jesus. It was a twofold gift. These seven stars are the priests of the houses of worship. He calls them stars, since they should sparkle on the planet. They don't create light; they simply mirror His Light to the world. Jesus said to light this light and set it on a slope where all can see. The darker the territory, the more imperative it is to sparkle His Light, so that those in murkiness can go to the Light.

Jesus is the Word of God. The Bible continued out of His mouth. The Bible is the composed Word of God. God is the author. People like Paul and John are only the penman, moved upon by the Holy Spirit to put it down for all to see. This Bible is the two-edged sword, Old and New Testament. This two-edged sword (law and effortlessness) is the main weapon that God's kin need.

The Bible itself says, "penetrating even to the isolating in half of the spirit and soul" Hebrews 4: v.12. The Word isolates great and evil. The bleeding edge of the Word some of the time even isolates families. One who trusts the Word can't retreat to their old, wicked lives, and this partitions families and companions here and there.

In John 1: v.1 We read. "Before all else was the Word, and the Word was with God, and the Word was God." This Word partitions the Spirit from the flesh. If you read it much, the Word will convict you of sin in your life. It will make you look for God and be saved. The Word is powerful. The force of Jesus is inconceivable. He is the Word. His Power, through His Word, has changed the entire world. He is Power. He is the wellspring of all force, vitality, and light. There is no force more powerful.

1:17 And when I saw him, I fell at his feet as dead. Furthermore, he laid his right hand upon me, saying unto me, Fear not; I am the first and the last:

John was completely overpowered by this vision of Jesus. The showed eminence of God was similar to a thousand suns and moons all in one! How would you see Christ? Do you consider Him to be a darling in the trough? Do you see Him just as He was the point at which He lived upon the earth 2000 years prior? On the other hand do you consider Him to be He truly is today, situated in force and superbness at His Father's side? You might have found out about Jesus all your life. You might even be spared and loaded with the Holy Spirit, yet have you truly gotten a disclosure of Him, "a drawing without end of the cover of haziness" to consider Christ to be He truly is? How would you see Christ?

John had never seen Jesus like this. He was so overcome with the vision of Christ that he: "fell at his feet as dead." When you truly get a dream of Jesus, you, as well, will be completely overpowered, when you truly comprehend His great force and superbness! God's message to you today, is the same as it was to His Apostle John: Fear Not! The same message the blessed messenger provided for Mary at the annunciation: Fear Not!

The expression "dread not": is utilized more than eighty times as a part of the Bible and by and large it is to calm the reasons for alarm of man in God's Presence. God is additionally saying to you today, as He did to John: don't fear your edgy circumstances. Try not to fear what's to come. The One who was dead however is currently alive is standing right close by! There is nothing to fear since Jesus has vanquished demise and hellfire. He has force and power over them. He has supreme force and power and He needs you to consider Him to be he truly is, high and lifted up, magnified most importantly things in paradise and on earth.

When you confront affliction, dissatisfactions, feelings of anguish, monetary issues, and family issues do you see Christ remaining adjacent to you as the Great High Priest making intervention for you? Do you see the Mighty Conqueror of death and damnation standing prepared to give you the triumph? Numerous adherents are living in thrashing in light of the fact that their vision of Christ is restricted to their characteristic personalities. God needs to take you past the confinements of your normal personality so you might consider Him to be He is and truly know Him in the completion of His showed power. The Apostle Paul supplicated that the Ephesians would get "a soul of insight and disclosure in the information of him". (Eph. 1 v.17) Paul was not discussing head learning, but rather a disclosure profound inside of their spirits. Jesus Christ, in His celebrated condition of superbness and force, is portrayed as remaining amidst His Church:

Prior we had seen Jesus remaining amidst the places of worship (candles). His appearance was: hair white as snow, eyes of flame, and feet of metal. An extremely marvelous figure. The greatness of His individual was overpowering. We see here the impact that this vicinity had on John. If we were to encounter Jesus, this is the impact it would have on us, also. When anybody experiences the vicinity of God, you can't stand. Stooping is not in any case enough. John fell level all over at His feet. He was completely humbled by this vicinity. This great appearance was a lot for John. He had all the earmarks of being dead.

Individuals experience issues bowing to God in church. Believe me, in the event that you are before Him, there is no trouble by any stretch of the imagination. He is God; we are simply individuals. Try not to give anybody a chance to convince you that you and I are on the level of God. It is not true. We are currently and dependably will be, subordinate to Him.

We see here that Jesus has sympathy on John and comes to and touches John with His privilege hand. Just one touch from Jesus quiets the biggest reasons for alarm. He consoles John when Jesus says to him, "Apprehension not". Jesus is dependably there ameliorating and empowering Christians.

Generally as Jesus said in John part 14:1, "Let not your heart be harried".

Trepidation is not of God. Peace is the thing that Jesus brings. We simply need to trust Him. The apprehension we need is of God, nobody or nothing else. The trepidation of God could be better expressed as reverence. Here we find in red Jesus discussing Himself, "I am the first and the last:".

This is like what God told Moses when he asked God who might he be able to say sent him. He replied, "I AM" Exodus 3:14. Am is current state, no starting no end.

The earth is the main place that there is time, as we probably am aware it. In paradise there is no division of time by light and dark. There is one and only interminable day. God is time everlasting. This is troublesome for us to see simply because we are caught here with a cycle of time. twenty-four-hour day, seven day week, three hundred and sixty-five day year, twelve month year. Endlessness can't be comprehended by substance.

1:18 I [am] he that liveth, and was dead; and, view, I am alive for evermore, Amen; and have the keys of hellfire and of death.

Jesus is clarifying here. He is the same one who tackled the type of fragile living creature and kicked the bucket on the cross for our wrongdoings.

This is intriguing. We should not just trust who He is and that He spared us, yet we should trust that He became alive once again. His body is the thing that kicked the bucket and rose once more. Jesus, when He plunged into hellfire, removed the keys of damnation from the fallen angel. When He emerged, He got rid of death.

Passing was the last adversary to be done away with. The fallen angel can't place anybody in damnation. Jesus is the special case who can do that. Jesus has the key. Nobody can enter, or exit, without Him.

At the point when Jesus said "I am He that liveth", it is life forevermore. Jesus Christ, as without a doubt the living one, He has life in Himself, He is life, He is our wellspring of life, and He has control of everything, in paradise, earth, and damnation.

Jesus brought numerous souls out of hellfire when He lectured in damnation. Jesus is Life. He controls our fate. We pick (He controls) either paradise or hellfire interminably.

1:19 Write the things which thou hast seen, and the things which are, and the things which might be from this point forward;

Verse19 is the key verse that opens the way to the whole blueprint of the book. It is additional confirmation of the triple division of this incredible Revelation. John was advised explicitly by Christ to compose, what you have seen: To compose the things which were. The things he saw, every one of that was uncovered to him through the distinctive dreams.

What is currently: To compose the things which are, (alluding to the state of the houses of worship in Asia Minor around then), and what will occur later: To compose concerning the things which were to come: The occasions which would happen later on as God satisfied His end time arrangement. The strict interpretation of Rev. 4 v.1 peruses "things which should be after these things" implying that the things of Revelation sections 4-22 must be satisfied after the "things" uncovered relating to the houses of worship in Revelation parts 2-3.

John is authorized of Jesus to record these things with the goal that they will be useful to all who read it. He is likewise advising John not to forget anything.

1:20 The puzzle of the seven stars which thou sawest in my right hand, and the seven brilliant candles. The seven stars are the heavenly attendants of the seven temples: and the seven candles which thou sawest are the seven chapels.

A puzzle is a concealed message. Not for the world, but rather for the congregation. The secret is Jesus. For this situation it is the Truth and the Word that is kept mystery. Jesus is broadly declared, yet few truly have the understanding or knowing of Him.

The seven stars are the dispatchers (not blessed messengers since heavenly attendants are never pioneers in the congregation). These delivery people are the key senior citizens or clergymen speaking to each of those houses of worship.

Whoever, or whatever, they will be, they spread the Light. Jesus is the wellspring of this Light. He is holding and ensuring these stars in His right hand. On the off chance that these are pastors of God, they have no force in themselves. The Light that they give out originates from Him.

This is one reason that I trust evangelists ought to be moved upon by the Holy Spirit of God, and get their message for the congregation through the Spirit from God. I don't trust that pastors ought to purchase, or be sent, messages from other individuals to be utilized to provide for the congregation. Jesus' Spirit is in every congregation, on the off chance that we are His. He knows the issue of every particular church on a given day, and only he recognizes what message should be brought.

These seven candles, we are told here, are the seven holy places typical of all temples for then and now. A candle is not a light. It is the holder for the Light. These candles lift the Light up for all to see. That is the precise motivation behind the congregation, to hoist the Light, Jesus. These candles must be tended to and powered to have the capacity to smolder.

The pastor and the congregation are hard to separate. We know this is talking about the congregation and the service of the congregation. I trust that the stars are clergymen grasped.

I trust these letters were really composed to these specific holy places portraying conditions that were going on then. However, maybe a more critical message for us to see, is the message in each of them managing the issues in our chapels at this moment.

CHAPTER 2

The Messages To The Churches

When you read Revelation parts 2 and 3, it's essential to see there are four applications to the messages.

Every message was given to the seven holy places as initially tended to. What's more, these temples were in presence in Asia at the season of the disclosure. Numerous different holy places existed in Asia in the meantime, yet the chapels chose were illustrative of the otherworldly conditions which existed around then.

The message can likewise be connected generally. By, the Church has gone through times like what is portrayed in each of the seven houses of worship.

These messages can be connected to current houses of worship of today. These uncommon messages were composed to the particular holy places in Asia however the same qualities and shortcomings can be found in today's Body of Christ. (Today's Church)

The messages can be connected to each of us on an individual premise. Take a gander at the messages for every congregation amid that time and ask yourself how you measure up by and by today.

These messages were composed by John in 95 AD when the Church of Jesus Christ was around 66 years of age. The congregation had encountered huge development regardless of exceptional abuse. Under the principle of Rome, records show more than 45,000 Christians were killed by torturous killing, smoldered to death and tossed to wild creatures. Furthermore, debasement was springing up in the Church. At the point when John composed the messages to the seven chapels, numerous adherents were anxious about the uncertain future. They feared being sufficiently solid to face misfortunes that they would be confronting and on the off chance that they could persevere through the abuse. To these early Christians Jesus gave his end time arrangement through these messages.

John was advised to compose what he found in a book and send that book to the 7 holy places in Asia. (Rev. 1 v.11) The whole Book of Revelation which incorporates the uncommon messages to those 7 houses of worship, was sent to those holy places and a gift was affirmed upon all who might read, hear and keep the words contained in this prediction. Jesus needed adherents to realize that He knew precisely where they were. He saw their benevolent acts, dedication and tolerance despite abuse. He additionally saw the awful which incorporated their trade off, dereliction, lack of concern, and tepidness. Abandonment He needed them to realize that in spite of abuse from without and debasement from inside of, He remained in their middle as a powerful winner and that through Him they also could succeed.

Christ's motivation in sending those messages to the seven places of worship was to engage devotees to defeat the foe. His motivation was to ascend His kin in triumph, to make them solid. When we take the veil off, we see that today's Church in its current condition is not prepared for Christ's arrival. That is the reason Christ is again strolling amidst His kin setting up His Bride for His coming. By His Spirit, He is mixing us out of our lack of concern. He is uncovering and impugning sin, calling us to atonement, conveying us to another, more grounded position of devotion and responsibility, and discharging a crisp anointing of His Spirit upon us.

As Jesus strolls in our middle, He knows our individual and corporate qualities and shortcomings. His message to us today is the same as it was to the seven holy places in Asia. "He that has an ear, let him hear what the Spirit saith unto the places of worship."

As we study the messages given to each of these holy places, open your soul to hear what the Spirit of God is stating to you. Request that God uncover any issues that should be managed inside of your life. Yield yourself completely to the Holy Spirit and permit Him to cleanse anything from your life that is disappointing to Him.

Section 2

2:1-3 Unto the holy messenger of the congregation of Ephesus compose; These things saith he that holdeth the seven stars in his right hand, who walketh amidst the seven brilliant candles" "I know thy works, and thy work, and thy tolerance, and how thou canst not manage them which are detestable: and thou hast attempted them which say they are missionaries, and are not, and hast discovered them liars:" "And hast borne, and hast persistence, and for my name's purpose hast toiled, and hast not blacked out."

There are numerous things that we should note about these verses.

To begin with, they are in red, so this is the Lord Jesus speaking. Literally there was simply such a congregation sixty miles northeast of the isle of Patmos. So there was a strict church of Ephesus. Many trust that this specific church was typical of the biblical age from around 30 to 100 AD - It is known as the Apostolic Church. I accept subsequent to review it precisely, we can see a portion of the holy places in our own particular day falling into simply this category. Here once more, this message is sent to the serving soul of this congregation.

Second, we are reminded again here that Jesus holds these stars in His right hand. Jesus strolls amidst this congregation; so we know rapidly, it falls into the class of Christianity.

We would see this congregation situated amidst a common encompassing yet being a congregation holding up a standard against the insidious surroundings. This congregation would be an otherworldly church guided and taught through the Holy Spirit of God. This congregation will be discovered working when the Lord comes back. They have been loaded with the force and vicinity of God. Jesus first lets them know the great, then lets them know of their shortcoming, as we find in the following verse. Despite the fact that this congregation has buckled down and not surrendered, we will see here that they have a couple inadequacies.

2:4 Nevertheless I have [somewhat] against thee, on the grounds that thou hast left thy first love.

Our first love, on the off chance that we are devotees, is putting Jesus in front of everything else. This current church's issues profoundly, can be seen in a large portion of our places of worship today. God won't permit trade off, yet on each hand we see only that.

In II Timothy 3:5: It says, "Having a type of purity, yet denying the force thereof: from such dismiss." Probably this congregation has become excessively refined for recuperating and deliverance. Perhaps a percentage of the world's music has wormed in unaware. Perhaps this congregation has started to excite more than instruct. This congregation is more engaging the world than to God.

As we take a gander at all of these temples, we should inspect ourselves and our congregation and see exactly what class we fall into.

Our first love, in the event that we are devotees, is putting Jesus in front of everything else. This present church's issues, profoundly, can be seen in a large portion of our chapels today. God won't permit trade off, however on each hand we see only that.

2:5 Remember along these lines from whence thou craftsmanship fallen, and apologize, and do the main works; or else I will come unto thee rapidly, and will evacuate thy candle out of his place, with the exception of thou repentance.

There is not a viable replacement for unified, intense, undying affection for Jesus Christ. Jesus cautioned the congregation at Ephesus to "apologize, and do the main works; or something bad might happen, I will come unto thee rapidly, and will uproot the candle, out of his place, with the exception of thou atone" He cautioned that in the event that they didn't atone, judgment would fall. They would never again be a genuine light and witness to the world.

What number of our houses of worship today are dormant, dull, and mechanical? What number of do not have the light and witness of Christ and His energy? The condition in this congregation, and in our temples and individual lives, did not occur without any forethought. It was a continuous procedure whereby adherents left their "first" love, their enthusiastic "wedding" love for Christ. The "principal affection" to which Christ called the congregation in Ephesus to return can be with the "wedding" love in a marriage relationship.

Another lady is so enamored with her spouse that he is the focal center of her life. When she takes her wedding pledges, she guarantees to neglect all others and give herself exclusively to him. She avidly foresees his wishes and affectionately tries to address every one of his issues. She goes through each conceivable minute with him. In this "wedding love" relationship, there is a unique closeness that creates between the spouse and her groom. She yearns to know everything conceivable about him. She opens her heart to him, uncovering her deepest mysteries and cravings. While they are separated from each other, she yearns for him and energetically expects when she will be with him by and by. On account of her affection, the lady puts her husband initially, before all else, including her own needs, longings, and aspirations.

It is this kind of immaculate, intense, benevolent" "wedding love" for Christ that made the pupils willing to give themselves 100% for the reason for Christ. It was this sort of adoration that consumed their own egotistical goals, spurred them to serve Christ with single hearted dedication, and made them willing to set out their lives for the reason for Christ. It is this kind of affection that we should have blazing inside of us to empower us to satisfy the reasons of God in these last snippets of time before Christ's arrival. Pretty much as Christ called the congregation in Ephesus to come back to their first love, He is strolling among us today, calling us to atone and come back to our first love.

Here are seven cautioning signs that flag that a congregation or individual has left their first love.

Christ is no more the focal center in your life.

You disregard your association with the Lord and invest less energy in request to God, adore and the Word.

You permit family, companions, work and your own goals to interfere with you and your association with God.

There is lost closeness in your association with God.

You are gotten in a cycle of dead works

You are more tolerant of sin

You will no more have a blazing energy for the lost

Your works were persuaded by exceptional affection and dedication to the Lord. Analyze your adoration for the Lord today with what it was then. Has your adoration become more profound or has it lost its intensity? Are your works persuaded by an energetic affection for God or would you say you are doing them only out of a feeling of obligation? Approach the Lord to forget you for leaving your first love. Start to do your first works once more. Make another responsibility to the rudiments of petition to God, venerate, and the Word. Stoke the fire of the withering ashes of your first love through reestablished fellowship with the Lord. This intense adoration is required of each one of the individuals who fit in with the Lord. Jesus called this the first and incredible instruction:

"Thou shalt love the Lord thy God with all thy heart, and with all thy soul, and with all thy mind. This is the first and incredible edict." (Mat. 22 v.37-38)

2:6 But this thou hast, that thou hatest the deeds of the Nicolaitans, which I additionally loathe.

Notice here that Jesus, as this congregation, abhors the transgression and not the miscreant. The deeds are despised, not the doer. There is by all accounts no record of the Nicolaitans aside from this notice here. It is conceivable to loathe shrewd and still not be carrying on with a satisfying life in God's sight. Experience is something we should maintain a strategic distance from completely.

Nicaulous and Baalam are in the same category. Probably malicious with no specific root. The tenet of Baalam, Nicaulous, and the Jezebel church imagined that being Christians liberated them from the ethical law. They trusted that misguided admiration and carnal things would not be held against them, since they had been sans set by Christ. Some of the progressivism we find in the houses of worship today originate from this very conviction.

Such a large number of are attempting to convey Jesus down to our level or to hoist us up to His level. This is an exceptionally risky principle to make ourselves into divine beings. That is the reason Lucifer was tossed out of paradise. Experience must not be blended in with love of God. We should not take part in this, as well as really abhor this practice.

2:7 He that hath an ear, let him hear what the Spirit saith unto the houses of worship; To him that overcometh will I provide for eat of the tree of life, which is amidst the heaven of God.

We all have ears, however this is talking about that inward ear of the heart that gets reality. Note here that Spirit is promoted importance God's Spirit. This is any soul, as well as the Holy Spirit of God. We likewise see here, that He is identifying with the places of worship, and abruptly bounced to people in the congregation when He says, "to him that overcometh".

We are not spared by and large but rather as people. We as people must choose who we will take after. We see here likewise that there is something to succeed. We should overcome prurient allurements of the tissue.

All adherents to Jesus will eat of the tree of life. Jesus is the Tree of Life. Heaven will be paradise, not hellfire, the same number of trust today. At the point when Jesus told the cheat on the cross, "Verily I say unto thee, Today shalt thou be with me in heaven." Luke 23:43. Many attempted to make it fit in with Jesus' body being in the grave. Jesus' Spirit went to paradise specifically from the cross, as our soul will leave our body the moment we kick the bucket.

Jesus said, "Father, into thy hands I compliment my soul:" Luke 23:46. The Spirit of Jesus went to God promptly. His Spirit rejoined His body three days later. Forty days after the fact Jesus' body and Spirit were taken to paradise on a cloud.

God is a Spirit; Jesus is a Spirit who was housed in a body for His keep focused We are a soul, also, housed in a body. If we are an adherent, our soul will instantly go to paradise when it leaves our body. The body will ascend at revival and rejoin our soul. Jesus' Spirit and the soul of the cheat on the cross were in paradise quickly. The tree of life is in heaven. Paradise is the patio nursery in paradise. This is a sublime rebuilding of the Garden of Eden. The radiant, being much more great.

2:8-9 And unto the blessed messenger of the congregation in Smyrna compose; These things saith the first and the last, which was dead, and is alive;" "I know thy works, and tribulation, and neediness, (yet thou craftsmanship rich) and [I know] the sacrilege of them which say they are Jews, and are not, but rather [are] the synagogue of Satan."

100 to 313 AD - The Persecuted Church

Situated around 35 miles north of Ephesus, Smyrna was a rich and delightful business city in Asia Minor and was perceived by Rome as its dedicated partner and a focal point of head love. In His message to this congregation, the Lord again lauded their acts of kindness, "I know your works, tribulation, and neediness". These devotees were oppressed and frequently lost their method for occupation as a consequence of their dedication to the Lord.

Making an open admission of their confidence implied neediness, craving, detainment, and some of the time passing. "Tribulation" utilized here paints a photo of a gigantic rock smashing whatever lies underneath it. The word passes on serious and consistent weight. Can you relate to that? Huge numbers of you are encountering "extreme and steady weight". You aren't overlooked! Jesus sees and knows.

It is intriguing to me that Jesus calls Himself contrastingly here than at the congregation of Ephesus. In the Ephesus letter He says, "he that holdeth the seven stars in his right hand, who walketh amidst the seven brilliant candles" Here at Smyrna He calls Himself, "the first and last, which was dead, and is alive"

The assignment here is this message is not from the Father or the Holy Spirit, but rather from God the Son, Jesus as we probably am aware Him. We see from this that God does not bargain precisely the same with everybody. He manages us at the level of our comprehension.

You find in the synagogue in Jerusalem, when Jesus called them "whited dividers" Matthew 23:27, clean on the outside and dingy within. Jesus said, "Trouble unto you, copyists and Pharisees, wolves in sheep's clothing!" Jesus called them an era of snakes, Matthew 23:33.

You see not every one of the individuals who case to be Christians are really Christians. In the event that we are not watchful, we will be similar to these Jews. We might say we are a Christian, and the world may really trust that we are a direct result of our outward appearance. Jesus takes a gander at the heart. We read in Matthew 7:22 "Numerous will say to me in that day, Lord, Lord, have we not forecasted in thy name? what's more, in thy name have thrown out fiends? what's more, in thy name done numerous brilliant works?" Matthew 7:23 "And afterward will I declare unto them, I never knew you: leave from me, ye that work wrongdoing." Their Christianity was a front for some narrow-minded thought process.

The contrition and salvation that truly include is the thing that goes on the heart. It is similar to having another recovered heart put within you, washed in the Blood of the Lamb. Being conceived again is having a fresh out of the box new heart, having no yearning to sin. The heart is either frantically shrewd or clean in Jesus. Some call it a change of heart. Whatever dedication is made must be made in the heart.

At the point when Jesus talks about His being "the first and last", He is discussing His interminable Spirit.

When He talks about "which was dead, and is alive", He is discussing His body which restored from the grave.

Jesus knows all; He was strolling, and is strolling in the midst of the houses of worship. These eyes of flame see everything, even in our hearts. He has only great things to say in regards to this congregation in Smyrna. To know them is to cherish them. Jesus knows how hard they have functioned for the kingdom. He realizes that they are rich in support of Him. They are rich in information of His Word. They have tenaciously looked for Him in His Word. They are rich in the endowments of the Holy Spirit. They have been through incredible tribulation. Tribulation comes to make you solid. They are solid, since they have been attempted and they have not fizzled God.

Maybe, their destitution talked about here shows that they are not fixated on having common riches. They are not rich in things the world would class as wealth. Their riches is of profound things. The fortune that we ought to all be looking for is the fortune amassed in paradise.

On the off chance that there is a congregation in this gathering we ought to all need to be similar to, it would be this congregation at Smyrna.

This "synagogue of Satan" that comes against them is the thing that we were examining some time recently. These are religious individuals with an outward appearance of conviction however with no internal conviction. This exacting church at Smyrna had numerous saints who remained against the malevolent, adoring individuals around them even unto the passing.

In our day it is the same situation. If we are in God's armed force, we should will to remain for what is correct even unto demise. The Spirit and the tissue (world) will be secured fight until the arrival of Jesus. The world and its framework, and even the barbarian church is against genuine exemplary nature and sacredness. Jesus is returning for a congregation that is without spot or wrinkle.

2:10 Fear none of those things which thou shalt endure: see, the demon should cast [some] of you into jail, that ye might be attempted; and ye might have tribulation ten days: be thou loyal unto passing, and I will give thee a crown of life.

He said they would endure. He is letting them realize that He and the Father thoroughly understand their agony. They should stay loyal unto the end, and awesome prizes will be theirs in paradise. Jesus cautions them they will be tossed into prison. We know from history that these devotees, in the strict church of Smyrna, were tossed into jail. Numerous in our day are being tossed into jail for their faith. It is getting to be increasingly hard to be a Christian, and much more hard to be a clergyman. The congregation is under assault of the fallen angel.

The importance of Christ's words to this congregation, that they would have tribulation for "ten days", might allude to the way that the Early Church endured ten noteworthy oppressions under Nero, Domitian, Trajan, Marcus Aurelius, Severus, Maximum, Decius, Valerian, Aurelian, and Diocletian. There were likewise some striking oppressions in the nearby Smyrna Church which kept going "ten days" (One day frequently is figured as one year in scriptural prediction).

It is anything but difficult to take after Jesus when everything is going great. The genuine test is, will you stay when all chances are against you? At the point when your companions and relatives have surrendered, will you stand? In the event that we are dependable and stand, there is a crown of life anticipating us. The crown of life is the one the Lord Himself gets ready for us. Crown of life signifies; "administering over death". There will be no more demise, neither should there be distress. "neither distress, nor crying, neither might there be any more agony: for the previous things are passed away." "See, I make all things new" Revelation 21:4

5. Numerous should be martyred before the arrival of Christ.

Christ's message to you today, amidst your agony, enduring, mistreatment, and testing is "Trepidation Not!" No matter what you are confronting, ailment, ailment, family issues, or even the likelihood of death, don't fear since "God hath not given us the soul of apprehension; but rather of force, and of adoration, and of a sound personality." (2 Tim. 1 v.7)

2:11 He that hath an ear, let him hear what the Spirit saith unto the places of worship; He that overcometh should not be harmed of the second passing.

We hear once more, take out the plugs in your inward man and get from God His truths. There is an extraordinary guarantee to the overcomers. The demise connected with hellfire, won't happen to them. They have been delegated with everlasting life.

The best blessing that we could ever get is the endowment of everlasting existence with Jesus. To know we would be isolated from Jesus for all of time everlasting would be more hellfire than I would care to hold up under. The main life worth having is with Him. I can't say enough great in regards to this congregation at Smyrna. There are just two in the seven that God has no censure for. Smyrna is one of them. Under awesome mistreatment this congregation stands, and having even confronted demise, still stands. If you somehow happened to depict this congregation in present day English, you would simply say that the unadulterated Word of God is lectured individuals who will acknowledge the Truth.

The pastor sustains the group the Word a few times each week. The assemblage concentrates on the Scriptures, ever anxious to take in more so they can be more in the will of God. They are not shaken by winds of false precept, for they test everything and everybody against the Scriptures. They have overall reinforcement of God. They are loaded with the Holy Spirit and work in the blessings of the Spirit.

They understand there is a fight continuing for the souls of men, and they have enrolled in God's armed force to battle underhanded at each hand. They are willing to surrender homes, family, whatever it takes to serve God. They tally the everlasting life more than the short life here. Pretty much the same number of were martyred

2:12 And to the heavenly attendant of the congregation in Pergamos compose; These things saith he which hath the sharp sword with two edges;

313 to 590 AD - The State Church. Here we have THE DANGER OF DOCTRINAL COMPROMISE

Situated around sixty miles north of Smyrna is Pergamos, which at one time was the official Asian community for the magnificent religion. It was additionally the focal point of love for four of the most essential agnostic cliques of the day: Zeus, Athene, Dionysos and Asklepios Jesus, once more, calls Himself by an alternate name. Here He is said to have "the sharp sword with the two edges" The sword with two edges is, obviously, the Bible with the Old and New Testament.

They were not overlooked. Jesus perceived their reliability in spite of the otherworldly environment in which they lived. In the first Greek, the words, "holdest quick" signifies "to clutch urgently with the greater part of one's energy." These Christians were clutching their confidence with all that they had and Jesus complimented them for their dependability.

There are such a variety of approaches to see these, as I have said before. For our study, we will endeavor to utilize the issues of this congregation to let us know what not to do in our congregation today.

God never shows signs of change. The things He was against a great many years back are the very things He is against today. God never shows signs of change; we change. If we are not cautious, these progressions will make us smug about the transgression in our life.

2:13 I know thy works, and where thou dwellest, [even] where Satan's seat [is]: and thou holdest quick my name, and hast not denied my confidence, even in those days wherein Antipas [was] my loyal saint, who was killed among you, where Satan dwelleth.

Jesus not just knows their works, He knows every little thing about them. Judgment starts at the place of God, since Jesus strolls forward and backward looking at them consistently.

Jesus says that He knows where they abide. He is alluding to the exceptionally detestable environment. This was an instructive focus. There were incredible libraries and spots of common training.

This congregation is submitting sin; trading off with the rapscallion around them. Commonly common shrewdness and loyalty to God are not firm. The Bible says that "The lewd personality is hatred against God" Romans 8:7.

Confidence is not truth. The informed personality needs to demonstrate by realities. Confidence, I say once more, is not truth; Hebrews 11:1 "Now confidence is the substance of things sought after, the proof of things not seen." Hebrews 11:2: "For by it the older folks got a decent report."

The brain and heart, despite the fact that physically a couple crawls separated, are miles separated in the Spirit.

Jesus knew this congregation in Pergamos would have a hard time. The malice outside the congregation and the trade off in the congregation tries to draw a greater amount of these individuals out of the church. Maybe they had great aims, however they got terrible results. Jesus goes so far as to call this underhanded city, "Satan's seat". We know by this that abhorrence won.

Jesus says to this congregation, you have My name on your congregation and I likewise am mindful you have not denied Me. Jesus even advises them that He knows that Antipas was martyred due to his awesome confidence in Jesus. This Satanic impact had come against Antipas and murdered him. We should understand that we should not cooperation with those of unbelief. We should witness to them, and afterward go home. Fellowshipping with the world brings trade off. The disgrace is that some of this has crawled into this congregation as we find in V-14.

2:14 But I have a couple of things against thee, on the grounds that thou hast there them that hold the principle of Balaam, who taught Balac to cast a stumbling block before the offspring of Israel, to eat things yielded unto symbols, and to confer sex.

Be that as it may, the Lord additionally criticized them for permitting individuals who rehearsed the "regulation of Balaam and the Nicolaitans" to stay inside of their assemblage.

In his message to Pergamos, Jesus looks at the behavior of some of these devotees with the activities of the Israelites who traded off with the Moabites. He likewise censured them for permitting the precept of the Nicolaitans to stay in their middle.

"Nicoliatane" originates from two Greek words, one signifying "to overcome" and the other signifying "the common people." It is typical of the advancement of a clerical request which led over the common people rather than Christ's order with respect to serving each other given in Mat. 23 v.8-9: The headship of Christ had been put aside for a religious progressive system.

2:15 So hast thou likewise them that hold the convention of the Nicolaitans, which thing I despise.

II Peter 2:1 "However there were false prophets likewise among the general population, even as there might be false instructors among you, who privily should acquire abhorrent apostasies, notwithstanding denying the Lord that purchased them, and bring upon themselves quick demolition." II Peter 2:2 "And numerous might take after their malevolent routes; by reason of whom the method for truth should be shrewd talked about."

In spite of the fact that they were successful in keeping their confidence amid abuse, they opened the way to profound decimation when they traded off with the world. Disaffection - Various Religions, Cults Compromise is mixing two thoughts together. The word reference says it is "to expose to threat." In profound matters, any position of trade off opens you up to peril and debasement.

Bargain is wild all through the Body of Christ and the Spirit of God is calling us to permit the "sword of the Spirit", the Word of God, to uncover and uproot trade off generally as a specialist evacuates a dangerous development. God can't endure trade off! He despises it.

Indeed, even the littlest bargain opens the ways to extra trade off, which prompts much more noteworthy bargain and in the long run, otherworldly passing. On the off chance that you have traded off in any part of your life, you should do what Jesus told devotees at Pergamos:

2:16 Repent; or else I will come unto thee rapidly, and will battle against them with the sword of my mouth.

Apologize intends to be genuinely sad and move in the opposite direction of evil. Go another bearing. Stroll in right remaining with the Lord. The sword that Jesus battles with is His Word. There is nothing more intense than the Word of God. Jesus has not abandoned them. He simply needs them to change their ways.

Jesus issued a stern cautioning to the congregation at Pergamos: "Apologize; or else I will come unto thee rapidly, and will battle against them with the sword of my mouth." Although most of the congregation at Pergamos were not misled and were not taking after the regulation of the Balaamites and the Nicolaitans, they were blameworthy of lack of interest toward the transgression inside of their congregation.

In any case, there were some who slipped in unnoticed, and conveyed false teaching. If you need to know more about the majority of this false educating, simply read all of section two of Second Peter.

2:17 He that hath an ear, let him hear what the Spirit saith unto the temples; To him that overcometh will I provide for eat of the concealed sustenance, and will give him a white stone, and in the stone another name composed, which no man knoweth sparing he that receiveth [it].

As we said some time recently, hear with our internal man. There is a fight, and we are God's soldiers. The Spirit and the tissue are secured fight. When we permit the Spirit of God to control our tissue, then we are His. He is our God, and we are His kin.

The stone said in V-17, most believe was a precious stone. It was likely the stone worn by the consecrated cleric that had God's name on it. It was escaped perspective alongside the heart behind the Urim and the Thummim. The others' stones were typical for the Tribes of Israel, and every one of them 12 were on the breastplate of the esteemed cleric.

We have gotten the name of Jesus Christ on the off chance that we are really His. We are Christians. Whatever the stone is, I am glad to realize that our name will be on it.

Jesus will nourish us His concealed manna. Manna tumbled from paradise inexplicably and sustained the Israelites on their way to the Promised Land in Exodus 16:14-15. This sustenance was typical of Jesus who is the Bread of Life. We will eat of the Tree of Life (Jesus) and live for eternity.

Whether this is otherworldly or physical, I don't generally care. It will be everything we need to maintain us. The first Ark of the Covenant, which the natural Ark was designed by, has dependably been in paradise, covered up to natural eyes.

The secret Jesus is uncovering is Himself in His totality.

He is the Tree,

He is the Bread,

He is the Manna,

He is LIFE.

We, as well, as Pergamos must atone and come to Jesus with all that we are or ever want to be. We are nothing until He fills us with Himself.

2:18-19 "And unto the heavenly attendant of the congregation in Thyatira compose; These things saith the Son of God, who hath his eyes like unto a fire of flame, and his feet [are] like fine metal;" "2:19 I know thy works, and philanthropy, and administration, and confidence, and thy tolerance, and thy works; and the last [to be] more than the first."

590 to 1517 AD - The Papal Church - THE DANGER OF MORAL COMPROMISE

The city of Thyatira was a crucial business and exchange focus situated around 40 miles southeast of Pergamos. Jesus recognized the congregation here at Thyatira for its acts of kindness.

Numerous Christians don't know that they are worshiping icons. Some are so brimming with pride and self trickiness that their otherworldly eyes are blinded from seeing the parts of their lives where they have declined to let Jesus rule as Lord. Numerous devotees today have made good bargains. They no more hold exclusive expectations of uprightness. On the off chance that you are blameworthy of good trade off, profound infidelity, then you should do what Jesus advised these adherents to do: Repent and after that hold quick! Clutch your respectability. Watch your Godly gauges. Try not to fall prey to good trade off.

Discussing icons, what could some of these be? Material belonging, different desires, amusement, excitement, vocation and narrow minded aspiration. (abide precisely as you consider the answer)

He said: "I know thy works, and philanthropy, and administration, and confidence, and thy persistence, and thy works; and the last to be more than the first". (Rev. 2 v.19) But at the end of the day, Jesus sees past this outward show of benevolent acts and uncovered a fortification of Satan right amidst the congregation. The congregation of Pergamos was permitting a lady who called herself a prophetess to instruct others that it was okay to blend agnostic religions with Christianity. She was instructing and enticing individuals to confer sex and bargain ethically.

The congregation at Thyatira, numerous accept, is illustrative of the Roman Catholic Church and the time of that chapels' prominence. I would not harp on that point.

We are taking a gander at the otherworldly and attempting to see the greater part of the seven houses of worship in our advanced holy places today. Wherever conceivable, not directing fingers or calling names. We should analyze ourselves before we begin directing fingers.

Jesus demonstrates this congregation His entering eyes which can even observe the aims of the heart. With His feet of fine metal, He demonstrates to them that He really is the last Judge.

It appears this congregation here in Thyatira has extraordinary affection and empathy and is a working church attempting to enhance the state of the less blessed around them. This congregation is understanding, which is picked up by much tribulation. This is not a hardened chilly church, as a percentage of alternate holy places may be, yet is a cherishing minding church. It appears that the works of this congregation enhance as they come, in light of the fact that the latter is more than the first.

This is truly an extremely pleasant articulation that Jesus made about them.

2:20 Notwithstanding I have a couple of things against thee, on the grounds that thou sufferest that lady Jezebel, which calleth herself a prophetess, to instruct and to allure my workers to submit sex, and to eat things relinquished unto symbols.

All through the Old Testament, this union of that which is blessed with that which is sullied is considered by God as profound infidelity. It was an evil entity in His sight!

This false educator is alluded to as "Jezebel," which could conceivably have really been her name, however absolutely alludes to her soul. It references Jezebel in the Old Testament, who was the wife of King Ahab. She was an adoring lady with corrupt strategies, to sustain her energy. Jesus cautioned the congregation of Thyatira of coming judgment to this false educator and each one of the individuals who confer otherworldly infidelity by good bargain.

This "Jezebel" was offered time to atone, however cannot. (Rev. 2 v.21)

Presently, the individuals who had been cheated by her instructing were given the decision to atone or confront serious judgment. In the Church today, most devotees are not enticed to love agnostic symbols of wood or stone, however they do love different icons!

This is one of the sacred writings that is regularly utilized by specific groups to say that ladies ought not instruct and preach. If we precisely take a gander at this, we will understand that Jezebel here is not a lady really, but rather an arrangement of shrewdness, whether taught by men or ladies. Sex is the issue here, not that there is a lady in the congregation. Generally as the Nicolaitans were not so much a specific nation and Baal was an image of malice and not a particular spot and individual.

We have to take a gander at sex and see what it is. Fornication is inbreeding or infidelity of either sex that are enjoying unlawful desire.

Everybody would concur that any clergyman of God who advanced any of these transgressions would be a Jezebel to Jesus.

Men and ladies who are professors in Christ are all the Bride of Christ. I don't trust that this Jezebel is all ladies who serve the Word of God, however simply the individuals who show detestable desire.

In Galatians 3:28, we read that with God there is no male and female. "There is neither Jew nor Greek, there is neither bond nor free, there is neither male nor female: for ye are each of the one in Christ Jesus." The same Paul that composed for ladies to be noiseless in chapel, in I Corinthians 14:34, composed this in Galatians.

We additionally need to take a gander at Acts 2:17-18. Acts 2:17 "And it might happen in the most recent days, saith God, I will pour out of my Spirit upon all substance: and your children and your girls should forecast, and your young fellows should see dreams, and your old men should dream dreams:" Acts 2:18 "And on my hirelings and on my handmaidens I will pour out in those days of my Spirit; and they should forecast.

There is something we are not understanding, or else the Bible negates itself. We know the Bible does not repudiate itself. We should look all the more deliberately at what the Scriptures mean. The blunder comes in malevolence messages that a few ladies or men bring. The Jezebel here could be a lady, however in the event that she is, it is not the way that she is a lady that isn't right, it is a shrewd message that isn't right. We should take a gander at one more Scripture in Acts.

Acts 21:8 "And the following [day] we that were of Paul's organization withdrew, and came unto Caesarea: and we went into the place of Philip the evangelist, which was [one] of the seven; and homestead him." Acts 21:9 "And the same man had four little girls, virgins, which did forecast." There are numerous samples simply like this of Philip's little girls.

We should all be watchful about censuring others in their service. Take a gander at the setting it is composed in, before revolting against others.

Jezebel calls herself a prophetess. It shows up whoever this is or whatever gathering this speaks to, they are advancing sentiments of the tissue not the Spirit.

All through the Bible we are cautioned not to eat things yielded to icons purposely.

2:21 And I gave her space to atone of her sex; and she apologized not.

We should deliberately take a gander at what must be atoned of. The wrongdoing here is sex. She was not to apologize of lecturing, but rather atone of sex. In the days that

John composed this, there were shrewd temples that even had prostitutes working in the congregation for the accommodation of the individuals.

In our day the evil houses of worship advance sex. Some chapels show that homosexuality and lesbianism are exchange ways of life. My Bible says they are a cursed thing to God, Leviticus 18:22.

You can without much of a stretch see profoundly this congregation in Thyatira in these temples. Did Thyatira need to atone, as well as cutting edge places of worship who instruct this anathema.

2:22 Behold, I will cast her into a bed, and them that submit infidelity with her into awesome tribulation, aside from they atone of their deeds.

Here this could be both physical and otherworldly infidelity. The general population who get included in these sex sins are liable, also. It is no reason to sin in light of the fact that your clergyman lets you know that you are not blameworthy. Attempt each message you hear by what the Bible teaches. Do not be betrayed by any false prophet, male or female. Their contrition is of their deeds, not whether they were male or female.

2:23 And I will murder her kids with death; and all the temples should realize that I am he which searcheth the reins and hearts: and I will give unto each one of you as indicated by your works.

The word interpreted reins signifies "the inward most personality", maybe the subliminal personality. The heart will be judged. The thought process behind our deeds is pretty much as vital as the deed.

In the Scripture above, we see that God won't generally ignore sin in the congregation. At the point when His judgment falls, it will start in the congregation. Discipline will be quick thus serious that different houses of worship will look and tremble at the discipline.

The works discussed here are the works of the heart and psyche which come to development in genuine deeds. Good or fiendishness really starts in the brain and heart. Generally as lovely words can't originate from a detestable heart, delightful deeds can't either. What we are inside will appear in what we accomplish for God.

2:24-25 "Yet unto you I say, and unto the rest in Thyatira, the same number of as have not this regulation, and which have not known the profundities of Satan, as they speak; I will put upon you none other weight." "However that which ye have [already] hold quick till I come."

What teaching is talked about here? The regulation of carnal desire and sex. The principle that says you can do what you please the length of you are purified through water. Jesus needs a virtuous virgin for a bride. Jesus needs us to be sacred as He is holy. Sin must not be drilled, on the off chance that we are Christians.

Jesus will excuse us of our transgressions on the off chance that we ask Him, yet we should not backtrack into that wrongdoing over and over. Our heart must longing to live above sin.

Notice here, additionally, that despite the fact that this specific church talked about is advancing sin, an individual can atone and be spared even in this circumstance. God does not pass judgment on gatherings. Jesus passes judgment on us each one in turn. It would be a shocking weight to have no other church to go to than one that taught sex. He instructs them to hold quick to sound teaching until He comes.

2:26-27 "And he that overcometh, and keepeth my works unto the end, to him will I give control over the countries:" "And he might lead them with a pole of iron; as the vessels of a potter should they be broken to shudders: even as I got of my Father."

You see here that Jesus indicates His works are what can anyone do. It additionally implies that we ought not simply do a little and get smug, yet stay with the Lord's work to the very end. Just as Jesus told the story of the great worker in Luke part 19, we should be a decent hireling and convey the our rewards for all the hard work to Jesus.

Jesus says, the worker, in Luke, was to lead more than ten cities. In V-27 He additionally guarantees that His loyal will rule. Remember the force is Jesus'. He gives us our energy. This force is to do His will as we rule. We are working under Jesus' direction. He is our pioneer. The "pole of iron" means the guideline will be solid, inflexible.

The standard will be as a shepherd leads on the off chance that they take after Jesus, yet in the event that not, they should be broken to pieces. This pole discussed could be a shepherd's or a king's. Whichever it is, the bar of amendment will be utilized as a part of affection. Jesus was given all force on earth, under the earth, and in paradise by the Father.

2:28 And I will give him the morning star.

Jesus is the Bright and Morning Star. He guarantees to offer Himself to the individuals who will tail Him.

2:29 He that hath an ear, let him hear what the Spirit saith unto the places of worship.

See again this message is not simply given to this one church of Thyatira, however to holy places, plural. We should take notice to the notices. Open the ears of our heart and get Jesus in His Fullness.

CHAPTER 3

The Danger Of Spiritual Death

3:1 And unto the blessed messenger of the congregation in Sardis compose; These things saith he that hath the seven Spirits of God, and the seven stars; I know thy works, that thou hast a name that thou livest, and craftsmanship dead.

Sardis: The Danger of Spiritual Death - 1517 to1790 – The Reformed Church

This congregation at Sardis is seen by numerous as the transformation church. In this study we will take a gander at this congregation in the light of our cutting-edge houses of worship.

Sardis is found 35 miles southeast of Thyatira. It was the capital of Lydia and was previously a picture of quality, fruitfulness, and riches. Heathen worship and corruption were its notoriety. The congregation at Sardis had "a name," a great notoriety, and it gave off an impression of being alive. Be that as it may, in actuality, there was only internal deadness. Their deadness was at any rate halfway because of some kind of debasement on the grounds that the Word says there were just "a couple" which had not been contaminated. (Rev. 3 v.4)

These individuals frantically required the service of the Holy Spirit. The notice of the "seven Spirits of God" is a reference to the sevenfold service of the Spirit found in Isaiah 11 v.2: "And the soul of the Lord should rest upon him, the soul of insight and comprehension, the soul of direction and might, the soul of information and the trepidation of the Lord." This congregation required the service of the Holy Spirit in these territories. In the event that you are profoundly dead, you require these services too:

The Spirit of Wisdom: A dead kicking the bucket church or individual needs to look for the knowledge of God.

The Spirit of Understanding: A dormant biting the dust church or individual needs a genuine comprehension of their condition so they can adjust it.

The Spirit of Counsel: A dormant biting the dust church or individual needs to regard the guidance of God.

The Spirit of Might: An inert passing on chapel or individual needs new quality to go into its dormant body.

The Spirit of Knowledge: An inert biting the dust church.

The Spirit of Fear of the Lord: An inert biting the dust church or individual needs their trepidation of the Lord revived.

On the off chance that you feel profoundly dead or your congregation is kicking the bucket corporately, then you should take after the fivefold arrange for that the Spirit provided for the congregation at Sardis in Rev. 3 v.3:

1. Be Watchful: The opened up Bible says to "Stir yourself and keep conscious." It is the ideal opportunity for us to wake up, get to be aware of the indications of the time, and be dynamic for God as at no other time.

2. Fortify: Take hold of the things that remain and are prepared to bite the dust in your life and reinforce them through petition to God and the Word.

3. Keep in mind: Reflect back on the guarantees of God -what you have gotten and heard in times past.

4. Hold Fast: Hold quick to your confidence and God's Word.

5. Apologize: Repent so you will be prepared for the arrival of Christ and not got uninformed.

This congregation is extremely evident to me. When I was a youngster, I went to a specific category church. This specific church was apparently exceptionally solid in the Lord. Individuals yelled and said so be it. Individuals were petitioned God for who were wiped out. At that point out of the blue, something many refer to as the National Council of Churches was shaped and my congregation, I had cherished so profoundly, changed. The National Council of Churches looks to physically make the congregation one. God's arrangement from the earliest starting point has been for the chapels to be one in Spirit. You can't enact Christianity.

In my congregation we no more taught Sunday school from the Bible, yet we got lessons from home office that we were to use. As best I could see, they had dropped a considerable lot of the Biblical teachings and went all the more too showing social change.

What had been a lifestyle for me for about all my life had changed. The yelling halted; the congregation turned out to be excessively formal for the so be it corner. The main thing I knew, I ended up in a cool formal church, not the warm minding church I had cherished so well. Church never challenged keep running more than fifteen minutes; we needed to remain focused. Book of scriptures studies got to be less and less. The assemblage was not in any case made mindful of how vital Bible perusing and learn at home was. It appeared my congregation, which adored every single Christian people, had made a temporary route.

I truly trust that houses of worship such as this, is the thing that the congregation at Sardis is about. They began simply awesome; yet as time went on, they faded away.

Notice in the verse over that Jesus talks about the seven Spirits of God. At the point when the blessings of the Holy

Spirit are denied and even talked malice of, the genuine church will become scarce. The force of God is in His Spirit. This is the reason Jesus addresses this congregation subsequently. The Spirit has gone. This congregation is as yet flying the banner of Christianity, however denying the force thereof.

I utilize this sacred text in Second Timothy a ton yet it flawlessly depicts the time we are living in and portrays this congregation under the most favorable conditions of all.

II Timothy 3:1 "This know additionally, that in the most recent days hazardous times should come."

II Timothy 3:5 "Having a type of righteousness yet denying the force thereof: from such dismiss."

Numerous groups would have us trust the blessings of the Spirit are not in operation today. In the event that they are not, it is a direct result of our absence of confidence. God never shows signs of change; we change.

A man without a soul is similar to a steed who has lost his wind. A congregation without the Spirit is gradually passing on.

God does not need us to deliberately go to chapel since it is anticipated from us once a week. He needs us to anticipate fellowshipping with Him. The adoration in our heart for Jesus ought to make us craving to go to chapel and get all that He has for us.

3:2: Be vigilant, and reinforce the things which remain, that are prepared to bite the dust: for I have not discovered thy works immaculate before God.

Jesus lets them know here; there is still some great in this congregation, expand upon those things. Indeed, even the positive qualities in this congregation is being diluted to the point, that even it is going to bite the dust. I trust the works here talked about are not saying they are not doing works, but rather that their works are inclined more toward the world than toward

God. This congregation, on the off chance that I comprehend it, is extremely social minded and helps nearby government with their activities.

On the off chance that you took a check of what number of genuine changes were made inside of the most recent year, you would be stunned at the shortage. You see, what we call benevolent acts and what God calls acts of kindness are two totally distinctive things. God takes a gander at the Spirit, and we tend to take a gander at the physical.

3:3 Remember accordingly how thou hast got and listened, and hold quick, and apologize. In the event that accordingly thou shalt not watch, I will go ahead thee as a criminal, and thou shalt not recognize what hour I will happen upon thee.

Here again Jesus is stating, your message toward the starting was okay, backpedal to that, the unadulterated Word of God. Some new Bible interpretations are diluting Jesus to the point that He is not God in them.

Some Bible universities would have their kin trust that: Jesus was not conceived of a virgin, that the Red Sea did not part, that Jonah was not genuinely gulped by a vast fish, and numerous more things.

They are diminishing the phenomenal workings of God and attempting to investigate them with what they call exploratory knowledge. This is simply one more assault of Satan to pulverize the magnificence of Christianity. These are essential to confidence in salvation through Jesus Christ. On the off chance that a unimportant man kicked the bucket for your wrongdoings, you are lost. Jesus was God show in the tissue. He was the ideal Lamb of God. He was and is LIFE. To deny that He was conceived of a virgin, denies that He is God the Son. His Father must be God.

These false instructors say the Red Sea did not part, but rather was only a boggy zone. In the event that this is genuine, disclose to me how the Egyptian troopers were suffocated.

The entire thing is an intrigue to prevent the god from securing Christ. This is extremely perilous. On the off chance that we deny Him, He will deny us before the Father, Matthew 10:33.

Obviously, these false teachings incorporate a showing that there is no paradise and no hellfire. That they are only a perspective. The Bible talks unequivocally about both and even lets us know what they will be similar to. The greater part of this is somewhat unbelievable.

We should trust the Bible completely or not trust it by any means. Concerning me, I trust it in its entirety. Jesus was Emmanuel, God with us. I accept to deny Jesus as the Christ, the Son of the Living God, is to deny salvation through Him."

3:4 Thou hast a couple names even in Sardis which have not debased their pieces of clothing; and they should stroll with me in white: for they are commendable.

Jesus is stating here there are a couple individuals even in this congregation of Sardis, or our fallen away church now that are still solid in the Lord. They trust reality instead of an untruth.

A polluted article of clothing is one not washed in the blood of the Lamb. The white that we should wear is a white robe made more white than snow by being washed in the blood of the Lamb. This is our robe of honorability that we will wear in heaven. "Honesty" implies in right remaining with God (Right standing with God).

The vast majority of the places of worship now that are similar to this congregation in Sardis, don't care to lecture or educate on the blood of Jesus. It was the shed blood that crushed Satan and obtained our salvation. We read in Hebrews, exactly how critical this shed blood is. Hebrews 9:22 "And everything is by the law cleansed with blood; and without shedding of blood is no abatement."

If we are not washed in the blood of the Lamb, then we are strolling in sin. We will concentrate on in a later lesson, in part seven of Revelation, about the colossal number from all countries remaining around the throne in their white robes. Disclosure 7:14 "And I said unto him, Sir, thou knowest. What's more, he said to me, these are they which left awesome tribulation, and have washed their robes, and made them white in the blood of the Lamb."

To prevent the force from claiming the blood, would deny us our entitlement to remain before the throne of God. Try not to be deceived. Believe the Word of God, the Bible. Give nobody a chance to convince you that it is not genuine.

3:5 He that overcometh, the same should be dressed in white clothing; and I won't abrogate his name out of the book of life, however I will admit his name before my Father, and before his blessed messengers.

This is one of the best guarantees in the Bible. We should Overcome the world and its teachings to acquire everlasting life. If we do succeed, our name will be composed in the Lamb's Book of Life, which will safeguard us unceasing life in paradise with Jesus.

On the off chance that we admit Jesus before men, He will admit us before His Father. Jesus is the Judge. We stand or fall by His summon.

You see from the announcement over that overcoming is not a luxurious situation, but rather a fight. Jesus won the war. We should enroll in this armed force of Jesus. We should battle until the very end, if important, for the standards He has taught us in the Bible.

Be solid; don't be driven away by all these new teachings of paradise on earth before Jesus comes. The main time the earth will be similar to paradise is the 1000 year rule of Jesus here. Withstand the villain and he will escape from you. Be a piece of the choose who can't be hoodwinked.

3:6 He that hath an ear, let him hear what the Spirit saith unto the houses of worship.

Again we are advised to hear what the Spirit said to the temple (churches).

3:7 And to the blessed messenger of the congregation in Philadelphia compose; These things saith he that is sacred, he that is genuine, he that hath the key of David, he that openeth, and no man shutteth; and shutteth, and no man openeth;

Philadelphia: The Danger of Failing to Advance - 1790 to 1900 AD - The Missionary Church.

The city of Philadelphia was 25 miles southeast of Sardis on a 800 foot rise. To this congregation, which Christ says has a little quality, the Lord comes to open a road of chance that no power in damnation can close. "Having the key of David" implies that He has the power to open this otherworldly entryway. The reference to the individuals who "say they are Jews and are not" alludes to all who reject Jesus Christ. Romans. 2 v.28-29 clarifies what constitutes a Jew:

For he is not a Jew, which is one apparently; nor is that circumcision, which is outward in the tissue: But he is a Jew, which is one internally; and circumcision is that of the heart, in the soul, and not in the letter; whose applause is not of men, but rather of God. (Romans 2 v.28-29)

Jesus demonstrates to Himself to this congregation of Philadelphia in the exceptionally same way that they adore Him.

1. He is Holy. Jesus instructs us to be Holy even as He is Holy, Leviticus 11:44, I Peter 1:15.

2. He demonstrates to Himself as truth. He is the Way, The Truth, and the Life, John 14:6.

Jesus is the one that opens the way to paradise or damnation for us. JESUS IS THE DOOR TO HEAVEN. He is the special case who can close or open either entryway. He removed the keys of hellfire from the fallen angel when Jesus went there and lectured. Jesus is the last Judge for everybody's resting place.

This congregation in Philadelphia and its typical church today, are very much aware of who Jesus is, as well as they are designing their lives after His. They are the very elect. Full of the Word, so full that it would be horrendously hard to mislead them.

God guarantees these devotees that He will keep them from the hour of enticement which will happen upon all the world. Note that the occasion talked about:

Is an unequivocal time period - "the hour."

Is a time of trial.

Was future from the season of John's composition.

Was to be around the world.

The guarantee, in Greek, was to "keep thee out of" the hour.

These realities make it obvious that the occasion alludes to the Great Tribulation portrayed in Mat. 24 v.15-22. Tribulation, Purpose of these adherents at Philadelphia who have just a "little quality" have in any case kept God's Word and have not denied His Name. God guarantees that they will get to be columns in the sanctuary of God. (Rev. 3 v.12) This congregation might have been little in number or in material assets, however God was going to make them solid. They are guaranteed an open entryway. In Scripture, an open entryway alludes to Christ (John 10 v.7), an opening to lecture the Gospel (Acts 5 v.19-20), and the bliss of the Church (Rev. 4 v.1). Each of these might be deciphered as the "open entryway" guaranteed to this congregation, even as each can be connected to the Church today.

In these end times, God is opening numerous enormous entryways of chance and there is dependably an inborn risk of neglecting to progress at Christ's order. You might feel you have just a little quality, yet God can make you a solid and powerful column in His Kingdom, an otherworldly warrior why should capable stroll through each entryway He opens. Give me a chance to ask you: What is keeping you away from satisfying God's require your life?

Dread?

Your accounts?

Your wellbeing?

Your associations with others?

God has set before you an open entryway which no man can close. Every one of the evil spirits in damnation can't close it. Jesus is the way. All you should do is stroll through those entryways in the all-powerful force of God.

3:8 I know thy works: observe, I have set before thee an open entryway, and no man can close it: for thou hast a little quality, and hast kept my assertion, and hast not denied my name.

Jesus knows about everything the houses of worship are doing. He has direct information, since He strolls in the church. Jesus is the entryway and has given Himself to us to experience to paradise. The entryway that Jesus opens must be shut by Him. Jesus tends to His own.

It is exceptionally intriguing here that He says this congregation has a little quality. This is valid for every solid devotee. In our shortcoming, Jesus is solid. The quality that supports us and sees us through is His, not our own. The great articulation Jesus makes about this congregation is that they have kept His Word.

We, as well, should be mindful so as to protect the Word of God. The Bible is our direction book for living. In the event that we transform it in any capacity, the directions won't work. Be that as it may, numerous have diluted the Word until it has been shortcircuited and lost force. We should not mess with the power. This congregation specified here may be little in size, yet huge in affection and the Holy Spirit. Once more, we see such a large number of preventing the name from claiming Jesus. I accept here that the name they are denying is that Jesus was God. We touched on it some time recently, however it merits saying again. Most temples today need to call Jesus: Prophet, Teacher, Healer, Man. Not very many understand that He was God show in the substance (God the Son). This is a critical thing, and will be said more as we go.

3:9 Behold, I will make them of the synagogue of Satan, which say they are Jews, and are not, but rather do lie; view, I will make them to come and love before thy feet, and to realize that I have cherished thee.

There is no distinction, truly, in somebody who takes after Satan and somebody who claims to be a Christian and is not. Both are lost.

The "synagogue of Satan" is only a position of love where God is not Lord. A Jewish synagogue could be of Satan if detestable won. An assortment of Christians meeting could likewise be a synagogue of Satan, if the genuine Word of God is not taught and got.

There will come a period when the Truth will win. The congregation, which does not trade off and wins unto the end, should rule with Christ. Jesus is simply reassuring this congregation that has made a decent attempt, that there will be a day of prize. The Christians will govern over the individuals who have rejected Jesus for a long time here on this planet, as we will see later on in Revelation. Jesus adores the unwavering. He has His ear swung to our requirements.

3:10 Because thou hast kept the expression of my understanding, I additionally will keep thee from the hour of allurement, which should happen upon all the world, to attempt them that abide upon the earth.

Trials, tribulations, and enticements come to all. It appears the gathering here specified, have been tried and found to remain in their allurement. There is a period of testing, and a period of triumph, or annihilation. Jesus was enticed forty days and evenings and turned out triumphant. At the point when trials come, we can do one of two things. We can remain against the allurement and experience triumph, or we can take the path of least resistance and succumb to enticement and tumble to crush. On the off chance that you are a Christian and if the enticement wins, then you will experience this specific allurement again and again until you remain against it and Overcome it.

It creates the impression this gathering said here has remained against these allurements, so their guarantee from Jesus is that they won't be required to experience the considerable enticement. There is a period determined of God when the enticements, tribulations, and trials will be great to the point that it will be by difficult to stand. A hour with God can be a particular time. God's chance and our time is not the same. This hour specified here unquestionably does not mean a hour, but rather a timeframe. (The Tribulation) There will be seven years of tribulation toward the end of the Gentile age. The last three and a half years of this will really be the rage of God. God has guaranteed the professors in the Lord Jesus Christ that we will be spared from the fury to come.

I trust this is the situation here. Temptation here, I accept, is the same as tribulation. Revelation 7:9 and 7:13-14 recounts the Christians who are spared from the insufferable enticement toward the end of three and a half years of tribulation.

Disclosure 7:9 "After this I observed, and, lo, an extraordinary large number, which no man could number, of all countries, and kindreds, and individuals, and tongues, remained before the throne, and before the Lamb, dressed with white robes, and palms in their grasp;"

Disclosure 7:13 "And one of the senior citizens replied, saying unto me, what are these which are displayed in white robes? What's more, whence came they?" Revelation 7:14 "And I said unto him, Sir, thou knowest. What's more, he said to me, these are they which left awesome tribulation, and have washed their robes, and made them white in the blood of the Lamb."

These are devotees to Jesus the Christ (the spared) who have been brought out (spared in) of incredible tribulation.

Matthew 24:21-22 depicts the seriousness of this incredible tribulation.

Matthew 24:21 "For then might be extraordinary tribulation, for example, was not following the start of the world to this time, no, nor ever might be." "And aside from those days ought to be abbreviated, there ought to no tissue be spared: yet for the choose's purpose those days should be abbreviated."

This is the hour of allurement, I trust, this Scripture in Revelation 3:10 is talking about. The professors in Jesus will be taken out just before this starts.

3:11 Behold, I come rapidly: hold that quick which thou hast, that no man take thy crown.

This announcement in V-11 is simply checking what we said over, that there is a test time for the devotees. We will be required to stand; and when we do, then we will be raptured and spared from the horrors.

3:12 Him that overcometh will I make a column in the sanctuary of my God, and he should go not any more out: and I will compose upon him the name of my God, and the name of the city of my God, [which is] new Jerusalem, which cometh down out of paradise from my God: and [I will compose upon him] my new name.

Again we see here that there is something that we should succeed. A man commonly is talked about as a mainstay of the group, or a mainstay of the congregation, which just means, that they are solid and are holding up the congregation. These individuals would be similar to establishing fathers, high in standards. They would be the ones who might see to it that the congregation remains focused ground.

This composition of the name of God just implies that we are fixed into His kingdom.

If we somehow managed to peruse all that much about this city, we would find that occasionally it is talked about as a bride. The adherents to Jesus are the lady of Christ. This name of the city being on the devotees just demonstrates that we are the spouse of Christ.

This new name of Jesus that is composed upon us is demonstrating that we are Jesus' ownership. We are His; we have been purchased and paid for with His blood.

When it says we should no more go out, it implies that our everlasting home arrives with Jesus.

Verse 12 is stating that we, the devotees, have put our trust and confidence in Jesus and continued hardship. We then have an unfathomable length of time of only unadulterated euphoria in this New Jerusalem with Jesus. Once we have gone from death into life through tolerating Jesus as our Lord and Savior, we are fixed by Jesus Himself. We fit in with Him. No one can grab us move in an opposite direction from Him. Jesus has the keys. Look to Him and no other. He is salvation.

3:13 He that hath an ear, let him hear what the Spirit saith unto the places of worship.

By and by we are advised to hear what the Spirit said to the places of worship by Jesus Himself who talked these words as these messages to these holy places are imprinted in red. He reminds us at the end of the day here to open the ears of our comprehension to His teachings.

3:14 And unto the blessed messenger of the congregation of the Laodiceans compose; These things saith the Amen, the unwavering and genuine witness, the start of the formation of God;

The Danger of Luke Warmness - 1900 AD - Current - The Apostate

Voyaging 45 miles southeast from Philadelphia, one would touch base at the invigorated city of Laodicea where a few noteworthy streets join. Prescription, creation of eye salve, fleece appropriation, assembling, and managing an account conveyed popularity to this city. It is fascinating to note how Christ related His message to these characteristics of the city in verses 17-18. The general population of Laodicea felt they don't required anything. They bragged of their wealth, yet they were profoundly poor. In spite of the fact that they were popular for their eye ointment, they were profoundly visually impaired. They were known for their fine fleece, yet they were profoundly bare. How would you know whether you are tepid? Put forth these inquiries:

It is safe to say that you are focused on evangelism and missions?

It is safe to say that you are focused on carrying on with a blessed life?

It is safe to say that you are focused on your neighborhood church partnership?

It is safe to say that you are focused on investing energy in petition to God, revere and the Word?

It is safe to say that you are focused on different adherents to the Body of Christ?

It is safe to say that you are effectively supporting God's work with your funds?

The general population at Laodicea were profoundly tepid and Christ said their condition must be cured. He ordered them to do three things which we additionally should would on the off chance that we like to kill our tepidness:

1. Purchase of me Gold, Tried in the Fire Gold is refined by the flame. Give the Word of God a chance to refine you profoundly and consume with extreme heat the Luke warmness in your life:

The expressions of the Lord are immaculate words: as silver attempted in a heater of earth, decontaminated seven times. (Psalms 12 v.6)

2. Purchase of me White Raiment - Allow God to change you by making a reestablished duty to exemplary living:

Furthermore, that ye put on the new man, which after God is made in honesty and genuine heavenliness. (Esp. 4 v.24)

3. Anoint your Eyes so You Can See - Receive the intense disclosure of God through Jesus Christ which will open your blinded eyes and impact genuine change in your life:

For God, who instructed the light to sparkle out of haziness, hath sparkled in our souls, to give the light of the information of the magnificence of God notwithstanding Jesus Christ. (2 Cor. 4 v6).

The book of Colossians, and in addition this message here, was to the Laodiceans. We find in Colossians 4:13 and 16. They were an extremely noticeable region. It appears that Paul and Jesus (in the book of Revelation) cautioned them about their absence of enthusiasm in their congregation.

In V-14 above Jesus is called "Amen". This is an exceptionally strange name for Him. I trust that it implies when He has said something, it is last. There is no space for talk. His announcements are supreme.

Jesus is talked about as "faithful". He is deserving of our confidence in Him.

Jesus is Truth. His witness is genuine on the grounds that He Himself experienced it. It doesn't falter. It is fact. He made everything in the earth as we probably am aware it. We can undoubtedly see from John that Jesus made everything. John 1:1 "At the outset was the Word, and the Word was with God, and the Word was God." John 1:2 "The same was in the first place with God." John 1:3 All things were made by him; and without him was not anything made that was made."

Jesus is the Creator for goodness' sake.

3:15 I know thy works, that thou workmanship neither icy nor hot: I would thou wert chilly or hot.

The Laodicean church was self-satisfied. They experienced the custom of chapel. They felt in the event that they went to chapel maybe a couple hours a week, they had done their obligation toward God. Vain love is far more terrible than not being spared at all. If we are not spared, in any event we understand it. Someone could lead us to God.

In the congregation at Laodicea, and in our defector temples today, they felt no requirement for more than they had. They were not in any case mindful that salvation was not as of now theirs.

Jesus had told the copyists and Pharisees that the publicans and mistresses will probably acquire paradise, Matthew 21:31. The individuals who trust they needn't bother with a doctor might pass on of some fear ailment before they considerably find they have it. Those who know they have a terrible malady can start to attempt to dispose of it.

When somebody has been acquainted with Jesus and starts to underestimate Him, it is exceptionally pitiful. This is the thing that I find in this congregation at Laodicea and in our formal temples of today.

Second Peter 2:21 is a sacred text we have to take notice of. "For it had been exceptional for them not to have known the method for nobility, than, after they have known [it], to turn from the sacred precept conveyed unto them.

A little learning is bad. We should be ablaze for God to satisfy a blessed God. Jesus must be Lord of our life. He will acknowledge no less.

3:16 So then since thou craftsmanship tepid, and neither chilly nor hot, I will spue thee out of my mouth.

Who needs tepid espresso or tea? No one. Jesus is stating, If you don't quit being languid in your love, I will heave you out. This is a solid cautioning that Jesus is disappointed. Jesus does not need only listeners to the Word, but rather doers. Don't be a seat hotter, get included.

3:17 Because thou sayest, I am rich, and expanded with products, and have need of nothing; and knowest not that thou workmanship vomited, and hopeless, and poor, and blind, and exposed:

Riches can once in a while give us a misguided feeling of security. It is exceptionally troublesome for an extremely affluent individual to be modest and understand a requirement for God. It is not unthinkable, simply troublesome. Some huge houses of worship can meet a fabulously expansive spending plan in light of the general population of awesome riches who go to. I find that it is much harder to tithe on a wage of 500,000.00 every year than it is on 5,000.00 for every year. The individual giving is not understanding that all he has fits in with God. He just takes a gander at the expansive "blessing" and says that is sufficient.

God favors a happy supplier, not a hesitant giver. God guarantees again and again to meet our needs. This congregation and its kin have no physical need. They think they can pay out of anything. It is for certain that we appeared on the scene bare, and that is the way we will clear out.

We will leave all the huge autos, enormous houses, and precious stone rings behind. God won't be awed by how much natural riches you have obtained. He claims everything. Your tiny bit in correlation won't awe Him, regardless of the possibility that you include it the billions.

We all face Jesus with only our confidence and works accomplished for Him to affirm of us. There is no fortune that will check then, however the fortune that we have accumulated in paradise.

This congregation and these rich individuals should be felt sorry for by us. Their smug state of mind keeps them from developing in the Lord. A Christian never stops; on the off chance that we are not developing, then we are falling ceaselessly. This congregation is oblivious in regard to the truth of their condition. They are oblivious to the necessities of others. Unless you have felt need yourself, you can't identify with it.

3:18 I direct thee to purchase of me gold attempted in the flame, that thou mayest be rich; and white garment, that thou mayest be dressed, and [that] the disgrace of thy bareness don't show up; and anoint thine eyes with eyesalve, that thou mayest see.

"Gold tried in the fire" means pure gold. Jesus is speaking of being rich in the sight of God. We need to be rich in good works laying up our treasures in heaven "where moth nor rust doth not corrupt. ..", Matthew 6:19-20.

The only riches worth having are the ones that we can collect on in heaven.

White raiment garments are only available if we are washed in the blood of the Lamb. Christians who are dressed in white robes standing around the throne of God are wearing garments Jesus has purchased with His own precious blood. We do not have enough money to buy them. They are a free gift to all believers in Jesus. In the sight of God, we are all naked until we are clothed in this white robe.

It is a very serious mistake to trust in uncertain riches. The rich young ruler who came to Jesus to find what he must do to be saved, went away sorrowful when he found he must give away his gold, which was wealth, Matthew 19:16-24.

The young man traded all of eternity with God for momentary wealth here on earth. We are all naked before God, because He can see right through us into our heart. Wash your eyes out where you can see clearly.

3:19 As many as I love, I rebuke and chasten: be zealous therefore, and repent.

Jesus says here that He rebukes this church because He loves them. Proverbs 19:18 "Chasten thy son while there is hope, and let not thy soul spare for his crying."

Jesus tells this church to get excited about serving Jesus and repent of their lukewarmness. When Jesus returns, we must be found working. Work for the night is coming when man's work is done.

Just as a fruit tree produces much more fruit after it is pruned, Jesus here is pruning the church so it will produce much fruit. Tribulation comes to make us strong. Perhaps this church would be stronger if it faced a little tribulation.

As many as I love, I rebuke and chasten: be zealous therefore, and repent.

In the closing appeal of these messages to the churches, Jesus issues a final call as we see in the next scripture.

3:20 Behold, I remain at the entryway, and thump: if any man hear my voice, and open the entryway, I will come into him, and will sup with him, and he with me.

Here we see a horrible scene. Jesus is outside attempting to get in. Jesus will thump for some time, yet there will come a period, in the event that we don't permit Him to come in, that He will stop knocking. Jesus needs to come and live within each of us. We have to permit Jesus to survive us.

Galatians 2:20, "I am killed with Christ: by and by I live: yet not I, but rather Christ liveth in me: and the life which I now live in the tissue I live by the confidence of the Son of God, who cherished me, and gave himself for me."

Our substance is nothing. It will soon pass. The Spirit which stays in us is the essential thing; it is unceasing.

In V-20 Jesus says "will sup with him". He is talking about His fellowshipping with us. He cherished us so much that He passed on for each of us. He needs to be our companion.

3:21 To him that overcometh will I allow to sit with me in my throne, even as I additionally succeeded, and am set down with my Father in his throne.

Jesus is sitting at the right hand of God the Father in paradise. On the off chance that we live satisfying to Him, we should be situated on thrones with Jesus.

Luke 22:29-30 "And I name unto you a kingdom, as my Father hath designated unto me;" Luke 22:30 "That ye might eat and drink at my table in my kingdom, and sit on thrones judging the twelve tribes of Israel." Jesus' arrangement for every one of us, is that we will be situated with Him in great spots. Jesus conquered the world when He presented His will to the Father's will. He overcame sin and passing on the cross. We will be an overcomer when we present our will to His.

"Not my will but rather thine O Lord" ought to be the cry of each adherent to Christ.

3:22 He that hath an ear, let him hear what the Spirit saith unto the places of worship.

This is the last time that Jesus Himself will identify with the holy places. Every congregation has its own independence. Did you see yourself or your congregation in any of them?

At the end of the day, toward the end of this message, Jesus instructs them to hear and comprehend; on the grounds that this message, as every one of the others, originated from the Spirit.

Since Christ cherishes us, He reproaches us. Since He tends to us, He cautions us of particular risks in these end days of time.

The Danger of Diminishing Love (Represented by the congregation at Ephesus)

The Danger of Fearing, Suffering (Represented by the congregation at Smyrna)

The Danger of Doctrinal Compromise (Represented by the congregation at Pergamos)

The Danger of Moral Compromise (Represented by the congregation at Thyatira)

The Danger of Spiritual Death (Represented by the congregation at Sardis)

The Danger of Failing to Advance (Represented by the congregation at Philadelphia)

The Danger of Luke Warmness (Represented by the congregation at Laodicea)

In these end entries we see a photo of:

The standing Christ, symbolizing His preparation to enter our individual lives and corporate church associations to amend each insufficiency.

The thumping Christ, who looks for us constantly, He continues thumping.

The arguing Christ, persistently addressing us, charming us to a more close association with Him.

The infiltrating Christ, who as we open the entryway of our lives to Him enters in.

The sidekick Christ, getting a charge out of sweet cooperation and fellowship with us, get ready and preparing us for His soon return.

Here are Nine Promises to Overcomers Jesus is not returning for a powerless, pallid, vanquished Church. He is returning for a strong effective Church made out of men and ladies who have figured out how to succeed. In each of His messages to the seven houses of worship, Jesus gave a particular guarantee to the individuals who succeed.

1. Overcomers Will Eat of the Tree of Life. -"He that hath an ear, let him hear what the Spirit saith unto the places of worship: To him that overcometh will I provide for eat of the tree of life, which is amidst the heaven of God" (Rev. 2 v.7). The individuals who Overcome will acquire interminable life. They will live until the end of time!

2. Overcomers Will Not be Hurt by the Second Death. - "He that hath an ear, let him hear what the Spirit saith unto the temples; He that overcometh might not be harmed of the second demise." (Rev. 2 v.11) Those who Overcome have their names written in the Book of Life and are a piece of the primary revival. The "second passing" is recognized in Rev. 20 v.14 as the pool of flame. The second passing has no control over the exemplary who are a piece of the principal restoration: "Favored and sacred is he that hath part in the main revival: on such the second demise hath no force, yet they should be clerics of God and of Christ and might rule with him a thousand years." (Rev. 20 v.6)

3. Overcomers Will Eat of the Hidden Manna. "He that hath an ear, let him hear what the Spirit saith unto the holy places; To him that overcometh will I provide for eat of the shrouded nourishment." (Rev. 2 v17) The "shrouded sustenance" alludes to Christ since He is the Bread of Life. (John 6 v.33 35) Jesus, in all His totality, will be showed to the individuals who Overcome and they will share of all that He is and has!

4. The individuals Who Overcome Will be Given a New Name. - "I will compose upon him the name of my God, and the name of the city of my God, which is new Jerusalem, which cometh down out of paradise from my God: and I will compose upon him my new name". (Rev. 3 v.12) To "compose the name after something" is a typical Hebrew expression used to show taking supreme ownership of something. Christ will compose His Name upon the temples of the individuals who succeed, perpetually recognizing them as His own particular ownership.

5. Overcomers Will Be Given Power Over the Nations. - "And he that overcometh, and keepeth my works unto the end, to him will I give control over the countries." (Rev. 2 v.26) Overcomers will rule with Christ and sit in judgment over the countries. (Rev. 20 v.4)

6. Overcomers Will Be Clothed in White Garments. - "He that overcometh, the same should be dressed in white attire; and I won't rub out his name out of the book of life, however I will admit his name before my Father, and before his blessed messengers". (Rev. 3 v.5) The white pieces of clothing that Overcomers will wear speaks to the uprightness of the holy people: "And to her was allowed that she ought to be displayed in fine material, perfect and white; for the fine material is the exemplary nature of holy people" (Rev. 19 v.8) John saw the reclaimed remaining before the throne of God, dressed in white robes with palms in their grasp. (Rev. 7 v.9)

7. Overcomers Will Be a Pillar in the Temple in the New Jerusalem. - "Him that overcometh will I make a column in the sanctuary of my God, and he might go not any more out: and I will compose upon him the name of my God, and the name of the city of my God, which is new Jerusalem, which cometh down out of paradise from my God: and I will compose upon him my new name." (Rev. 3 v.12) A column is perpetual, so Christ's guarantee to the individuals who Overcome implies He will give them a lasting spot in the New Jerusalem. Literally nothing will have the capacity to expel them from their place in great Jerusalem!

8. Overcomers Will Sit With Christ on His Throne. - "To him that overcometh will I allow to sit with me in my throne, even as I additionally succeeded, and am set down with my Father in his throne." (Rev. 3 v.21) Those who Overcome will sit with Christ on His throne and rule with Him until the end of time!

9. Overcomers Will Inherit All Things. -"He that overcometh might acquire all things; and I will be his God, and he should be my child". (Rev. 21 v.7) This guarantee is the summation of the considerable number of gifts God can offer. Like a child taking ownership of his legacy, the individuals who Overcome will take ownership of all their Heavenly Father has arranged for them.

Your Are Called to Overcome. - Beloved, these guarantees don't have a place with apathetic, uncommitted, trading off, frightful, unfaithful adherents, yet to the individuals who succeed! "Overcome" in these verses is interpreted from the Greek work, "nikao," which signifies "to win." When Christ calls us to succeed, He is calling us to vanquish by finding our foe, drawing in him in battle, and crushing him! We are called to Overcome and CONQUER the tissue!

"Because then as Christ hath languished over us in the tissue, arm yourselves similarly with the same personality: for he that hath endured in the substance hath quit sin; That he no more ought to experience whatever is left of his time in the tissue to the desire of men, yet to the will of God? (1 Peter 4 v.1-2)

We are called to Overcome and Conquer the world! Jesus said: "on the planet ye should have tribulation: yet be of encouragement; I have Overcome the world."

We are called to Overcome and Conquer sin! "For sin should not have domain over you: (Romans 6 v.14).

You can Overcome the substance, the world, sin, Satan and his abhorrent realms as a result of Jesus Christ who lives inside of you! In the Spirit, John witnessed the colossal triumph that fits in with God's kin and proclaimed, "And they overcame him by the blood of the Lamb, and the expression of their affirmation; and they adored not their lives unto the demise." (Rev. 12 v.11) We are called to Overcome and Conquer Satan! "Ye are of God, little kids, and have Overcome them: on the grounds that more prominent is he that is in you, than he that is on the planet." (1 John 4 v.4)

Christ has succeed, and by His Spirit living inside of us, we can do likewise: "For at all is conceived of God overcometh the world: and this is the triumph that overcometh the world, even our confidence. Who is he that overcometh the world, yet he that believeth that Jesus is the Son of God (1 John 5 v. 4-5).

You don't Overcome due to who you are. It is not as a result of any value of your own, your benevolent acts, your quality, or whatever else you have. You can Overcome the substance, the world, sin, Satan and his shrewd realms in view of Jesus Christ who lives inside of you! In the Spirit, John witnessed the immense triumph that has a place with God's kin and announced, "And they overcame him by the blood of the Lamb, and the expression of their confirmation; and they adored not their lives unto the demise." (Rev. 12 v.11) We are called to Overcome and Conquer Satan! "Ye are of God, little kids, and have Overcome them: in light of the fact that more prominent is he that is in you, than he that is on the planet." (1 John 4 v.4)

Darling, you are an overcomer and more than a victor through Him who adored you. (Romans 8 v.36) Your triumph is fixed with the confirmation of the blood of Jesus Christ!

Our Yea and Amen - The last awesome anointing that will fall on this planet before the arrival of Jesus Christ is the supplication to God anointing. In Rev. 3 v.14, there is a regularly disregarded, yet lovely photo of Jesus' part as your request to God accomplice.

Jesus proclaims, "These things saith the Amen" which means He is the "So be it". The Hebrew rendering of Isaiah 65 v.16 additionally calls God "the God of Amen." What does this mean? The first importance of the verb "to so be it" is utilized to attest that somebody is solid, dependable, and honest. It is utilized as a part of the Old Testament in two ways:

It echoes a pioneer's request to God or applause. It signifies "Yes, in reality" or "might it be so in extremely truth." (For illustrations, see Psalms 41 v.13; 72 v.19; 106 v.48; 1 Chronicles 16 v.36; and Nehemiah 8 v.6)

It is utilized as the consent of an audience to a regal announcement or reason. (For samples, see 1 Kings 1 v.36; and Jeremiah 11 v.5)

At the point when Scripture announces that Jesus is the "So be it," it implies that He is the awesome "Yes" to the petitions to God of God's kin at whatever point they are made as per God's will:

"For every one of the guarantees of God in him are yea, and in him Amen, unto the wonderfulness of God by us". (2 Cor. 1 v.20)

Picture this: Jesus is situated at the Father's side. As you enter the throne room in supplication to God to intervene as indicated by the will of God helped by the Spirit indwelling you, Jesus joins His omnipotent mediation with yours, then He swings to the Father and seals it with His "Yes and Amen!" The "So be it", so be it, is articulated to the Father through Christ as we claim God's guarantees in petition to God!

To close this part I need to you to peruse Rev. 1 verse 3 once more:

Favored [is] he that readeth, and they that hear the expressions of this prescience, and keep those things which are composed in that: for the time [is] within reach.

Parts 2 and 3 are 2 of the most essential sections in the Book of Revelation in my brain. I prescribe you re-read these and study them, then contrast them with your congregation. Not all houses of worship are similar and much false educating or instructing about common hobbies rather than the gospel message is being taught today in numerous congregations.

CHAPTER 4

The Door Opened

4:1 After this I looked, and, view, an entryway [was] opened in paradise: and the principal voice which I heard [was] in a manner of speaking of a trumpet chatting with me; which said, Come up here, and I will shew thee things which should be in the future.

What do you believe is being discussed in this first verse? (Some trust this is delineating the Rapture)

The entryway implies passage by method for disclosure into paradise. The charge "Come up here most likely does not allude particularly to the Rapture, yet rather to the adjustment in scene for John who is to get disclosure about future occasions. This starts the last area of the book portraying the occasions that take after the congregation age.

Matthew 24:31 - And he might send his blessed messengers with an extraordinary sound of a trumpet, and they should assemble his choose from the four winds, from one end of paradise to the next. All the choose are accumulated and gathered before Christ. This is the zenith of world history, introducing the millennial rule of Christ.

This will be the trumpet of get together (the silver trumpet of recovery) "four" means the whole world. We've all heard the colloquialism: "from the four corners of the earth I'm certain. This get together won't be just Americans, yet the genuine devotees from each nation of the world. These "blessed messengers" are serving spirits who do these requests of their Lord and Master. The "He" here is Jesus (Messiah), however now He is Lord of rulers and King of rulers.

This "sound of a Trumpet" could be a strict trumpet blowing, or it could be the voice of our Lord seeming like a trumpet. This is the last sequential notice of silver in the Bible. There will be no silver in paradise. "Silver" means recovery, and there is no silver there; on the grounds that we have as of now been reclaimed. There is just gold in paradise. In the Holy of Holies, there was gold, in light of the fact that in the vicinity of God, there was just gold. This assembling of His choose is what is generally alluded to as the satisfaction of the congregation. His congregation has no section. It is "all" who genuinely have confidence in the Lord Jesus Christ.

1 Corinthians 15:52 In a minute, in the twinkling of an eye, at the last trump: for the trumpet should sound, and the dead might be raised ethical, and we should be changed.

I Thessalonians 4:16-17 "For the Lord himself might slip from paradise with a yell, with the voice of the chief heavenly messenger, and with the trump of God: and the dead in Christ should rise first:" "Then we which are alive [and] remain should be made up for lost time together with them in the mists, to meet the Lord noticeable all around: thus should we ever be with the Lord. To truly comprehend read the greater part of this record. I have picked only two verses from the record for here. This will happen so rapidly that you would not have sufficient energy to flicker your eye.

The "I" in verse 1 is obviously John who is composing this. Jesus has been talking in the past part directly. Now we get notification from John about the things he saw. This is after Jesus completes His messages to the seven places of worship.

We will see the number "seven" all through Revelation. Seven signifies "profoundly complete". Perhaps in this number, God is stating, this is it. There is nothing else to read. If you can't get the message in Revelation, you can't get it.

John investigates paradise and is startled "see". The entryway of paradise is open. Jesus is the way to paradise. The entryway of paradise is not shut to the devotees to the Lord Jesus Christ. Jesus opened the route to the very throne of God, when the sanctuary window ornament was torn from the top to the base (opening the path to the sacred of holies), when He passed on the cross, Matthew 27:51.

"Looked" is essential also. We should look for before we can discover. Jesus is returning for the individuals who are searching for Him.

Notice, this entryway was "opened" in the previous tense. It is not going to be opened. Jesus opened it for us. It is currently open to devotees. Paradise is in a matter of seconds the home of God. It will likewise be our interminable home.

There are a few different occasions in the Bible where the entryway of paradise was opened. Numerous prophets, additionally, have seen a dream of the superb.

Ezekiel talks about his investigate paradise. Daniel had a look into paradise. At the point when Stephen was stoned to death, he saw into paradise.

At the point when Stephen investigated paradise, he saw Jesus remaining at the right hand of God. Most times Jesus is situated at the right hand since His work is finished, however I trust that He was remaining to get His loyal worker, Stephen, home.

This entryway has never been shut to the genuine adherents.

The principal voice that John hears in V-1 is either the voice of Jesus Himself, or the voice of Jesus' very own messenger. It has no effect; the message itself is from Jesus. At the point when the Lord calls us to meet Him noticeable all around, when the congregation is gotten away, we will hear the trumpet; the silver trumpet of recovery.

In Both Matthew 24:31 and I Thessalonians

4:16 I read at first the voice and the trumpet appear to be exchangeable. The voice of Jesus and His own holy messenger are a touch of befuddling, also. Whichever way the message is from Jesus. This trumpet was conversing with John.

The voice that John heard was similar to a trumpet. This is an effective voice; it gives a genuine sound. This voice is conversing with us, and John.

The voice said, "come up here" to John, however is continually saying to us, "come up here". Get your psyche off the things of this world and look heavenward. The call of Jesus has dependably been "come". In this particular sentence, He tells John "come up here", then includes why.

Jesus, the voice, says, "I will shew thee things which should be hereafter." John will be demonstrated an investigate the future. John could have had a dream of this, or he could have been transported into paradise for a minute so as to see all of this. We do realize that review something from the earth makes us see only the without further ado. From a magnificent point, we can see yesterday and tomorrow.

Notice that these things of the great beyond should be. Why must they be? Since God requested it from the earliest starting point of the world and God never shows signs of change. We should change to fit His arrangement, not the a different way.

John is not told a particular time in the great beyond, just that it will be later than the present time he is in.

John is presently seeing into the future, after the professors in Christ are raptured into paradise, in this specific scene.

4:2 And quickly I was in the soul: and, observe, a throne was set in paradise, and [one] sat on the throne.

John was at that point in the Spirit we know from a past lesson, however this implies a more profound involvement in the Spirit. A twofold measurement of the Spirit, you might say.

John was changed or transported, in a flash. This throne, as we said some time recently, has been seen by numerous in the Bible. "One" does not truly signify "one" but rather, I trust it implies the solidarity of the trinity.

God the Father God the Son or God the Word God the Holy Spirit "Sat" is characteristic that the work is finished.

A throne demonstrates rulership and power. Notice that the "throne" was "set in paradise"; set is past tense. This throne is involved even now in paradise, where Jesus sits at the right hand of the Father.

4:3 And he that sat was to look upon like a jasper and a sardine stone: and [there was] a rainbow indirect the throne, in sight such as unto an emerald.

The "jasper and sardine stone" were the most valuable of all stones. The excellence of God was dazzling to the point that John couldn't depict Him. The jasper was the last and the sardine the principal stone in the breastplate worn by the esteemed cleric, Exodus 28:17-20. These stones are in the establishment of the new Jerusalem, Revelation 21:19-20.

The precious stone and ruby are implied by these stone. These stones are known for their clearness and splendor.

There was a precious stone between the breastplate and the heart of the consecrated cleric. The name engraved on this stone, I accept, is the unspeakable name of God Almighty. The jewel stone beside the heart remained for immaculateness and leniency.

The emerald is another valuable stone, green in color. Green signifies "natural or of the earth". The emerald was additionally part of the breastplate, and of the establishment of New Jerusalem.

The estimation of these three distinct stones is more prominent than different stones. These are named valuable stones and are extremely costly.

This rainbow is green (natural) to demonstrate the pledge in the middle of God and man. The principal rainbow said was an indication of a guarantee from God to man. God would never again demolish the earth by water. Sometimes it is known as a bow, and at times a rainbow. The rainbow encompasses the throne as a consistent suggestion to God and man of the contract. This is an excellent incredible beautiful sight to behold.

4:4 And indirect the throne [were] four and twenty seats: and upon the seats I saw four and twenty older folks sitting, dressed in white attire; and they had on their heads crowns of gold.

The twenty-four seats were really thrones. Miniature thrones in power, subordinate to God, yet all things considered they encompass the throne of God.

The twenty-four seniors who speak to the recovered in paradise recognize that people were made by God for His great delight. Their reaction of commendation perceives the sway of God over our lives.

A standout amongst the most disputable inquiries raised by this vision of the throne of God is the character of the 24 senior citizens.

In Rev. 5 v.9 the Scriptures lets us know the four and twenty senior citizens sung another tune. "Also, they sung another tune, saying, Thou are qualified to take the book, and to open the seals thereof: for thou wast killed, and hast reclaimed "us" to God by the blood out of each related, and tongue, and individuals, and country.

Notice "and hast recovered us" along these lines uncovering their human instinct. These 24 senior citizens are recovered men. Once their human instinct was affirmed, it got to be clear that the Rapture was imagined by Rev. 4 v.1 as happening before the Tribulation. Happiness For this scene, which is of the throne of God in paradise just before the 7-year Tribulation as characterized in sections 6-19, pictures twenty-four men or "senior citizens" in the vicinity of God.

Twelve is an otherworldly number which needs to do with representation. The number twenty-four, I accept, could be two twelve's.

One twelve for the Old Testament

One twelve for the New Testament

The twelve prophets speak to the devotees of the Old Testament. The twelve supporters speak to all devotees from the New Testament.

There are numerous different schools of thought on the twenty-four.

John, "the devoted witness" watches these occasions quickly after the congregation age has been finished up and only before the start of the Tribulation. These men, whether 12 who speak to Israel and 12 who speak to the congregation, or 24 exceptional Christian pioneers in all congregation history, has no effect, they all are reclaimed men! They are reclaimed holy people who are in paradise just before the disclosure of the Tribulation that takes after. Like John, they are a piece of the pre-tribulation bliss in their celebrated bodies worshiping every one of the three individuals from the Trinity.

This scene in paradise does not happen amidst the Tribulation or at its end, however before it starts.

These Old Testament devotees were anticipating Messiah and were lectured, when Jesus lectured in damnation and carried imprisonment hostage out with Him.

See every one of the twenty-four were wearing white robes. White robes are worn by professors in Jesus, who have washed their robes in the blood of Jesus and are made white as snow. All through the Old Testament individuals like David were searching for the Savior. They accepted, despite the fact that they were looking forward rather than in reverse to Him.

There are more than thirty-seven Old Testament sacred writings which specify the happening to Jesus Christ. These were satisfied, each one. It is not preposterous to talk about Old Testament devotees.

These crowns that they had on their heads were gold. This demonstrated they don't had anything to do with these crowns being put on their heads. Gold means the virtue of God. God set these crowns on their head. The beauty of God set these crowns on their head. They don't did anything to gain them. It was a free blessing from God for accepting. Crowns show rulership, and we adherents are guaranteed that we will rule with Jesus.

4:5 And out of the throne continued lightnings and thunderings and voices: and [there were] seven lights of flame blazing before the throne, which are the seven Spirits of God.

The "lightnings and thunderings" demonstrated the grandness and greatness of God. Lightning, tremors, and thunderings all through the Bible have been an outward decree of God. Indeed, even at the foot of Mount Sinai the general population feared God, as a result of simply such appearances.

The "seven lights" are a typical number covering every one of the workings of the Spirit of God.

The seven spirits of God alludes to according to the Lord or attributes of God. (Zech. 4:10 and Isaiah 11:2) "the seven Spirits" mean the total of the force of the Spirit is show there at the throne and radiates out to the twenty-four or all Christendom. Fire all through the Bible has been typical of God, as in the blazing hedge, Exodus 3:2. In Hebrews 12:28-29, we are advised to serve God with veneration and Godly apprehension, since God is a devouring flame.

We don't totally comprehend God, yet we should acknowledge and trust God. This Spirit of God which is smoldering is to light up the psyches and Spirits of all who will acknowledge it. Jesus is the Light.

Somehow, all three are present in these lamps (Spirit) that illuminate.

4:6 And before the throne [there was] an ocean of glass such as unto precious stone: and amidst the throne, and circuitous the throne, [were] four monsters brimming with eyes before and behind.

This "ocean of glass" helps us all that much to remember the laver in the sanctuary in the wild. Generally as this symbolized sanctification in the sanctuary, this, as well, could symbolize the requirement for absolution while in transit to the throne.

All around the throne were the four beasts. Probably somewhat better interpretation would have been living ones. The number "four" demonstrates the comprehensiveness of these monsters or living beings. In Isaiah 6:2-13 and in Ezekiel 1:5-28, these living creatures are likewise called "seraphim" and "cherabim". These brutes, or living creatures, encompassing the throne are loaded with eyes which implies their shrewdness was overpowering.

The 4 Beasts or living Creatures are most likely blessed messengers who protect the throne of God. The eyes symbolize shrewdness, and the wings delineate movement. They revere God as did the seraphim in Isaiah's vision. (Isaiah 6 v.1-3) The lion speaks to quality, (Psalms 103 v.20) The calf administration, (Heb.1 v.14) The substance of a man insight, (Luke 2 v.52) and the falcon quickness. (Dan 9 v.21) The heavenly vision has a solid implication to Ezekiel 1 v.4-14.

The eyes signify shrewdness or intelligence. These creatures looking "before and behind" means they think over into times past and, likewise, look forward into things to come. These living ones, or living creatures, likewise indicate the four accounts, Matthew, Mark, Luke, and John.

Those books really are brimming with insight. Matthew looks back at the historical backdrop of Jesus, and part 24 looks ahead to the final days.

4:7 And the main monster [was] like a lion, and the second brute like a calf, and the third mammoth had a face as a man, and the fourth monster [was] like a flying hawk.

The four living creatures demonstrate the four accounts: Matthew Jesus is appeared as the Lion of the tribe of Judah. The parentage of Jesus is in Matthew, demonstrating that Jesus genuinely was the Lion of the tribe of Judah.

Mark -Jesus is appeared as the worker of man (calf).

Luke - Jesus is appeared as a man

John - Jesus is shown as God (eagle).

In John 1:1, Jesus, the Word, is in fact God the Word, God the Son. God in the flesh of man. Despite the fact that the four accounts recount the same story basically, they additionally indicate four distinctive personalities. You can without much of a stretch see why these brutes, living creatures, are typically the four accounts.

4:8 And the four mammoths had each of them six wings about [him]; and [they were] loaded with eyes inside: and they rest not day and night, saying, Holy, sacred, blessed, Lord God Almighty, which was, and will be, and is to come.

Sacred, heavenly, blessed. This is the cry of these radiant animals who know God as He truly seems to be. It has been recommended that every "heavenly" is coordinated to one of the individuals from the Trinity. At that point these animals help us to remember the One who "is to come." The arrival of Christ is ensured in the expressions of these magnificent hosts. In Acts 1:9-11 celestial creatures depict how Christ will truly return "in like way as ye have seen him go". Here these holy messengers in paradise reaffirm that guarantee.

The six wings discussed in Isaiah 6 appear to show lowliness, submission, and adoration to God. The number six makes me accept, likewise, that these wings show work and action (six-day work). It appears to be here that one of their errands was to broadcast the sacredness of God. I truly trust the three "sacred" and "Master God Almighty" demonstrate Father, Word, Holy Ghost.

The "which was, and will be, and is to come" just promotes that idea and demonstrates to us the unfathomable length of time of this three in one. We do know from First John 5:7 that there are three in heaven. "For there are three that bear record in paradise, the Father, the Word, and the Holy Ghost: and these three are one."

4:9And when those mammoths give radiance and respect and because of him that sat on the throne, who liveth for ever and ever,

This "when the monsters give eminence and respect and much appreciated" is a ceaseless thing. The four accounts have broadcasted this before, are announcing it now, and will declare it for all of time everlasting.

"The giving of "honor" continues forever and on. The giving of "much obliged" is to the Spirit of God, the Trinity.

The tune of the living creatures is giving gestures of recognition then, not seconds ago, as well as but continuously.

We see by this honor given it ought to be all greatness and all honor, and so forth. The unending length of time of God is so troublesome for us to comprehend on the grounds that our psyches are customized to an existence of just shy of one hundred years here on the earth.

4:10 The four and twenty seniors tumble down before him that sat on the throne, and love him that liveth for ever and ever, and cast their crowns before the throne, saying,

At the vicinity of God it is a typical thing to tumble down prostrate at His feet. The "four and twenty older folks tumble down before" demonstrates their awesome quietude at the vicinity of God. A profound regard and respect ought to be given God.

"him that sat on the throne" is extremely interesting. God the Father is on the focal throne, however instantly on His right hand sits God the Son, Jesus. The "throne" incorporates both the Father, and the Son, and the Holy Spirit.

"Worship" has been misconstrued by so many. We sing about it in our tunes and utilize it in our prayers. Do we genuinely know how to love? Our places of worship call Sunday administrations, venerate, yet once more, next to no genuine love goes on. The word that was interpreted "love" here signifies "total veneration to God, to worship Him". One of the implications of the word intends to "kiss", such as a pooch licking his expert's hand. Supreme quietude and love of God is the thing that it truly implies. Do we go to chapel to submissively revere and worship our God? A profound regard and respect ought to be given God.

Why do they "cast their crowns before the throne"? These crowns are the successful crowns that Jesus has put on their head. They, or we, have done nothing to win the crown. These crowns fit in with Jesus, not us. He won the victory. He set them on our head. Everybody profits by the triumph, yet Jesus won it. This is another demonstration of modesty on their part. When they toss the crowns at Jesus' feet, they are letting him know that they are His since He won them.

4:11 Thou craftsmanship commendable, O Lord, to get radiance and respect and power: for thou hast made all things, and for thy joy they are and were made.

We see here the value of God and why He ought to be adulated. It is, in our general public, the mainstream thing to love the made as opposed to the Creator. We are cautioned about this again and again all through the Bible. Not just as far as getting our needs stirred up and thinking a lot of cash, gems, family, homes, cars, and entertainment (which can absolutely turn into a God to us), however numerous are really loving the sun, moon, stars, and rivers.

In far too many Christian homes today we see totem poles, Buddah's and all sorts of horoscope paraphernalia.

God is an envious God. He won't permit the devotee to mess around with false gods. How might we be able to contrast the Creator of everything with His creations? We should perceive God to be preeminent to all others in each way. Before the world existed, He talked, and it got to be. The force of his Word made all that we know.

I trust it regards comprehend why He didn't simply let it be, and live as He seemed to be, and not trouble with all of this. We have been such an issue and anguish to Him. The earth and all that is on it, was made for God's pleasure. He made us so He could partnership with us. We are to Jesus such as our kids are to us. They are incredible euphoria, however at the extremely same time, they can bring us hurt. The delight far exceeds the hurt. Perhaps that is how it is with God managing us. The delight exceeds the distress. We see here that the entire universe was made for God.

CHAPTER 5

A Rolled Up And Sealed Scroll

5:1 And I found in the right hand of him that sat on the throne a book composed inside and on the posterior, fixed with seven seals.

We are not told particularly anyplace what this book contains. This is one of the puzzles that will stay until we are in paradise with Him and ask Him face to face. We realize that the Right Hand of God is Jesus Christ, so whatever this book is, (really the book is a parchment that is moved up and fixed) Jesus is holding it. This book is filled to flooding and has something even on the back could mean the completion of time. Perhaps on the converse side would be "it is done" or "the end".

"fixed with seven seals" just implies that it is shut in fulfillment. These seals could be opened each one in turn or at the same time.

They maybe, if opened each one in turn, could uncover a bit every time a seal is uprooted.

5:2 And I saw a solid holy messenger broadcasting with an uproarious voice, Who is qualified to open the book, and to free the seals thereof?

I trust the reason a "solid blessed messenger" is said here is to demonstrate that all the natural and brilliant quality, beside God's, can not open this book or these seals.

The "boisterous voice" is as though the holy messenger is shouting to see who will approach to open the book.

5:3 And no man in paradise, nor in earth, neither under the earth, could open the book, neither to look subsequently.

There are a few things that man can't do. This one proclamation here demonstrates that Jesus was, and is, no negligible man. This says paying little mind to where he is found, man does not have the ability to open this book. There are a few things, similar to judgment, that are held for Jesus to do.

The seven-fixed parchment is thought to be the title deed to the earth. In Practical terms seems God the Father holds this title deed, awaiting the return of His Son, Jesus Christ, to the earth. This powerful scene in heaven indicates that only Christ, who died to redeem mankind back to God, is qualified to open the seals of this scroll and claim His kingdom over all the earth.

One and only with the best possible power could open the book by loosing or uprooting its seals (Isaiah 29 v.11).

The inquiry is, "Who has the privilege to judge the world?" - That is to uncover what is covered up in the parchment and to execute what is composed. No man, actually, "Nobody" could be found among humanity or heavenly attendants who had the power to uproot the "seals" and read the parchment.

5:4 And I sobbed much, on the grounds that no man was discovered qualified to open and to peruse the book, neither to look subsequently.

John started to cry since it appeared that there was nobody to open this book. Truth be told, these unworthy men were even kept from taking a gander at the book.

5:5 And one of the seniors saith unto me, Weep not: view, the Lion of the tribe of Juda, the Root of David, hath won to open the book, and to free the seven seals thereof. Keep in mind the twenty-four senior citizens were delegates of the congregation. It truly doesn't make a difference which one of the twenty-four this is.

"The Lion of the tribe of Judah. (Juda)" the names of our Lord are never given coincidentally, however all pass on a piece of His inclination. Subsequent to the lion is the lord of brutes and since Judah is the decision tribe of Israel, this demonstrates Christ is to come as King to rule over human undertakings.

The "Lion of the tribe of Juda" is Jesus, obviously. In Matthew, we are demonstrated Jesus as the Lion of the tribe of Juda. It is fascinating to note that despite the fact that Jesus is dropped from David in the tissue, He is additionally David's God.

"The Root of David." This, obviously, alludes to Jesus' incarnation on His first conception with His roots in the group of David.

This "hath won" just shows that Jesus won the fight. He came against Satan and Jesus won. He won in a way that nobody expected when He kicked the bucket on the cross. Jesus is the stand out qualified to open the book. He was triumphant over sin and Satan. Only he lived upon this world free from sin. He is worthy. Probably these seals would be uprooted each one in turn.

One and only with the best possible power could open the book by loosing or uprooting its seals (Isaiah 29 v.11).

The inquiry is, "Who has the privilege to judge the world?" - That is to uncover what is covered up in the parchment and to execute what is composed. No man, actually, "Nobody" could be found among humanity or heavenly attendants who had the power to uproot the "seals" and read the parchment.

5:6 And I viewed, and, lo, amidst the throne and of the four mammoths, and amidst the older folks, stood a Lamb as it had been killed, having seven horns and seven eyes, which are the seven Spirits of God sent forward into all the earth.

This is John taking a gander at the extremely same scene with all the more being uncovered to him as he looks. It is nearly as though he is astounded when he says "lo".

Here we see Him at the throne, and extremely close are the twenty-four delegates of all Christendom. This is an abnormal thing here, for Jesus is the Right Hand of God. This book is really held by Him, but, we see Him go to take the book and open it. As in dreams, numerous imageries are available here.

Where might the Lamb, Jesus, be however in the midst? We found in a past lesson how He was amidst the church. Here we consider Him to be the ideal Lamb sacrifice. Everything that He is encompassed by is noteworthy to His church. Jesus is the focal figure in the majority of this.

We know likewise that Jesus is unquestionably amidst the four accounts. He is the focal topic of every one of the four books.

Ordinarily, contemplations come to us (as we are survey something) that are not something we see with the eye. Here we see John understanding the passing of the Lamb, and additionally Him restored.

"A sheep, looking as though it had been killed." When Christ finished the work of reclamation, He earned the title deed to the earth; as by Adam came sin, so by Christ came recovery. It is a lovely picture that we see here! Despite the fact that the blessed messenger alludes to our Lord in His wonderfulness as a Lion, showing His energy and might, John considers Him to be a conciliatory Lamb, for John sees Him through eyes of confidence. The individuals who reject Christ will consider Him to be a Lion when He comes to judge and to rule over them. The individuals who put stock in Him will consider Him to be their conciliatory Lamb.

The "seven horns" demonstrate that all force has a place with Him showing that the Lamb is not frail. A horn as Scripture shows its energy (see Zech. 1 v.18). At the point when Christ came the first run through, as a Lamb, however He showed certain forces, He didn't show the majority of His energy. When He comes whenever, as a Lion, at His Glorious Appearing, it will be in the indication of His transcendence, His everything expending power.

In Matthew 28:18, we see this checked. "What's more, Jesus came and spoke unto them, saying, All force is given unto me in paradise and in earth." This announcement is imprinted in red which implies Jesus Himself talked these words. This was spoken after His resurrection.

The "seven eyes" just means that He possesses all wisdom and understanding. "Seven eyes, which are the seven spirits of God sent out into all the earth." These eyes speak of the judgment of our Lord, including the seven characteristics of the Holy Spirit that rests on Him without measure (Isaiah 11 v.2; John 3 v.34).

At the point when our Lord comes, He will know all that people have ever thought or done. Each deed will be brought into judgment. Note that seven is God's number of flawlessness; thusly when Christ, the Lion of the tribe of Judah, comes to judge the world toward the end of the Tribulation, it will be as the ideal judge, who has all force and who thoroughly understands mankind. It ought to additionally be borne at the top of the priority list that He was the conciliatory Lamb, yet individuals rejected him.

The Seven Spirits of God - The seven Spirits don't mean seven unique Spirits, however the seven qualities of the one Holy Spirit. It ought to be borne personality a primary concern, that these attributes are not restricted to His part in paradise, His part amid the Tribulation, or His part amid the Church Age, however are an endless part of the Holy Spirit. In this way, when we are loaded with the Holy Spirit, notwithstanding the product of the Spirit found in Gal. 5 v.22, we ought to hope to show these attributes:

1. The Spirit of the Lord

2. The Spirit of astuteness

3. The Spirit of comprehension

4. The Spirit of advice

5. The Spirit of force

6. The Spirit of Knowledge

7. The Spirit of the apprehension of the Lord

The "seven spirits of God" just implies that every one of the Spirits of God abide in Him. He has all the completion of the Godhead staying in Him.

These seven Spirits of God sent forward into the earth are the profound endowments to offer the Christians some assistance with mentioning in I Corinthians section 12. It starts, "Now concerning otherworldly blessings, brethren, I would not have you oblivious." Then it goes on and records the endowments that will be of assistance to us Christians.

1. Word of Wisdom

2. Knowledge

3. Faithful

4. Healing

5. Miracles

6. Prophecy

7. Discernment

8. Tongues

9. Interpretations

There are significantly more than seven. Seven is only a profound number importance the fulfillment, or totality of the Spirit. If you needed to, you could name a hundred all the more, for example, philanthropy, tolerance, and so on.

5:7 And he came and took the book out of the right hand of him that sat upon the throne.

As I said some time recently, this is Jesus, the Lamb, taking the book from His own particular self, since He is the Right Hand of God.

5:8 And when he had taken the book, the four mammoths and four [and] twenty older folks tumbled down before the Lamb, having each one of them harps, and brilliant vials loaded with scents, which are the supplications to God of holy people.

All of Christendom will bow before the Lamb. We read that each knee will bow and each tongue admit to God, Romans 14:11.

It is a genuine solace to realize that each request to God that we ever implored is put away in paradise

5:9-10 "And they sung another tune, saying, Thou workmanship qualified to take the book, and to open the seals thereof: for thou wast killed, and hast reclaimed us to God by thy blood out of each related, and tongue, and individuals, and country;" "And hast made us unto our God lords and clerics: and we should rule on the earth."

This delightful new melody, declaring how commendable Jesus is to get our reverence, will be a heavenly sound. All voices will be in accord. This melody commending Jesus for reclaiming us from sin and passing will be joined by the excellent music of the harp in the verse some time recently.

The shed blood of Jesus was, and is, the reclaiming factor. I cherish the way that nationality, or shading, or sex, or whatever other detachment that man has won't be a component here. Salvation is for everybody who will acknowledge it. Jesus passed on for every one of us whether we are Americans, Indians, Africans, Chinese, Russian or something else. It is our decision whether to acknowledge, or dismiss, the endowment of salvation. No other barriers exist.

In V-10, talking about "lords and clerics" could be rendered kingdoms and ministers in that kingdom. We will see later on in Revelation that Christians will rule with Jesus 1000 years on the earth as subordinates to Jesus. Just as there were ministers with an esteemed cleric over them, our decision will be under His tenet.

We might rule on the earth. A comparable guarantee is given to that "huge number, which no man could number (Rev. 7:9) when revived after the Tribulation (Rev. 20:4). Together the Christians, who were spared before the Tribulation, alongside the holy people spared out of the Tribulation will "administer and rule" amid Christ's one thousand-year kingdom.

5:11 And I viewed, and I heard the voice of numerous holy messengers indirect the throne and the brutes and the senior citizens: and the quantity of them was ten thousand times ten thousand, and a huge number of thousands;

This number is not a strict number and would not be further bolstering our good fortune to make sense of. It just means a number too huge to check. This is a vast organization of serving spirits, angels. The voice must be boisterous to be such a large number. Heavenly attendants 10,000 x 10,000 = 100 Million + 1000's and 1000's.

5:12 Saying with a boisterous voice, Worthy is the Lamb that was killed to get influence, and wealth, and insight, and quality, and respect, and brilliance, and gift.

The intriguing thing here is that this immense social affair was all maxim the same thing. It was complete reverence and acknowledgment of Jesus of who and what He was. Not that they could give Jesus anything, but rather they understood that it was right for Him to have all things.

5:13 And each animal which is in paradise, and on the earth, and under the earth, and, for example, are in the ocean, and all that are in them, heard I saying, Blessing, and respect, and superbness, and power, [be] unto him that sitteth upon the throne, and unto the Lamb for ever and ever.

Jesus made everything and everyone. This equitable implies that trees, creatures, fish, fowl, and every living being, for example, creatures and individuals, all shouted out gifts to God.

The "him that sitteth upon the throne" could be God the Father and God the Son. Likely the Elohim God, due to the partition of the gift a short time later unto the Lamb. This commendation was not temporarily, but rather was to venture into all of time everlasting. "Sitteth" implies persistent sitting.

5:14 And the four mammoths said, Amen. Also, the four [and] twenty older folks tumbled down and venerated him that liveth for ever and ever.

These agents of the Christians are stating, so be it (so be it). Our love of Him will never stop. Indeed, even in paradise, we will be commending and revering Him. In shutting section 5 we saw three upheavals of applause and love are coordinated toward Christ and the Father.

(1) The mammoths and the seniors laud the Lamb for having reclaimed them through His blood (v.8,9) and for giving them power (later on) to rule on the earth (v.10);

(2) Myriads of heavenly attendants likewise laud the Lamb for His brilliance and knowledge (v.11, 12); and

(3) Every territory of creation loves both the Father and the Lamb (v.13,14). The supplications to God of holy people (v.8) might be requests to God for the satisfaction of the messianic kingdom (6:9, 10; 8:3).

CHAPTER 6

The Four Horsemen
Of The Apocalypse

6:1 And I saw when the Lamb opened one of the seals, and I listened, so to speak the commotion of thunder, one of the four mammoths saying, Come and see.

The Lamb here is Jesus Christ, the stand out qualified to open the seals. This commotion as thunder demonstrates God uncovering something to His kin. Ordinarily all through the Bible, God's voice has been mixed up for thunder. Here one of the four brutes, or four living creatures, says "Come and see". Obviously, the greater part of the four accounts say "Come and see". We are welcome to investigate the glorious stage and see things never told upon the earth as of not long ago. We will find in the opening of this first seal, the triumph of Christ and His congregation.

This part starts what is called "The Four Horsemen of the Apocalypse". The four horsemen present the photo of man's cruelty to man. They appear to be a perfect forecast of the issues of mankind that will bring about much human enduring. This is not new, for those in control of the issues of this world have a background marked by bringing on their kindred individuals much enduring, with bogus any expectations of peace took after by wars, starvations, and demise.

One of the most exceedingly terrible revulsions of the Tribulation is the numerous sicknesses that will strike the world's kin, especially the individuals who dismiss the Savior and decline to have their name written in the Lamb's Book of Life. The judgments are begun with the 7 seals.

The seals speak to the start of Christ's judgment of unbelievers on the earth amid the Tribulation period. There is a nearby similitude between these judgments and the occasions anticipated by Christ in Matthew 24:4-31. The motivation behind the Tribulation period is to rebuff unbelievers for their wrongdoing and dismissal of Christ and to convey the remainder to confidence in Christ.

6:2 And I saw, and see a white steed: and he that sat on him had a bow; and a crown was given unto him: and he went forward overcoming, and to win.

The First Seal: A White Horse (The first of the 4 horsemen of the Apocalypse is white). The rider has a bow however no bolts, demonstrating that in spite of the fact that he is militarily solid, to start with he does his vanquishing by tact. Since he wears a crown, we know he is fruitful in his endeavors. What's more, who is the rider on the white stallion? There can be probably the Antichrist, through misleading and smart moving will convey a false peace to the world.

(Antichrist) But that peace won't last.

6:3-4 "And when he had opened the second seal, I heard the second mammoth say, Come and see." "And there went out another steed [that was] red: and [power] was given to him that sat subsequently to take peace from the earth, and that they ought to kill each other: and there was given unto him an incredible sword."

The Second Seal: John composes of the second horseman, "It was allowed to the person who sat on the red steed to take peace from the earth, and that individuals ought to kill each other; and there was given to him an incredible sword."

John is urged to "Come and see". We, as well, might get a look through the eyes and the pen of John. This red steed implies war. This war could be twofold in nature. There is a consistent assault of the fallen angel and his evil spirits on Christians, yet I trust this goes much more distant than this. This red steed (as I would like to think) shows an extensive war.

This red steed likewise implies the saints who kicked the bucket holding up the name of Jesus. Blood ran uninhibitedly all through the Bible. Adherents to a few sections of the world are notwithstanding being made saints now. War is on each side. In Israel and Lebanon nowadays there are numerous killed each day. Ireland has what they call a blessed war going on. Indeed, even these are not the degree of what I trust this Scripture implies. I truly trust this red steed needs to do with a worldwide war of extraordinary greatness. The Spirits of war.

We trust this seal speaks to an extraordinary blaze we may call World War III. Whenever Daniel's "three lords" restrict the Antichrist, he will react in fatal manner, quickly smashing his foes and conveying demise to earth on an enormous scale at no other time known. Just since the approach of the nuclear age has it been conceivable to present this sort of incredible, quick devastation as a powerful influence for generally scattered bits of the globe.

His motivation is to make "humanity butcher each other" The Greek word that is utilized, furthermore the verb, signifies "to butcher, butcher or slaughter somebody". This contains a reason condition which uncovers that peace is taken from the earth for the very reason that humankind ought to butcher one another. Also, in the rest of the Revelation's Seals, Trumpets and Golden Bowl Judgments, humankind does this to himself with heartless aptitude.

We read in Zechariah about these four stallions, and we can without much of a stretch see what it is on account of the Bible lets us know. Zechariah 6:1 "And I turned, and lifted up mine eyes, and looked, and, see, there came four chariots out from between two mountains; and the mountains [were] piles of metal.

"Metal" means judgment. The number "four" implies this is an all inclusive message. Zechariah 6:2: "In the principal chariot [were] red steeds; and in the second chariot dark stallions;" Zechariah 6:3 "And in the third chariot white steeds; and in the fourth chariot grizzled and cove stallions."

This is a dream of the same stallions that we are perusing about in Revelation. To comprehend the whole message, you have to peruse section 1 and part 6 of Zechariah. Zechariah 6:4 "Then I addressed and said unto the holy messenger that chatted with me, What [are] these, my ruler?"

At the point when Zechariah asked the heavenly attendant what this implied, this is the answer he got. Zechariah 6:5 "And the holy messenger addressed and said unto me, these [are] the four spirits of the sky, which go forward from remaining before the Lord of all the earth." We see again the soul of war in this red steed.

6:5-6 "And when he had opened the third seal, I heard the third brute say, Come and see. What's more, I viewed, and lo a dark stallion; and he that sat on him had a couple of parities in his grasp." "And I heard a voice amidst the four brutes say, A measure of wheat for a penny, and three measures of grain for a penny; and [see] thou hurt not the oil and the wine".

The Third Seal: A Black Horse - Rampant swelling -a typical result of war -Famine is proposed by John's words, "A quart of wheat for a denarius, and three quarts of grain for a denarius; and don't hurt the oil and the wine."

Following in scriptural days a denarius was a typical compensation for full time work, and a quart of wheat or three quarts of grain are fundamentally subsistence diets, John is demonstrating that a man will need to work throughout the day just to get enough nourishment to eat, with nothing left over for his family or the elderly.

In the anecdote of the vineyard, Matthew 20:2, full time work was a penny. This "penny", in the verse above, means an entire day's pay. I trust this implies a chunk of bread will be so swelled in value, as a result of lack of nourishment, that it will take an entire day's wages of a man to purchase one piece.

We definitely realize that it is a "measure", which is a little sum. Grain is by all accounts a third the cost, so maybe a small supper of grain for three could cost an entire day's wages.

The starvation will be great to the point, that nourishment will be weighed by the ounce and administered deliberately. This starvation will likely be as terrible as the starvation that was in Egypt in Joseph's opportunity. Most likely dry spell will trigger yield disappointments in numerous spots. Just the extremely rich will have the capacity to purchase food. Personally, I trust, God will train Christians, who are completely sold out to Him. They will know when to plant and precisely what to do, as Joseph was told, of God, what to do.

This is fled swelling to its most exceedingly awful conceivable conclusion. In numerous parts of the world expansion is now to that awful compelling. I simply read in a few sections of Africa where the expansion rate is more than 1200%.

At the point when expansion is combined with starvation, we see a circumstance more shocking than we want to imagine. We should stay intently tuned in to God. In the event that He instructs us to burrow a profound well, we should do that. In the event that He instructs us to plant a greenery enclosure, we should do that. It will be critical to have the capacity to take day by day direction from God. Not to address, simply do it. I trust God is even now setting up spots of shelter for Christians.

Then again, the call to not "hurt the oil and the wine," are images of riches, shows that the rich will do fine and dandy. Then again it could mean something alluding with Spirit-filled Christians. Oil and wine are typical of the Holy Spirit of God. That His Hand will be on the Tribulation Saints ensuring them amid the tribulation.

I can't sufficiently stretch, that this starvation may not be simply physical but rather profound, too. Amid this time, I trust, that numerous houses of worship will instruct false teachings. Indeed, even now there is a horrible starvation of truth in the congregation. At no other time have such a variety of denied: the virgin conception of Christ, the Red Sea separated, Jonah being gulped by the huge fish, God as Father. Jesus is God with us, "Emmanuel",

Numerous chapels are appointing gay people to lecture. Common Humanism makes man a divine being.

The amount more starvation of the Spirit would we be able to take? Truly there will be a physical starvation, as well. Stay tuned to the voice of God. He will see you through it all.

The third horseman of the Apocalypse, who rides out right on time in the Tribulation, will take an overwhelming toll in passings and ailment. The dark stallion he rides is a conspicuous image of starvation and malady, which frequently take after war.

This could be a message of harsh times for all of humankind. "dark" symbolizes:

burden

grieving

fright

starvation, physical or otherworldly

malicious

inverse of goodness

everything that contradicts God

Christian Saints will be spared IN the starvation and not FROM the starvation. Noah was spared IN the surge, not FROM the flood. God can rain nourishment from paradise if fundamental. I trust God will set up spots of asylum where devotees can run, so they can have physical and profound sustenance.

God won't neglect the exemplary.

6:7-8 "And when he had opened the fourth seal, I heard the voice of the fourth brute say, Come and see." "And I looked, and observe a pale stallion: and his name that sat on him was Death, and Hell took after with him. Also, power was given unto them over the fourth part of the earth, to execute with sword, and with craving, and with death, and with the brutes of the earth."

The Fourth Seal - A Pale Horse - This stallion speaks to death.

John says the rider who sat on this stallion "was Death, and Hades took after with him. What's more, power was given to them over a fourth of the earth, to execute with sword, with craving, with death, and by the mammoths of the earth." One quarter of the world's populace, well over a billion individuals, will bite the dust as a consequence of WWIII.

I trust this needs to do with wars, for example, the one in Israel now, starvation and dry spell around the world, and demise from many different things. A sample is the plant in Russia, Chernobyl, which blasted. "Chernobyl" implies wormwood. The Bible says 33% of water will get to be wormwood, Rev. 8:11. I truly trust this happens later in the situation.

That Hades takes after Death demonstrates that those killed are unbelievers, for upon death adherents don't go to Hades yet straight to the Savior's side.

This "pale" here, means a wiped-out shading, a debilitated green shading, as though wiped out to the death. "Passing, and Hell" are assembled, which means an end of natural dwelling. Death is unavoidable for each one of us. Passing of the body, that is. Hell awaits a few, yet paradise anticipates Christians. Damnation is now and then a word utilized for the grave. In that specific occasion, Hell would take after death, on the grounds that our bodies lie in the grave until revival day. Demise and genuine hellfire is saved for the lost.

I truly trust this is a period at last that is discussed as a period when men's hearts will come up short them because of a paranoid fear of things that are happening upon the earth, Luke 21:26. We have the ability to thump the earth off of its hub with the atomic bombs. Fear is widespread here in the U.S., as well as around the globe. All it would take is for one insane man to push the wrong catch and aggregate annihilation would happen.

6:9 And when he had opened the fifth seal, I saw under the sacred place the souls of them that were killed for the expression of God, and for the affirmation which they held:

At the point when the fifth seal is broken, John sees "under the sacred place the souls of the individuals who had been killed for the expression of God and for the affirmation which they held."

Soon after the start of the Tribulation there will be an incredible "soul harvest" in which millions will come to confidence in Christ, Many as an aftereffect of the proclaiming of the 144,000 witnesses portrayed in Rev. 7.

The greater part of these Tribulation holy people will be slaughtered by the powers of Antichrist. These martyred souls will shout out for God to vindicate their passings, however they will be advised to "rest a short time longer," until both the quantity of their kindred workers and their brethren, who might be killed as they were, was finished.

Envision! In spite of the frantic abhorrence of the Antichrist, notwithstanding the detestations of war and starvation and plague and demise, God is still such a great amount in control of natural occasions that even the quantity of trusting saints has been settled by celestial announcement.

God, as the witness Paul reminds us: "It is an equitable thing with God to reimburse with tribulation the individuals who inconvenience you, and to give you who are beset rest with us when the Lord Jesus is uncovered from Heaven with His strong holy messengers, in flaring flame taking retribution on the individuals who don't know God, and on the individuals who don't comply with the good news of our Lord Jesus Christ." (2 Thess. 1, v.6-8)

Such a large number of houses of worship have overlooked that oppression goes to the genuine devotee. Numerous show that on the off chance that you are not living prosperously, both physically and profoundly, that you are not in right standing. That is unquestionably just not really, an incredible inverse is valid.

We should be killed with Christ. We should get our tissue under subjection. In Galatians 2:20 "I am killed with Christ: all things considered I live; yet not I, but rather Christ liveth in me: and the life which I now live in the tissue I live by the confidence of the Son of God, who cherished me, and gave himself for me."

The Christian has tribulation which makes him solid. We are no superior to our Master. In the event that He endured, we will endure. The distinction in our agony and His, is that our affliction is for the most part not unto the passing.

6:10 And they cried with an uproarious voice, saying, How long, O Lord, blessed and genuine, dost thou not pass judgment on and retaliate for our blood on them that harp on the earth?

John did not see these souls with his physical eye, but rather saw them in the Spirit. These souls were sitting tight for the Judge of all the earth to interfere with the fiendishness of the fallen angel and his oppression of the holy people who stayed there. Their cry was the same, one might say, as the Christians who say, come rapidly Lord Jesus.

This is not a censure of the Lord, but rather only an arguing for it to all be over. These souls are not searching for retaliation, but rather are simply shouting out for the Lord to end every last bit of it and set up His kingdom. Who better can sympathize with our era of saints than the saints of the past? A percentage of the saints of today are not physically killed, but rather are mistreated by their associates.

6:11 And white robes were given unto each one of them; and it was said unto them, that they ought to rest yet for a little season, until their fellow servants additionally and their brethren, that ought to be executed as they [were], ought to be satisfied.

These are the ones who were martyred amid the tribulation and have washed their robes and made them white in the blood of the Lamb." White robes are the uniform issued to all professors in the Lord Jesus.

At the point when the totality of time comes, the time that God has picked, Jesus will show up in the mists and blow the silver trumpet of reclamation. He will assemble all devotees with Him in paradise. He won't come one hour early or late. He will be on time. It will be at the particular time He browsed the establishment of the earth.

These saints are our kindred servants. They landed in paradise the same way we will, through their confidence unto the passing. The white in these "white robes" demonstrates that these have been successful over the issues in this world.

6:12 And I viewed when he had opened the 6th seal, and, lo, there was an extraordinary seismic tremor; and the sun got to be dark as sackcloth of hair, and the moon got to be as blood;

The Great Earthquake - The initial four seals depicted judgments to a great extent delivered by man; the 6th seal portrays a judgment unmistakably heavenly in cause. John recounts a tremor so enormous that "each mountain and island was moved out of its place."

Maybe John is alluding to gigantic volcanic action, for he says "the sun got to be dark as sackcloth of hair, and the moon got to be similar to blood." Particulate matter scattered in the climate after a volcanic emission has frequently turned the sky dark and made the moon appear to turn red.

The 6th seal brings regular debacles of different sorts (Matt. 24:7, 29). The earth and the radiant bodies will go into shakings. Joel 2:30, 31 predicts a considerable lot of these judgments in nature as indications of the day of the Lord.

This appalling tremor is told about in Isaiah 2:19, "And they should go into the openings of the stones, and into the caverns of the earth, because of a paranoid fear of the Lord, and for the eminence of his loftiness, when he ariseth to shake unpleasantly the earth."

In Ezekial 32:7-8, we read about the murkiness of the sun, moon, and stars. In Matthew 24:29, we read of this same thing in the heavens. "Instantly after the tribulation of those days should the sun be obscured, and the moon might not give her light, and the stars should tumble from paradise, and the forces of the sky should be shaken:"

6:13 And the stars of paradise fell unto the earth, even as a fig tree casteth her unfavorable figs, when she is shaken of a strong wind.

The fig tree (physical Israel) rejected Jesus and His Holy Spirit. In Acts part 2, we read of the sound as of the surging relentless wind that came and filled them with the Holy Ghost. This compelling wind is of God. Commonly when we read of the strong wind it is an indication of the Holy Spirit of God. The Holy Spirit can be lovely, as we read in Acts 2, or alarming to the individuals who don't accept.

The Old Testament and the New Testament concur that there will be a period when the sky will be shaken. Isaiah sections 7, 13, 17, Matthew 24 and no less than twelve more parts in the Old and New Testaments concur that there will be a day, generally as this one talked about that John saw, when the sky will be shaken.

We read, additionally, of the profound shaking that will take place. We read that there should be an awesome falling without end in the congregation just before this happens. II Thessalonians 2:3 "Let no man delude you by any methods: for [that day might not come], with the exception of there come a falling endlessly to start with, and that man of sin be uncovered, the child of destruction.

As should be obvious, devotees will be attempted and numerous will fall away. In Luke part 21, we read what number of will be double-crossed by those of their own family unit.

Luke 21:25-26, we read again of the hullabaloo in heaven. "And there might be signs in the sun, and in the moon, and in the stars; and upon the earth trouble of countries, with perplexity; the ocean and the waves thundering;" Luke 21:26 "Men's hearts falling flat them for trepidation, and for taking care of those things which are going ahead the earth: for the forces of paradise should be shaken." You can without much of a stretch see this is forecasted of John, as well as by many pens all through the Bible.

6:14 And the paradise withdrew as a parchment when it is moved together; and each mountain and island were moved out of their places.

This quake will be strong to the point that mountains will straighten out and islands will vanish. A seismic tremor of this greatness would promptly set up a screen of smoke that nothing in the sky would be obvious. We read in Isaiah 34:4, a comparative Scripture as above.

"And all the host of paradise should be broken up, and the sky might be moved together as a parchment: and all their host might tumble down, as the leaf falleth off from the vine and as a falling [fig] from the fig tree." Whatever this is, it is of awesome greatness.

I remind you once more, that Revelation is not composed in sequential request. The happenings in the verses above are long after the devotees are in paradise. We, Christians, ought not fear things we see happening that is in satisfaction of these sections. We ought to turn upward and cheer toward the start of any of these things, in light of the fact that our recovery draweth near, Luke 21:28.

6:15 And the lords of the earth, and the colossal men, and the rich men, and the boss commanders, and the powerful men, and each bondman, and each liberated individual, concealed themselves in the lairs and in the stones of the mountains;

This truly is the time when much silver and gold won't have the capacity to spare individuals from the Wrath of God.

Stowing away in "caves and in the stones" will be of no utilization in light of the fact that these openings will quit for the day the earthquake. Men will look for death, however passing won't come, Rev. 9:6.

6:16 And said to the mountains and rocks, Fall on us, and conceal us from the substance of him that sitteth on the throne, and from the fury of the Lamb:

The general population of earth will unmistakably perceive these marvels as originating from the hand of God, for they are said to shout out to the mountains where they take spread, "Fall on us and conceal us from the substance of Him who sits on the throne and from the fury of the Lamb!

All of a sudden they understand who Jesus is, however it is excessively late. They have rejected Him Since it is past the point of no return, they understand their repulsive error of dismissing Jesus as their ideal Lamb sacrifice. They would rather bite the dust at this moment, than face Him and be recounted their forever in hellfire that anticipates them. They now even understand that Jesus sits on the throne. What an appalling arousing.

This that John sees is all that much like a fantasy, in that the things he sees are not especially in back-to-back request.

6:17 For the colossal day of his fierceness is come; and who might have the capacity to stand?

The response to that is "no one". The thing we should do is ensure that we are not left here to face these revulsions. The best approach to guarantee that is by offering out to Jesus NOW. Make Him Lord of your life NOW before it is past the point of no return.

As a consequence of these initial six seal judgments, numerous unbelievers will need to bite the dust and to escape God, yet will be not able. The colossal day of his rage is the day of the Lord, the anticipated time of God's judgment of the earth and its occupants (Joel 1:15; 2:1, 11, 31).

The day of rage is differentiated to the present "day of beauty." Is come means God's day of judgment "is here", it has at long last arrived, having started with the initial six seals.

The "immense day" talked about in V-17, starts three and a half years of the most exceedingly awful things you could ever envision. The most recent day must be the last judgment. Fate for the unbelievers.

Keep in mind, Revelation is composed to the congregation, the Christians. It urges us to anticipate heaven. It, additionally, lets us know the horrendous things we will be spared from when the Wrath drops on this planet.

Also, it drives genuine Christians to witness to their loved ones while there is still time. Recognizing what is coming, we unquestionably would prefer not to desert anybody behind.

CHAPTER 7

The First Six Seals

7:1 And after these things I saw four heavenly attendants remaining on the four corners of the earth, holding the four winds of the earth, that the wind ought not blow on the earth, nor on the ocean, nor on any tree.

This "after" will be after the happenings of the initial six seals. These heavenly attendants (serving spirits) were to accomplish something to the entire earth (four corners of the earth). These holy messengers were sitting tight for requests from God. Their occupation right now was to control these four winds until God said discharge them. The rage is kept down until the individuals who must be fixed are fixed.

The seal demonstrates proprietorship and security, as a ruler's seal ring was utilized to verify and ensure official reports. The 144,000 are all Israelites from the 12 tribes (12 times 12,000). This number might be taken truly, or metaphorically of a national transformation. Every one of the 12 tribes (Isaiah 11:11-13; Ezek. 37:15-28). There are no "lost tribes." In the rundown of tribes, Joseph remains for Ephraim, and Dan is missing, perhaps on the grounds that it was the primary tribe to go into heathen worship and heresy (Judges 18). The 144,000 will obviously be changed over and dispatched to be a light to the Gentiles amid the Tribulation.

Rev. 7 v.1-4 Suggest that before the world is dove into the sicknesses and catastrophes introduced by the 6th seal judgment toward the end of the main quarter of the Tribulation, God will raise up a multitude of 144,000 Jewish evangelists to spread over the globe and acquire a spirit harvest of unfathomable extents. Each of these "workers" of God will get a "SEAL" on his brow. While we don't know precisely what this seal will be, the content appears to propose it will be noticeable. (At any rate to Christians) Whatever the seal is, it manages these 144,000 Jewish witnesses "of the considerable number of tribes of the offspring of Israel" some sort of powerful insurance, in any event until the immense soul harvest of Rev. 7 v.9 can be proficient.

7:2-3 "And I saw another holy messenger climbing from the east, having the seal of the living God: and he cried with a noisy voice to the four blessed messengers, to whom it was given to hurt the earth and the ocean," "Saying, Hurt not the earth, neither the ocean, nor the trees, till we have fixed the workers of our God in their temples."

This holy messenger sent from God was most likely a chief heavenly messenger, or perhaps Jesus, Himself. This heavenly attendant is endowed with the employment of taking a seal and putting God's imprint upon the gathering that God will ensure amidst the anger of God.

Despite the fact that this gathering will be on the earth amid this repulsive anger that should fall on the tenants of the earth, they will be secured, for they are fixed with God's name on their brow in full view. This heavenly attendant originates from the east. This is the same area from which the light comes. This heavenly attendant has power over these four blessed messengers.

The "ocean" here could be an exacting ocean or as in different spots it implies substantial gatherings of individuals.

God has said again and again all through the Bible that there has been a remainder of Jews who have not bowed their knee to false divine beings. At a certain point in the Old Testament, He said that the number then was 7000. We read in the eleventh section of Romans that God told Elijah that there were 7000 who had not bowed the knee to Baal. Romans 11:4, "But rather what saith the answer of God unto him? I have saved to myself seven thousand men, who have not bowed the knee to the picture of Baal." You see, God has dependably had a remainder of physical Israel.

7:4 And I heard the quantity of them which were fixed: [and there were] fixed a hundred [and] forty [and] four thousand of the considerable number of tribes of the offspring of Israel.

"You Shall Seek Me and Find Me When You Search For Me with All Your Heart" - This is a guarantee from God Almighty (Deut. 4 v.29) - God has never been without a witness of His salvation on this planet. Since all adherents from this present age will have been all of a sudden and phenomenally uprooted by the occasion known as the Rapture, new witnesses must be raised up instantly.

Envision what might happen if, all of a sudden, amidst some exceptionally attempting times on earth, 144,000 Israelites in a flash and inexplicably got to be faithful devotees to Jesus as their guaranteed Messiah and Savior. This will happen much the same as Saul of Tarsus (Paul) was supernaturally conveyed to confidence headed straight toward Damascus. I don't recognize what will bring about the change, other than the force of the Holy Spirit.

Be that as it may, in numerous wonderful rates, 144,000 Jews will be gotten to confidence Jesus as the Messiah and Son of God, and will turn out to be intense evangelists. Picture 144,000 Hebrew Billy Grahams circling the world and conveying this marvelous sparing truth to a pained and befuddled people. That is exactly what's going to happen.

God's Special Protection for the 144,000 - Since these hirelings will be stamped men on earth, working straightforwardly counter to the hobbies of the worldwide pioneer, they will be "checked" men in more than one feeling of the word. They will be under steady assault by the Antichrist's powers and the evil forces unleashed upon the earth. At different times they will experience the ill effects of craving, presentation, disparagement, torment and detainment. Be that as it may, they all will be supernaturally protected to proceed with their witness all through the tribulation period.

At the very end, the 144,000 witnesses will stand triumphantly on Mount Zion with Jesus. Jesus alludes to them as "these siblings of mine". (Mat. 25 v.31-46) The way a man treats these evangelists amid the Tribulation will reflect whether he is a devotee to their message or not. Remember, it will be to a great degree dangerous to help and abet them. They will probably be on the Antichrist's "most needed rundown". Be that as it may, the lesson is that God's man or lady is indestructible until God is done with him here on earth.

Only the way that there is a particular number given lets you know that these are not the devotees. The devotees can't be numbered for huge number. The Christians are not from the tribes of Israel fundamentally. A number of them have no Jewish blood at all. In Galatians part 3, we read that devotees to Christ are Abraham's descendants on account of confidence, not blood.

In verse 8 of section 3 of Galatians the adherents are called pagan, which individuals of physical Israel are never called. Abraham is not the father of devotees due to blood line, but since they (the same as Abraham) are spared by confidence. Galatians 3:7-8, "Know ye in this way that they which are of confidence, the same are the offspring of Abraham." Galatians 3:8

"What's more, the sacred writing, anticipating that God would legitimize the rapscallion through confidence, lectured before the gospel unto Abraham, [saying], In thee might all

DR. JOHN THOMAS WYLIE

countries be honored." You see, the tribes we are going to see recorded are the greater part of the country of Israel. The main way this bodes well is that this 144,000 is the leftover of physical Israel that God has dependably had.

7:5-8 "Of the tribe of Juda [were] fixed twelve thousand. Of the tribe of Reuben [were] fixed twelve thousand. Of the tribe of Gad [were] fixed twelve thousand." "Of the tribe of Aser [were] fixed twelve thousand. Of the tribe of Nepthalim [were] fixed twelve thousand. Of the tribe of Manasses [were] fixed twelve thousand." "Of the tribe of Simeon [were] fixed twelve thousand. Of the tribe of Levi [were] fixed twelve thousand. Of the tribe of Issachar [were] fixed twelve thousand." "Of the tribe of Zabulon [were] fixed twelve thousand. Of the tribe of Joseph [were] fixed twelve thousand. Of the tribe of Benjamin [were] fixed twelve thousand".

A few researchers contend that the 144,000 evangelists aren't inexorably Jews? In any case, a perusing of Rev. 7 verses 4 - 8 lets us know they are incorrect. Those verses go ahead to recognize the "tribes" each of the 12,000 originates from. Most Jews alive today don't know which tribe they originate from. However, God does! Furthermore, He deliberately chooses 12,000 from each of the 12 tribes. You might see when you read Rev. 7 v.4-8 that 2 tribes are missing and 2 others have been substituted in their places. Why?

A few researchers trust the tribe of Dan is missing in light of the fact that the Jewish Antichrist, known as the False Prophet, will be a relative. This absolutely is by all accounts the importance of an antiquated prediction that Jacob gave about the tribes of Israel in the most recent days: "Dan will be a serpent in the way, a venomous snake by the way, that nibbles the stallion's heels so that his rider falls in reverse". (Gen. 49 v.17) We can anticipate that the Holy Spirit will proceed onward the hearts of individuals toward the start of the Tribulation and come full circle with the second happening to Christ.

Later in Revelation 14 we'll find another 144,000. Check whether you imagine that they are the same or distinctive.

From this rundown of 12 names both Dan (who we just talked about and Ephraim are discarded. Dan was overlooked in light of the shrewdness in his life. On the other hand, Levi, Joseph, and Manasseh make up the twelve. Levi was not recorded some time recently, on the grounds that he got no area. He was religious. God picks whom He will.

7:9 After this I viewed, and, lo, an extraordinary huge number, which no man could number, of all countries, and kindreds, and individuals, and tongues, remained before the throne, and before the Lamb, dressed with white robes, and palms in their grasp;

These are clearly the adherents to Jesus Christ (Lamb) who have been washed in the blood of the Lamb and raptured into paradise.

One soothing truth gathered from Revelation is that in spite of the fact that Antichrist will have control over all people groups and dialects, he won't trick each person. Verse 9 makes it clear that the proclaiming of the gospel by the 144,000 Jewish witnesses will achieve a large number that nobody can number, from each dialect, tribe, and individuals. Along these lines, even Satan's control won't keep individuals from accepting Christ independently.

This is as per the way it has been all amid the Christian allotment. Countries and people groups have rejected Christ, yet people have gotten Him. By 1 v.10-11, "He was on the planet, and however the world was made through him, the world did not remember him. He went to that which was his own, however his own particular did not get him." But rather the content proceeds: "Yet to all who got him, to the individuals who had confidence in his name, he gave the privilege to end up offspring of God." (v.12)

7:10 And cried with a noisy voice, saying, Salvation to our God which sitteth upon the throne, and unto the Lamb.

We can't assume acknowledgment for our salvation. Our salvation is a free blessing through elegance. Jesus merits all the credit. He acquired our salvation with His valuable blood. We should acclaim and love Jesus for only he merits all the credit. obviously, the triune God (Elohim) sits on the throne.

7:11 And every one of the blessed messengers remained circuitous the throne, and [about] the older folks and the four monsters, and fell before the throne on their appearances, and adored God,

This is another perspective of the throne area. obviously, Elohim God is on the inside throne. Jesus is sitting at the right hand of the Father.

The four living creatures are exceptionally close to the throne. The twenty-four senior citizens, illustrative of all Christendom, are exceptionally close, also. The holy messengers circle the throne. All fall before the throne of God altogether reverence and love.

7:12 Saying, Amen: Blessing, and brilliance, and intelligence, and thanksgiving, and respect, and control, and may, [be] unto our God for ever and ever. So be it.

7:13 And one of the elders answered, saying unto me, What are these which are arrayed in white robes? and whence came they?

This elder is certainly representative of the church. He must already know who these are. He probably asks this question to teach those who do not understand who these are.

Those which were "arrayed in white robes" cannot be the same people as those sealed in their forehead. Those sealed in their forehead would have no reason to be sealed, if they would be immediately transported to heaven. There are no winds of terror in heaven. There would be no purpose in putting the mark on them for heaven. This is certainly another group. They have been taken out of the great tribulation on the earth. The seven years are broken up into two 3 1/2-year periods. The first 3 1/2 years are called tribulation, and the last 3 1/2 years are known as the Great Tribulation.

Christians will know tribulation but will be saved from the wrath to come. I Thessalonians

1:10 "And to wait for his Son from heaven, whom he raised from the dead, [even] Jesus, which delivered us from the wrath to come."

I trust this joy, or getting without end of the Church, happens before these seven years. We read in Daniel 12:1-4 "And around then might Michael stand up, the considerable ruler which standeth for the offspring of thy individuals: and there should be a period of inconvenience, for example, never was following there was a country [even] to that same time: and around then thy individuals might be conveyed, each one that should be discovered composed in the book." "And huge numbers of them that rest in the dust of the earth should wakeful, some to everlasting life, and some to disgrace [and] everlasting scorn." "And they that be shrewd might sparkle as the shine of the atmosphere; and they that swing numerous to uprightness as the stars for ever and ever." "However thou, O Daniel, quiets down the words, and seal the book, [even] to the season of the end: numerous should rushed forward and backward, and learning should be expanded."

You see there is no doubt that this we read in Daniel is the same time as what we have been perusing in Revelation. In Daniel 12:9, "And he said, Go thy path, Daniel: for the words are quit for the day fixed till the season of the end."

Here is the reason a few individuals trust that the euphoria will happen toward the start of the Great Tribulation. In the event that we read whatever is left of part 12, verse 12 says: Blessed [is] he that waiteth, and cometh to the thousand three hundred and five and thirty days. (1335) This time I accept is toward the end of the season of the Great Tribulation, when the earth is reestablished and the sheep and the goats are isolated. Significance after the most recent 42 months, (thousand three hundred and five and thirty days. - 1335 days) an extra time (75 days) is included for this procedure.

Amid that timeframe the Julian schedule was utilized (just 30 days for each month) so the 1260 days is right.

7:14 And I said unto him, Sir, thou knowest. What's more, he said to me, these are they which left awesome tribulation, and have washed their robes, and made them white in the blood of the Lamb.

He unquestionably definitely knew who they were. This was simply underscoring a lesson to be learned. This white is such a splendid white, to the point that, I trust, it even shimmers as the Shekinah Glory of God. Here once more, white stands for honesty. We are upright since we have tackled Jesus' nobility. See additionally, that they were not spared from tribulation, but rather in it.

Bear in mind, each one of those new adherents will have been abandoned after the Rapture correctly in light of the fact that he or she had rejected God's offer of salvation up to that point.

The white robes depict a remaining of nobility, and the huge number gestures of recognition God particularly for their salvation. Note the sevenfold acclaim of verse 12.

The recovered Gentiles of this vision are either holy people who will be martyred amid the tribulation, or adherents who will survive the Tribulation and enter the Millennium in their common bodies, or both. The sanctuary might be either the natural, millennial sanctuary, or the throne and vicinity of God in paradise. Natural distresses will be more than (21:3, 4). Christ will give them profound sustenance. There will be truly no crying or distress in the vicinity of God, for He will have wiped away all tears from their eyes.

7:15 Therefore are they before the throne of God, and serve him day and night in his sanctuary: and he that sitteth on the throne should abide among them.

We, Christians, are before the throne since we chose to take after Jesus, to acknowledge His salvation, to be washed in His blood, and to trust in the restoration. We are to be His workers and to abide with Him until the end of time. It discusses "day and night" here, yet there is no night in paradise with Jesus. We are in the vicinity of the Light, and there is only one endless day with Him.

We read in Ephesians 5:27 "That he may show it to himself a grand church, not having spot, or wrinkle, or any such thing; yet that it ought to be sacred and without flaw."

Disclosure 21-3 talks about this very thing, "And I heard an extraordinary voice out of paradise saying, Behold, the sanctuary of God [is] with men, and he will stay with them, and they should be his kin, and God himself might be with them, [and be] their God." How a great deal more superb would it be able to be?

7:16 They should hunger not anymore, neither thirst anymore; neither might the daylight on them, nor any warmth.

On the off chance that we read in Isaiah

49:10 we will read, "They might not hunger nor thirst; neither should the warmth nor sun destroy them: for he that hath leniency on them might lead them, even by the springs of water might he control them."

Both of these help us to remember the 23rd Psalm. Jesus is the Shepherd. He sees to the requirements of His run.

Jesus is the Light, and there will be no requirement for the sun or the moon. There will be a vicinity of Light.

7:17 For the Lamb which is amidst the throne should bolster them, and might lead them unto living wellsprings of waters: and God should wipe away all tears from their eyes.

This is without a doubt paradise where there is endless peace and joy. Here once more, we consider Jesus to be the Shepherd of His sheep, accommodating everything our needs, and fulfilling us ecstatically. We have tears on earth yet not in paradise.

CHAPTER 8

The Seventh Seal,
7 Trumpets And 7 Angels

8:1 And when he had opened the seventh seal, there was quiet in paradise about the space of thirty minutes.

The Seventh Seal -"When he opened the seventh seal, there was quiet in paradise for around one-half hour".

That doesn't sound to terrible isn't that right? Yet, ...

The importance of this hush is twofold:

(1) It is completely inverse the typical sound example of paradise, and

(2) it is the consequence of the disclosure by Jesus Christ to the other-worldly has concerning what is going to fall on the earth. The opening of the seventh seal presents the 7 trumpet judgments, which are all judgments of God sent on the earth. In these judgments, God is solely the sender and individuals are only collectors. These judgments are terrible to the point that the holy messengers stand short of breath in amazement.

Do you think the individuals who reject Jesus Christ so effectively today would stay "quiet" in the event that they knew the awful fate of judgment that is happening upon this world and upon them since they are dismissing God's Redeemer, the Lord Jesus Christ?

In the earlier verses of Revelation paradise is seen to be a blissful and adoring spot, with melodies singing, Trumpets blasting, heavenly creatures shouting out, however abruptly there comes this dismal quiet.

As ghastly as the seal judgments were, the trumpet judgments will be more awful.

8:2 And I saw the seven blessed messengers which remained before God; and to them were given seven trumpets.

Whether this seven is strict, or not, doesn't make a difference (in this occurrence I trust they are literal). These "blessed messengers" are readied to do God's requests. These "seven trumpets" were to sound the alarm. Trumpets are noisy and convey an unmistakable note. There will be no doubt of the message. The trumpet all through the Bible is utilized for two particular purposes:

1: To amass the general population for love.

2: To amass the general population for war. At any rate, this is to alert and get ready, prepare.

This empowers the Christians and means judgment to the defector and common. The Wrath of God arrives.

As the seventh seal is broken, the seven holy messengers get trumpets. Tim LaHaye, (a Baptist evangelist with more than 40 years' experience and the writer of the Left Behind Series of Books) thinks the 7 seals happen in the main quarter (21 months) and the seventh seal starts the 7 trumpet judgments which start the following 21 months or second quarter of the Tribulation. "What's more, I saw the seven holy messengers who stand before God, and to them were given seven trumpets"

The opening of the seventh seal does not bring about the seven heavenly attendants to remain before God. Clearly they are dependably there, anticipating an extraordinary task from their

Creator. The opening of the seal results in every one being given a trumpet that will be blown in legitimate grouping, presenting a future type of judgment.

In the main time of the Tribulation the earth has known the fury of the Antichrist; now it will start to feel the rage of God Almighty.

8:3 And another blessed messenger came and remained at the sacrificial table, having a brilliant censer; and there was given unto him much incense, that he ought to offer [it] with the requests to God of all holy people upon the brilliant holy place which was before the throne.

Verse 3 lets us know this relentless holy messenger stands before the glorious brilliant sacred place of incense, which is before the Throne of the Almighty God. The supplications to God of the considerable number of adherents are blended with radiant incense and presented to God. These requests to God contain the saints' and the agony holy people's weeps for help and equity. The response to these requests to God is the Seven Trumpets and Seven Golden Vials.

We should understand that the sanctuary in the wild (with its Holy place and most Holy Place) was a scaled down of the course of action in paradise. The holy place developed by Moses for Israel's Tabernacle was replicated from this one.

At the point when Jesus passed on the cross, His blood must be conveyed to the benevolence seat in paradise, pretty much as the sheep in the sanctuary had its blood sprinkled on the kindness seat in the most Holy place.

The very throne of God is the most blessed spot in heaven. Jesus is our High Priest perpetually, who mediates for us at the throne of God.

This vessel must be made of gold to be in the nearby nearness of God. Pretty much as everything in the most Holy place in the Tabernacle in the Wilderness must be immaculate gold, or unadulterated gold overlay.

A percentage of the essayists trust "censer" here ought to be frankincense. That is not a horribly essential point. The "incense", in V-3, most likely indicates frankincense.

Notice that the supplications to God of the holy people with their offering is upon the brilliant holy place at the throne of God. Some of the time we feel our supplications to God go no place, however here we see them at the throne of God.

The brilliant holy place, too, was in the very vicinity of God and in this manner must be made of gold.

We were not imploring the heavenly attendant. The heavenly attendant's just occupation was to transport them and keep them safe until they were gotten. We should never appeal to a blessed messenger. Truth be told, we don't implore Jesus. We appeal to the Father for the sake of Jesus.

The vital thing, to see here, is that our supplications to God go to the throne of God, to the most Holy place.

8:4 And the smoke of the incense, [which came] with the requests to God of the holy people, rose up before God out of the heavenly attendant's hand.

The Bible talks about this as a sweet noticing relish, Ezra 6:10. The "heavenly attendant" was the delivery person who conveyed the requests to God.

8:5 And the holy messenger took the censer, and filled it with flame of the sacrificial stone, and cast [it] into the earth: and there were voices, and thunderings, and lightnings, and a seismic tremor.

The thunderclaps, lightnings, and tremor are the aftereffect of the flame from the holy place, demonstrating that the activity of paradise starts a responsive activity on earth. As the requests to God for the holy people for retribution are taken from the sacred place, there are unnerving sounds, flashes of light, and a tremor on the earth, presenting the way that the seven blessed messengers are going to sound their trumpets.

Fire from the sacrificial table of copied offering implies that God acknowledged the requests to God of the holy people. This "flame taken from the sacrificial table and cast to the earth" is the anger of God. Our God is a devouring flame. God is irritated, and He has chosen the time has come to rebuff those on the earth who have rejected Jesus Christ as their Savior.

Pretty much as God at last pulverized Sodom and Gomorrah when they would not apologize, there is a period when the flame of God will slide upon this world in discipline.

All through the Bible, these normal calamities specified in V-5: "thunderings, lightnings, seismic tremor" are God managing humanity. This is the same, and I trust these are exacting. A horrible tempest happens over the ground and a frightful shaking underneath happens, too. The Wrath of God has started.

Are the Trumpet Judgments Literal Judgments - The most ideal approach to choose if the trumpet judgments are exacting or typical is to study them regarding the infections of Egypt, as found in Exodus 7-11. Five of the diseases of Egypt are rehashed in the book of Revelation. Nobody proposes that what happened in Egypt was not exacting in its type of judgment on the insubordinate Egyptians; in this manner, we can presume that the same thing applies amid the Tribulation period and that the trumpet judgments present physical judgment on the earth. The main exemptions are those trumpets that present occasions outside human ability to comprehend, and even they influence individuals physically.

8:6-7 "And the seven blessed messengers which had the seven trumpets set themselves up to sound." "The primary heavenly attendant sounded, and there took after hail and fire blended with blood, and they were provided reason to feel ambiguous about the earth: and the third piece of trees was consumed, and all green grass was consumed."

The First Trumpet: Hail, Fire and Blood - Ice and fire downpour from the sky, consuming 33% of all the world's trees and the majority of its grass. This is a natural catastrophe without parallel to this point ever; its outcomes are limitless. To exacerbate matters even, John likewise includes that "blood" lands with the hail and fire, as the prophet Joel had anticipated: "And I will demonstrate ponders in the sky and in the earth: blood and fire and mainstays of smoke" (Joel 2 v.30) And this is just the primary trumpet!

We read here, as in V-2, of the seven holy messengers that had been holding up requests to move. They now are discharged and advised to do these things. A few religions will let you know that God never rebuffs, yet this is not true. This is discipline from God. The fiend is not doing this. It is done on requests from God. Another spot where this bizarre wonder of flame and hail combined falling is in Exodus 9:24 "So there was hail, and fire blended with the hail, extremely shocking, for example, there was none like it in all the place where there is Egypt since it turned into a nation." Both were disciplines from God. The distinction is that this one in Exodus was restricted. The one in Revelation is all the more widespread. One thing essential to recall is that the anger of God falls on them of unbelief.

Ezekiel 38:22 "And I will argue against him with epidemic and with blood; and I will rain upon him, and upon his groups, and upon the numerous individuals that [are] with him, a flooding precipitation, and incredible hailstones, flame, and brimstone."

It is the same God in Ezekiel that we find in Revelation.

We find in the greater part of this and the following few trumpets, most likely, uncover God's judgment which might be of nature as cataclysmic types of nature or might be as His permitting people to unleash nuclear or atomic weapons of war. The main trumpet is bad to the point that it slaughters 1/3 of all vegetation.

8:8 And the second holy messenger sounded, and so to speak an incredible mountain smoldering with flame was thrown into the ocean: and the third part of the ocean got to be blood;

Two Author's perspectives will be given for clarifications as to the Trumpet Judgments. Perused both then you choose which you accept.

The Second Trumpet: A Mountain of Fire - As in Sodom and Gomorrah (Gen. 19) Tim LaHaye sees this as truly incident.

At the point when the Second trumpet is blown, John sees "something like an extraordinary mountain smoldering with flame" - Tim Lahaye supposes it is likely a huge shooting star smashing through the air - "tossed into the ocean, and 33% of the ocean got to be blood." thus, 33% of everything living in the ocean passes on, and 33% of the boats on the ocean are crushed.

As of now the WHO (World Health Organization) states "about portion of the world's kin are influenced by ailments identified with inadequate and polluted water," which is the reason they are attempting to enhance the water supplies of the world. Think about the diseases that will be spread when the water supply turns intense, then to blood in the "colossal and repulsive Day of the Lord."

By Lindsey (The writer of the book "The Late Great Planet Earth") he supposes this will be an atomic holocaust. He expresses that in an atomic explosion, stickiness noticeable all around is in a split second compacted into water and driven straight up into the solidifying temperatures of the upper stratosphere. It then is immediately solidified and falls back to earth as goliath pieces of ice. This he states would represent the flame, blood and ice, and that with enough of the different underdeveloped nations who now have atomic abilities makes this surely a probability.

Consider the super dirtied air with radiation and now with 1/3 of all vegetation gone, the absence of oxygen they give. A considerably more noteworthy disaster is all the green grains are consumed. With starvation officially seething in numerous parts of the world and lack of nourishment all over the place else, this will seal the fate of millions. Maybe the fortunate ones will be the individuals who kick the bucket in the blasts.

8:9-11 "And the third part of the animals which were in the ocean, and had life, kicked the bucket; and the third part of the boats were wrecked." "And the third holy messenger sounded, and there fell an extraordinary star from paradise, blazing so to speak a light, and it fell upon the third part of the streams, and upon the wellsprings of waters;" "And the name of the star is called Wormwood: and the third part of the waters got to be wormwood; and numerous men passed on of the waters, since they were made astringent."

The Third Trumpet - A Star Called Wormwood - Tim Lahaye states that when the third holy messenger blows his trumpet, another shooting star collides with earth, "blazing like a light." It doesn't fall on the ocean however on 33% of the world's streams and springs, turning them "sharp" and harmful. As an aftereffect of this sickness, "numerous men" kick the bucket.

"Presently this will be the infection with which the Lord will strike every one of the people groups who have gone to war against Jerusalem; their tissue will spoil while they remain on their feet, and their eyes will decay in their attachments, and their tongue will spoil in their mouth." (Zech. 14 v.12)

This to Hal Lindsey implies atomic blasts. Hal states that maybe the most alarming disclosure is that humanity and his own particular innovations cause the majority of the worldwide holocaust.

His perspective on this is somewhat distinctive. The greater part of Revelation judgments he sees as being made by man and is atomic. In the second Trumpet the verse determines "something like an extraordinary mountain smoldering with flame." He sees this to be either a colossal meteor or, more probable, various H-bombs. A hydrogen or nuclear bomb blasted under the sea resembles a gigantic blazing mountain ejecting out of the ocean. Notwithstanding devastating 33% of every marine vessel, the "flaring mountain" will wipe out 33% of all marine life, turning the ocean dark red with the blood of the dead.

Why might such a weapon be shot into the sea? Straightforward he says. Today, maritime force, particularly super atomic submarines with ICBM dispatch ability, is seen as the eventual fate of fighting. Russia and the US both have more than 100 atomic controlled submarines each fit for terminating ICBM rockets with numerous nuclear warheads. The Russian Typhoon class atomic subs are the biggest, speediest, stealthiest, most profound plunging and deadliest on the planet. Everyone conveys as standard law 20 ICBMs with 10 warheads each. That is 200 warheads that can transform 200 extensive urban areas into endless crushed burial grounds. These can be dispatched from submerged and hit 95% of our real populace focuses in under 8 minutes from dispatch.

God has blessed man with awesome innovative capacity, yet as opposed to utilizing it for good; he regularly utilizes it to obliterate his planet and himself.

Man's most essential issue has never been an absence of knowledge or training, yet a nature that is fallen and ethically debased. Unless man encounters another conception, in which he gets a supernatural conception of another profound nature through which God speaks with him, he is bound to the ruinous impact of his fallen nature. The Third Trumpet is again atomic. He makes reference to Chernobyl concerning how water can be dirtied by a solitary atomic episode.

The greater part of this is discussing ghastly things connected with such a change in the earth that it is past our comprehension. I trust these Scriptures could have both an exacting and an otherworldly significance joined to them. From the profound point of view: as of late we have seen grand stars (well-known priests) falling.

One truly fascinating thing from the physical point of view: Chernobyl implies wormwood.

This mishap that happened in Russia influenced generally socialist nations (the individuals who deny God). This had a repulsive prompt impact of aftermath in huge numbers of the neighboring nations. Meat was not eatable and milk from creatures couldn't be drunk. Literally a huge number of individuals were loaded with malignancy bringing on aftermath.

Numerous years from now they will at present be seeing the outcomes from this frightful mischance. In a few places the radiation was 1000's of times the typical sum. "Wormwood" implies terrible water, and I figure on the off chance that you checked the water now on this planet now, you presumably would find that an extensive rate of it is awful.

8:12 And the fourth blessed messenger sounded, and the third part of the sun was stricken, and the third part of the moon, and the third part of the stars; so as the third piece of them was obscured, and the day shone not for a third piece of it, and the night in like manner.

The Fourth Trumpet - Darkness Descends - All life on this planet relies on upon the sun: If it were to blast, the earth would burn; if it somehow managed to go icy, the earth would solidify strong. Neither of those extremes is in perspective with the fourth trumpet judgment, yet somehow God reduces by a third the measure of brilliant vitality achieving earth from the sun and all other divine bodies. John composes, "33% of the sun was struck, 33% of the moon, and 33% of the stars, so that 33% of them were obscured; 33% of the day did not sparkle, and in like manner the night."

Tim LaHaye states that God who made light in any case can reduce it to 33%. Really, day and night will appear to be turned around, for there will be sixteen hours of dimness and eight hours of light.

This normally helps us to remember the disease sent on Pharaoh as portrayed in Exodus 10 v.21. "Haziness over the place where there is Egypt, obscurity which might even be felt." And it offers point of interest to our Lord's forecast, "There should be signs in the sun, and in the moon, and in the stars; and upon the earth misery of countries, with perplexity; the ocean and the waves thundering; men's hearts fizzling them for apprehension, and for taking care of those things which are going ahead the earth: for the forces of paradise might be shaken" (Luke 21 v.25-26)

8:13 And I observed, and heard a blessed messenger flying through the middle of paradise, saying with an uproarious voice, Woe, hardship, trouble, to the inhabiters of the earth by reason of alternate voices of the trumpet of the three heavenly attendants, which are yet to sound!

The last three trumpets will be particularly extreme, as reported by the triple redundancy of Woe, hardship, trouble. They will be coordinated toward the inhibitors of the earth, that is, the unbelievers still alive on earth. Both the most established and the lion's share of Greek compositions read "falcon" rather than holy messenger in the primary part of the verse.

Express gratitude toward God Christians will be saved the Wrath. It appears from the announcement in verse 6, the things which have as of now happened are presumably amid tribulation. From the "troubles", the fury is going to come.

Indeed, even the issues we have officially found out about are unpleasant, yet they deteriorate. Here once more, notice the mid-time partition of this, four holy messengers have sounded, and three more are going to sound.

This normally helps us to remember the disease sent on Pharaoh as depicted in Exodus 10 v.21. "Haziness over the place that is known for Egypt, obscurity which might even be felt." And it offers subtle element to our Lord's expectation, "There should be signs in the sun, and in the moon, and in the stars; and upon the earth pain of countries, with perplexity; the ocean and the waves thundering; men's hearts fizzling them for apprehension, and for taking care of those things which are going ahead the earth: for the forces of paradise should be shaken" (Luke 21 v.25-26)

8:13 And I viewed, and heard a blessed messenger flying through the middle of paradise, saying with a boisterous voice, Woe, trouble, hardship, to the inhabiters of the earth by reason of alternate voices of the trumpet of the three heavenly attendants, which are yet to sound!

The last three trumpets will be particularly serious, as reported by the triple reiteration of Woe, trouble, hardship. They will be coordinated toward the inhibitors of the earth, that is, the unbelievers still alive on earth. Both the most established and the lion's share of Greek original copies read "hawk" rather than heavenly attendant in the principal part of the verse.

Express gratitude toward God Christians will be saved the Wrath. It appears from the announcement in verse 6, the things which have as of now happened are likely amid tribulation. From the "hardships", the fierceness is going to come.

Indeed, even the issues we have officially found out about are horrible, however they deteriorate. Here once more, notice the mid-time partition of this, four holy messengers have sounded, and three more are going to sound.

CHAPTER 9

The Fifth Angel,
Fifth Trumpet And Demons

9:1 "And the fifth holy messenger sounded, and I saw a star tumble from paradise unto the earth: and to him was given the key of the unlimited pit."

We realize that Jesus Christ holds the way to the endless pit. He removed the key from Satan when He (Jesus) went there, lectured, and carried bondage hostage out with Him, Ephesians 4:8 The Fifth Trumpet - The ejection of Satan from paradise. The distinguishing proof of Satan in this entry is not hard to make. Isaiah anticipated this improvement in the very same way portrayed by John. "How you have tumbled from paradise, O star of the morning, child of the day break! You have been chopped down to the earth, you who have debilitated the countries!" (Isaiah 14 v.12)

Numerous individuals erroneously trust that all through mankind's history, Satan has as of now been expelled from paradise, or that he rules in some sort of kingdom in hellfire. That isn't valid. Satan has dependably had admittance to the Throne of God, where he serves as the standard informer of the holy people of God. "Presently there was a day when the children of God came to present themselves before the Lord, what's more, Satan additionally came among them." (Job 1 v.6)

Satan's entrance into God's vicinity changes here. Presently he is kicked out of paradise, and he is enraged. Note additionally that he conveys with him the way to the no-limit pit. (Rev. 9 v.1) He didn't have it before; it was given him by the One who holds the keys to paradise, damnation and to death.

9:2 "And he opened the unlimited pit; and there emerged a smoke out of the pit, as the smoke of an extraordinary heater; and the sun and the air were obscured by reason of the smoke of the pit."

Jesus gave Satan the keys with the goal that he could be discharged to complete this discipline. Generally as Satan needed to have authorization of God to beset Job, Satan brings these frightful things on the earth and his kin by consent of God.

The physical smoke that surfaces most likely will cloud the sun and decrease the light. In the otherworldly, it will decrease the Light, as well.

The pit is the home of Satan and the evil presences. At the point when Satan opens the chasm, here come the evil presences in power to mislead and wreck. They have such a horrendous nature, to the point that God needed to tie them to keep mankind from being destroyed before the selected time, however now the limits are off.

"Also, out of the smoke approached beetles upon the earth; and power was given them, as the scorpions of the earth have power. What's more, they were informed that they ought not hurt the grass of the earth, nor any green thing, nor any tree, yet just the men who don't have the seal of God on their brows.

The presence of these insects is both startling and loathsome (v.7-10), and they don't act in a sloppy path; truth be told, John says, "They had as lord over them the heavenly attendant of the unlimited pit, whose name in Hebrew is Abaddon, yet in Greek he has the name Apollyon" (v.11) Both names signify "Destroyer". This is by all accounts one of the maladies that God sends on the adherents of Antichrist to frustrate them from converting among the uncommitted of the world. It might likewise give Tribulation holy people some an opportunity to set themselves up for the repulsions of the soon to come Great Tribulation.

In the event that any religious action is as yet going ahead right now, there will be a surge of false convention and criticizing of the Lord Jesus Christ. It would be a sort of religion of the tissue, (anything goes religion). It sounds all that much like what is going on today in many holy places.

9:3 "And there left the smoke insects upon the earth: and unto them was given force, as the scorpions of the earth have power."

The depiction of the insects demonstrates that they are devils who are given physical structures so as to show their pulverization and torment. Stallions demonstrate their warlike character. Their crowns portray them as vanquishers. Human confronts show insight. Their female hair maybe makes them enchanting and appealing. The teeth of lions demonstrates to them to be damaging and harmful. Breastplates of iron make them indestructible. Wings symbolize quickness. The stings in their tails give them the ability to hurt. Luckily for humankind, their time of torment is constrained to five months. Yet, the following judgment is much more terrible.

Notice, these must be evil spirits as they had no force all by themselves. It was given unto them.

9:4 "And it was charged them that they ought not hurt the grass of the earth, neither one of the any green thing, neither one of the any tree; however just those men which have not the seal of God in their brows."

This is an assault on the individual, which makes us take another take a gander at it profoundly. They have orders not to hurt the vegetation or the 144,000 who have been fixed in their brows. Genuine grasshoppers would eat each green thing that they could discover, and they do. Taking a gander at this from the otherworldly outlook, these insects are evil spirit spirits turned free upon this world. The fallen angel, or his devils, can't generally hurt anybody secured in the blood of Jesus.

They were not allowed to kill anybody, but rather to torment for five months; and their torment was similar to the torment of a scorpion when it stings a man." (Rev. 9 v.3

5) God's directions are fundamentally, "You might torment the individuals who have the Antichrist's imprint, yet you may not slaughter them." Also, "you may not touch the individuals who fit in with Me." Satan's energy is under strict control over those fixed by God -both now and in the Tribulation. In spite of the fact that this will be a time of awesome anguish, it is truly the finesse of GOD at work. I'm certain that the LORD is trying to make humanity think in light of the fact that about this awful torment and to choose to come to Him. 9:5 "And to them it was given that they ought not kill them, but rather that they ought to be tormented five months: and their torment [was] as the torment of a scorpion, when he striketh a man."

Here once more, whether this is physical torment and torment from aftermath creating wounds and torment, or whether this is profound and awful enduring, it is brought on by consistent assault from the fallen angel for five months. It is frightful. As at Hiroshima, the individuals who survived the bomb, wished they were dead. Extraordinary wounds, distortions and torment outside our ability to grasp occurred. As a rule it took five months to kick the bucket. A shocking smolder would have the agony of a scorpion's sting.

As of right now, we should take a gander at something we've examined some time recently. Keep in mind the 144,000 where the four holy messengers kept down the winds until they had been fixed in section 7 verse 1?

Were the 144,000 fixed as well as the individuals who swung to Christ amid the Tribulation. Those are the Tribulation Saints and they too were fixed by God generally as all genuine Christians of today have God's seal on them.

9:6 "And in those days should men look for death, and might not discover it; and might longing to bite the dust, and demise might escape from them."

Passing would be an appreciated help to such an excess of torment. These strengths of shrewdness turned free (over the top) upon the earth, whether physical or profound, will be terrible to the point that men will ask to kick the bucket however will be not able amid this discipline.

This was the first of the three Woes!

9:7-8 "And the states of the insects [were] like unto stallions arranged unto fight; and on their heads [were] in a manner of speaking crowns such as gold, and their appearances [were] as the characteristics of men." "And they had hair as the hair of ladies, and their teeth were as [the teeth] of lions."

Here John portrays the insects (devils) as he gives a point by point depiction of their appearance in his vision. They are portrayed as grasshoppers as they will bring huge and obliterating judgment from God.

This devil host will be for all intents and purposes relentless and man will have no weapon that can hurt them or cure for the awful torment they will cause.

Their countenances of men demonstrate they are wise and reasonable creatures, not creepy crawlies. Having hair as being similar to the hair of ladies underlines their alluring quality. Maybe to bait clueless unbelievers to approach them before striking them.

Having teeth like the teeth of lions means they will be more savage, effective and fatal than lions.

9:9 "And they had breastplates, so to speak breastplates of iron; and the sound of their wings [was] as the sound of chariots of numerous stallions hurrying to fight."

Breastplates of iron symbolizes their resistance.

To put it plainly, they will be difficult to oppose or to obliterate. There will be no getting away from their overall attack as there will be no place to run or avoid them.

In a representation drawn from a combat zone, John looks at the sound of their wings to a moving armed force, taking note of that it was similar to the sound of chariots, of numerous stallions hurrying to hitter. The sound alone will be sufficient to place dread into the hearts of the unbelievers.

9:10 "And they had tails like unto scorpions, and there were stings in their tails: and their energy [was] to hurt men five months."

As these evil presences are contrasted with scorpions, it is clear that their central goal is to hurt men. The very way of this full scale evil torment that drives men to look for death and not discover it, or to seek after death and not get it, is not portrayed.

There are references in the book of scriptures where evil presences had individuals, for example, found in Matthew 8 v.28, Matthew 4 v.23-24, Matthew 8 v.6 and Mark 9 v.20-22.

These evil spirits are given the ability to torment unbelievers for 5 entire months with no alleviation for the tormented. This burdens God's sovereign control over the timing of their strike. In the end God will return them to the chasm with their shrewd expert, then send them to the pool of flame. (Part 20)

9:11 "And they had a lord over them, [which is] the heavenly attendant of the endless pit, whose name in the Hebrew tongue [is] Abaddon, yet in the Greek tongue hath [his] name Apollyon."

You can call him any name you want to. This is Satan. Lucifer was one of the blessed messengers near God in paradise. He was an exceptionally wonderful holy messenger before his fall. The greater part of the evil spirits were holy messengers in paradise until 1/3 of the holy messengers took after Lucifer and got to be devils.

Heavenly attendants, as we have said some time recently, are serving spirits. These fallen heavenly attendants (evil spirits) are serving agony and enduring. Their main goal is to obliterate. Their pioneer, Lucifer, is the exemplification of underhandedness. He has been their ruler since they were thrown out of paradise by God. Their dwelling place, they are not on a mission of pulverization, is in the void. This is the place they were loosed from in V-2. They are constantly bringing on war, both otherworldly and strict. Their central goal is to decimate any way they can.

This "ruler" in V-11 is the star we found in V-1, which was tossed out of paradise and has hellfire for a dwelling place. Pretty much as he lead these blessed messengers out of paradise, he drives them in this mission of decimation. Satan, despite the fact that fallen, must do everything the Lord orders him.

Keep in mind the majority of this happens on the grounds that God's rage is aroused. God alone can stop Satan. This time God would not like to stop him. God permits, and even requests, this to happen. Satan, Apollyon, Abaddon, Lucifer, the fiend, or whatever you want to call him, is still loyal to God. He, as we, or some other being, or blessed messenger, are made and subject to the goals of the Creator. God alone could stop this annihilation. "Apollyon" and "Abaddon" mean demolition.

Jesus had and has numerous names. Satan is a forger, so he has numerous names, also. Individuals all through history have attempted to put names of present day victors to these, however I don't trust that is proposed here.

9:12 "One hardship is past; [and], see, there come two burdens all the more in the future."

As though this is not sufficiently repulsive that we have been catching wind of, there are two more burdens. The open fighting in the city of Lebanon and Israel help us all that much to remember the things we read about in the last lesson. A mother here of the world has no clue when her family goes out whether they will return alive or not.

The descendants of Ishmael and Isaac (the fragile living creature and the soul) are still in mortal battle after all the 1000's of years that have passed. Pretty much as there is an otherworldly clash of the fragile living creature and the soul that we should confront every day, there is a physical fight in Israel between the Arab and the Jew. Ishmael was informed that his descendants would live around the Jews and would be battling consistently.

The Bible is valid. A burden is a shocking catastrophe.

9:13-14 "And the 6th heavenly attendant sounded, and I heard a voice from the four horns of the brilliant sacrificial table which is before God," "Saying to the 6th blessed messenger which had the trumpet, Loose the four holy messengers which are bound in the colossal waterway Euphrates."

The number six shows man or humanity. "Horns" mean force and quality. The number four means around the world. This "brilliant sacrificial stone" is the place God is. God is never connected with different metals.

The Sixth Trumpet - The Four Angels Released - At the blowing of the sixth trumpet, the second misfortune is discharged: the arrival of "the four heavenly attendants who are bound at the considerable waterway Euphrates" (v.14). The blessed messengers obviously lead a multitude of 200 million "horsemen" (evil spirits) who slaughter 33% of humanity through the infections of flame and smoke and brimstone.

God sees the Euphrates River as the isolating line in the middle of East and West. Indeed, the old Roman Empire likewise saw it that way. Everything east of the Euphrates was known as the Far East or Asia. The locale just toward the west of the colossal waterway was known as the Near East or Asia Minor.

9:15 "And the four holy messengers were loosed, which were readied for 60 minutes, and a day, and a month, and a year, for to kill the third piece of men."

At the point when these holy messengers are loosed, they instantly rouse the immense populace focuses of Asia to dispatch an assault on the Western and Middle Eastern fortifications. These devils are successful, on the grounds that they cause one and a half billion individuals, 33% of the remaining populace, to be executed in short request.

The Apostle John composed, "And the four blessed messengers, who had been readied for the Hour and Day and Month and Year, are discharged, with the goal that they may kill 33% of humankind. What's more, the quantity of the armed forces of the horsemen (evil spirits) was 200 million; I heard the quantity of them."

9:16 "And the quantity of the armed force of the horsemen [were] two hundred thousand: and I heard the quantity of them."

Presently notwithstanding the evil presences who have wandered the earth all through history, profound powers of mischievousness in the glorious spots (Eph. 6 v.12) as of late cast to earth (9 v.1 and 12 v.4) and the various evil spirits as of late discharged from the chasm at the sounding of the fifth trumpet, comes another wicked armed force that is two hundred million in number.

Some have proposed that the 200 million will originate from the Chinese who can at present field a multitude of that size. Be that as it may it is exceptionally farfetched this could be a human armed force because of the failure to prepare, nourish, transport, also the water it would take to backing that size unexpected. Those things thought about unequivocally propose this will be an extraordinary instead of a human power, particularly as the four heavenly attendants (devils) are charging this power.

When you consolidate this third with the quarter of humankind slaughtered in the seal judgments, by this point in the Tribulation half of the world's populace (after the satisfaction) as of now has been demolished. Tim LaHaye makes reference to the Chinese armed force which can raise a 200-million-man armed force now. That has provoked a few mediators to propose the 200 million would accompany the rulers of the east to do fight with Christ at the fulfillment of the end of this age, known as the Battle of Armageddon. While there is no doubt that the armed forces of the Orient going to that fight at the very end of the Tribulation will be gigantic, because of the unbelievable populace of those nations, they unquestionably are not the Rev. 9 v.16 armed force. Consider the accompanying reasons:

The 9 v.16 armed force goes out amid the sixth trumpet, which happens close to the center of the Tribulation; the 16 v.12 armed force goes out toward the end of the Tribulation.

The 200 million in 9 v.16 are not people but rather devils, doing things men can't do. These "horsemen" have a heavenly impact on the earth.

The Chinese armed force would incorporate every one of the men and ladies under arms in China, including their neighborhood state armies or resistance powers. It is highly unlikely the socialist government could hazard submitting all its military and combat hardware to the Middle East, for they know their opportunity hungry subjects would revolt before they returned. Also, the logistics of moving a multitude of 200 million from the Orient over the Euphrates and the Arabian Desert to the little place where there is Israel appears to be outlandish.

Tim LaHaye states that the 200 million are not to be taken as people. They are a strict unnatural, devil like underhandedness spirits that leave the pit, progressing under the administration of the four bound heavenly attendants. Just the unrepentant will be executed by this judgment.

For these and different reasons not specified, it is not sensible to expect that the armed forces of 16 v.12 are synonymous with those of 9 v.16. The 200 million horsemen who go ahead the scene will clearly be otherworldly, animals that are so amazing to look on that they really panic a few individuals to death. What's more, their sting "is in their mouth and their tails", and with them they murder 33% of the world's populace of the individuals who reject Christ and submit themselves to Antichrist.

9:17 "And in this manner I saw the stallions in the vision, and them that sat on them, having breastplates of flame, and of jacinth, and brimstone: and the leaders of the steeds [were] as the heads of lions; and out of their mouths issued fire and smoke and brimstone."

Stallions have been regularly connected with fighting in sacred text. It is clear these are not real steeds judging the heads were as the heads of lions.

Numerous have attempted to relate the importance of this sacred text with weapons of war, however this can't be. John would have no issue with partner a lion's head with what these seemed to resemble.

John saw three ways the evil presence steeds murdered their casualties and all ways portray the fierce and crushing fierceness of hellfire. They burned them with flame, then suffocated with smoke and brimstone which continued out of their mouths.

9:18 "By these three was the third piece of men murdered, by the flame, and by the smoke, and by the brimstone, which issued out of their mouths."

The final aftereffect of this satanic 200 million was that 33% of the remaining humankind would be slaughtered. Note that a quarter of humanity was executed amid the seal judgments, leaving seventy five percent of the remaining populace. As 33% is presently executed, half of humankind now has been murdered. (33% of 75 that was remaining is 25%)

The passing of 33% of the world's remaining occupants will be the most calamitous debacle to strike the earth subsequent to the surge amid the days on Noah.

9:19 "For their energy is in their mouth, and in their tails: for their tails [were] like unto serpents, and had heads, and with them they do hurt."

Not just were these evil steeds ready to execute with their mouths, additionally demise was in their tails. Their tails are similar to destructive noxious serpents. The steeds tails were not real serpents as the stallions were not genuine steeds.

However, these pictures are depicting the powerful destructiveness of this evil presence power in wording that one would ordinarily comprehend in the regular world.

Not at all like the wicked scorpion stings of the fifth trumpet judgment, the chomps of these evil creatures will be fatal.

9:20 "And whatever is left of the men which were not murdered by these maladies yet apologized not of the works of their hands, that they ought not revere villains, and symbols of gold, and silver, and metal, and stone, and of wood: which neither can see, nor listen, nor walk:"

It is unimaginable to the point that after numerous years of agony and demise at this point from the horrendous judgments of God, joined with the 144,000, the two witnesses, a heavenly attendant who gives the Word of God to people, also the endless number of Tribulation Saints, that whatever remains of humanity, who were not executed by these plaques, did not apologize.

These "men" are guys, as well as all of humanity. Ladies will need to respond in due order regarding their own behavior, and the men. What on the planet needs to happen before they will apologize? These things loved in verse 20 portrays our day. These are things of the world. Attempting to out do the neighbors with: a greater house - "wood or stone", better adornments - "gold and silver", costly trimmings - "metal" and love of the villain - "love fallen angels"

These things recorded are lifeless questions and have no energy to fulfill anything.

Anything or any individual who does not raise Jesus Christ to divinity is in mistake and adoring the fiend. Jesus said Himself that "He that is not with me is against me; and he that gathereth not with me scattereth abroad." Matthew 12:30.

We are either in favor of Jesus or the villain. There is no center ground. We are not to love God's manifestations. We are to adore the Creator.

9:21 "Neither apologized they of their homicides, nor of their divinations, nor of their sex, nor of their robberies."

At that future point ever, godlessness, supernatural quality, spiritism, satanism and all types of false religion will turn into the standard as devils lead individuals into more shrewd and horrible practices. Savage wrongdoings like homicide will be totally widespread. With no feeling of ethical quality, the insidious, unrepentant individuals will mimic the evil spirit swarm's lethal blood desire. Obviously, professors in God will without a doubt be their prime targets.

By and by, individuals will decline to apologize of their transgressions as the universe of unrepentant individuals seek the rare supplies of nourishment, apparel, water, safe house and meds.

Affected by the gigantic evil presence constrains that has been unleashed upon the world, false religion, murder, sexual depravity and wrongdoing will be unparalleled in mankind's history.

The Big Four Sins - Rev. 9 v.21 records the four most noticeable sins of the Tribulation period. The importance of these wrongdoings is incredible in light of present patterns on the planet. It's no occurrence that the four noteworthy sins recorded here are today four of the most difficult issues confronting law requirement.

(1) The first of these trademark sins is murder. For reasons unknown, societal tolerance, absence of discipline or absence of confidence, there has been a disturbing increment in homicide all through the US and the world. One element is the dismissal of total guidelines of good and bad. At the point when a judge who posts the Ten Commandments in his court is sued, you know society has its needs upside down. Any individual who was wakeful in the last part of the twentieth century could see the roughness around us. I don't think I have to expound on this point.

The homicide of unborn youngsters in our day is a stench in God's nostrils. Ladies and men ought to apologize of these homicides. Murder with a savage weapon is not generally with a firearm or a blade. A standout amongst the most pointless homicides in our day is tanked drivers killing individuals with their cars. Some are tanked on liquor and some on medications. These are pointless killings that don't finish anything.

President Clinton vetoed a bill, went with bi-divided backing in both the house and the senate, that would have precluded halfway conception premature births.

(2) The second unmistakable sin of the Tribulation period will be medication related mysterious exercises. The word magic works is utilized as a part of Rev. 9 v.21. It originates from the Greek word meaning drug store, and alludes here to the act of the mysterious attached to the utilization of medications.

Drug use in the 1990's multiplied from the 1960's and mid 70's. In 1997 more than 11% guaranteed to utilize medicates each month. By study by the Center on Addiction and Substance Abuse at Columbia University in New York, today's little girls are 15 times more probable than their time of increased birth rates moms to have started illicit medication use by age 15.

Another class of soaring use is in alleged planner medications, for example, methamphetamine. Charles Rangel, D-N.Y. expressed when Bill Clinton was pesident that "I have never, never, never seen a president who thinks less about this issue."

There is a solid connection between medication use and evil spirit ownership. As far back as 1971, the International Journal of Social Psychiatry managed the truth of evil presence ownership and how to analyze it.

There is a need to find out if there is any inclusion in medication enslavement, as it is basic that addicts, particularly with heroin and liquor, get to be included with dark enchantment and the other way around. Some have been known at times to have been extremely religious individuals who defaulted, and in this way left themselves open to some force other than God to control their lives.

Magic works can likewise be anything connected with the mysterious: palm perusing, horoscope, and so forth. Such a large number of individuals in our general public today are playing around with psyche control, supernatural contemplation, and other false religions. The majority of this sort of action is to undermine our confidence in God.

(3) The third noticeable sin of the Tribulation will be widespread indecency. "Porneia," the Greek word utilized as a part of this verse, alludes to a wide range of sexual action outside of marriage. Clearly, there will be a finished breakdown in the organization of marriage. Indeed, people, as anybody can obviously see, we're just about there!

More than 70,000 ladies are sexually ambushed each year in the US. (1 at regular intervals) It is the most quickly developing fierce wrongdoing in the nation.

Aggressive behavior at home is more across the board than any other time in recent memory. Every year somewhere around 2 and 4 million ladies are battered; 1,500 ladies are killed by their private accomplices; 1.8 million elderly are casualties of abuse; 1.7 million tyke misuse reports are recorded. Sex covers living with somebody before you are hitched. Sex spreads being hitched and dating another person. Sex covers all gay person and lesbian acts.

The US Supreme court rules as unlawful Colorado's Amendment 2 to the state constitution, a basic and famous endeavor to deny neighborhood governments from transforming gay people and other sexual goes amiss into the most recent ensured political class. By the court's thinking, as disagreeing Justice Antonio Scalia brought up, any express that bans Polygamy is likewise stuck in an unfortunate situation.

It's really a matter of open deliberation in the House of Representatives and US Senate, whether men ought to be permitted to wed men and ladies wed ladies. (1997)

(4) The fourth normal for the Tribulation will be burglary of different types. Wrongdoing in the majority of its signs is on the upsurge today. The specialists say a young wrongdoing emergency is right around the bend. At the present development rate, there will be almost one half million more preadult young men in the year 2010 than there are today. That pattern would mean there will be 30,000 more ceaseless adolescent delinquents in the city in 15 years. (from 1997) Though speaking to just 7% of every male adolescent, these constant guilty parties carry out 70% of all genuine wrongdoing in their age bunch.

At the point when a country, established as one country under God, surrenders its sway under God for "reliance" on the world, you can see where the future falsehoods. To be a companion of this future framework in the feeling of trading off God's perspective of life and letting the world crush you into its mold is to confer infidelity, profoundly talking. Keep in mind, additionally, that in a genuine association with God through Jesus Christ, adherents are seen just like the "Lady" of Christ (2 Cor. 11

v.2) That's another reason that playing around with false religion is seen all through the Bible as otherworldly infidelity.

Throughout the previous 30 years, America has been inundated in a society war that undermines the country's extremely establishment, its exceptionally survival. God's statement lets us know in Luke 12 v.48 that "For everybody to whom much is given, from him much will be required; and to whom much has been committed, of him they will ask the more."

The historical backdrop of the world has any country been more honored than the US? Yet there is dependably an expense to impropriety. What's more, today we are starting to pay it. In the previous 30 years there has been a 560% expansion in brutal wrongdoing. Illegitimate births have expanded 419%. Separation rates have tripled. The quantity of youngsters living in single guardian homes has tripled. The high schooler suicide rate has expanded 200%. Understudy Achievement Tests have plunged 80 focuses.

It ought not astonish us that Billy Graham said years prior that if God didn't pass judgment on America soon, he would need to apologize to Sodom and Gomorrah. In any case, it's not only the US. The whole world is in a headlong dive into the ethical quality of Sodom and Gomorrah and tragically into the same judgment.

CHAPTER 10

The Little Book

10:1 And I saw another strong holy messenger descend from paradise, dressed with a cloud: and a rainbow [was] upon his head, and his face [was] figuratively speaking the sun, and his feet as mainstays of flame:

At no other time does Christ show up as a holy messenger or made being after His revival. This blessed messenger is undoubtedly Michael, Gabriel, or a heavenly attendant equivalent to them who makes a solemn vow by Jesus Christ, demonstrating something noteworthy is going to happen. Heavenly attendants assume a conspicuous part in the Apocalypse, being specified sixty-six times.

The cloud, the rainbow, the sun, and the mainstays of flame might allude to divinity, however a parallel might likewise be drawn with the holy messenger Gabriel.

10:2 And he had in his grasp a little book open: and he set his right foot upon the ocean, and [his] left [foot] on the earth,

The "Little Book" that was found in paradise in verse 2 has a comparative mission as that given to Ezekiel 3 v.1-3 and Jeremiah 15 v.16. The prophetic Word, which is the thing that the "Little Book" is, contains the "sweet" message of God's great arrangement for humankind including the happening to Christ, the Millennium Kingdom, and Heaven, yet it likewise contains the Judgment of God on delinquents who don't atone and come to Him, and their definitive dispatch to hellfire.

Only the way that it is opened lets us know that it is to be uncovered to the individuals who will expend it. As adherents, we are advised to eat this book, pretty much as John was advised to eat it. This "little book", I accept, is the Word of God, the Bible.

The Bible (Word) is alive. When we eat the Bible it gives us the quality to live successful lives before Him. Jesus is in territory over everything. He is our wellspring of force. Examining the Bible is more essential to our life than our day by day bread. Praise God, the Bible is of no private understanding. God the Holy Spirit will instruct each of us what the Bible is stating to us.

The planting of the feet on the ocean and the earth (dry area) demonstrates Christ's power over the earth completely, and the apportionment of His guaranteed legacy as Messiah.

10:3-4 "And cried with an uproarious voice, as [when] a lion roareth: and when he had cried, seven thunders expressed their voices." "And when the seven thunders had articulated their voices, I was going to compose: and I heard a voice from paradise saying unto me, Seal up those things which the seven thunders articulated, and keep in touch with them not".

It appears that John was endeavoring to record everything as he saw it. This little book is not for the world to see. That is the reason Jesus talked in illustrations. Just the devotees to the Lord Jesus Christ should comprehend what is in the Book, and after that just through the direction of the Holy Spirit and Bible study. This message then from these voices is not for the world as a rule. Jesus, or God the Father, prevents John from uncovering these things by letting him know not to record this.

Thundering voices must come either from God or something exceptionally close Him. The voices that sound like seven thunders are an extraordinary element in the book of Revelation. John is readied to record what these thunder like voices say when he hears another voice instructing him to "seal up and not record what he listened".

This is the main announcement in the whole book of Revelation that is fixed up. With respect to the seventh heavenly attendant, the secret of God ought to be done I accept when the seventh coming dish judgment trumpet is sounded, is what is being alluded to here.

Both Daniel and John were told to seal up quite a bit of what they saw, holding the translation for the era to whom it would be self-evident: "I was going to compose; and I heard a voice from paradise saying, "seal up the things which the seven rings of thunder have talked, and don't think of them." And then, "But concerning you, Daniel, disguise these words and seal up the book until the end of time; numerous will retreat and forward, and learning will increment."

It ought to be evident to even the most easygoing of perusers this is the era in which information has expanded to the level important to comprehend the contrasts in the middle of images and substance. This is the era in which numerous will experience John's observer confirmation, to their everlasting misgiving! This is the Generation of End Times.

10:5-6 "And the holy messenger which I saw stand upon the ocean and upon the earth lifted up his hand to paradise," "And sware by him that liveth for ever and ever, who made paradise, and the things that in that are, and the earth, and the things that in that are, and the ocean, and the things which are in that, that there ought to be time no more.

Lifting the hand connotes taking a pledge (Gen. 14:22, 23; Dan 12:7). The declaration of the holy messenger is that there will be no more defer in the foundation of the millennial kingdom of Christ. This presumes a present deferral or delay of the guaranteed kingdom (between Christ's two approaches). With the sounding of the seventh trumpet (Rev. 11:15), the present puzzle type of the kingdom will be over (Rom. 11:25) and what God guaranteed to the prophets (Isaiah 11; Jer. 31; Ezek 36, 37; Dan 7; Zech. 14; Matt 6:10) will at last be finished. Christ's Coming Kingdom Time no more. This truly signifies "defer no more" and shows that the season of the end is quickly drawing closer. From the sounding of the seventh holy messenger's trumpet, the world will move determinedly toward the satisfaction of the considerable number of predictions of the Bible, finishing in the happening to Christ to the earth.

10:7 But in the times of the voice of the seventh holy messenger, when he might start to sound, the secret of God ought to be done, as he hath proclaimed to his hirelings the prophets.

This is when Jesus uncovers Himself to the Christians in paradise. The Bible says that when we get to paradise, we will remember Him, since we will be similar to Him. I John

3:2 "Dearest, now are we the children of God, and it doth not yet show up what we might be: but rather we realize that, when he should show up, we should be similar to him; for we should consider him to be he is."

You see this is a riddle to us now. When it is uncovered, it will be simple to the point that we will think, "Why didn't I think about that?" It is not for us to know this at this moment.

This seventh trumpet implies this is the last judgment. All through the New Testament, God talked in illustrations so the world would not understand. Just those to whom Jesus would uncover Himself would get it.

10:8-9 "And the voice which I got notification from paradise spake unto me once more, and said, Go [and] take the little book which is open in the hand of the heavenly attendant which standeth upon the ocean and upon the earth." "And I went unto the blessed messenger, and said unto him, Give me the little book. What's more, he said unto me, take [it], and gobble it up;

and it should make thy stomach biting, yet it might be in thy mouth sweet as nectar."

This is the third reference to the area of the blessed messenger who remains on the ocean and earth. (Verses 2, 5 and 8) This underlines unequivocally the surprising power he has over the earth.

John is advised to eat the little book, and when he does, it turns out to be sweet in his mouth (Ps. 119:103; Jeremiah 15:16) yet severe in his midsection. The demonstration of eating speaks to the comprehension and assignment of prophetic disclosure. The message is "sweet" on the grounds that finally the kingdoms guarantees are going to be satisfied. It is biting on the grounds that it must be proficient through more judgment and tribulation.

In Ezekiel parts 2 and 3, we see that physical Israel declined the New Testament and its educating of Jesus. This sweetness is the excellent message got, yet the sharpness is the failure when they reject the message. This intensity is the shocking judgment, too.

10:10 And I took the little book out of the heavenly attendant's hand, and gobbled it up; and it was in my mouth sweet as nectar: and when I had eaten it, my gut was biting.

The demonstration of eating the book (scroll) symbolizes the retaining and acclimatizing God's Holy Word. The Bible At the point when John expended the book, the words that were composed were sweet as nectar. (extremely satisfying)

Yet, for the individuals who might be tormented in hellfire for whatever remains of time everlasting, which was going to happen, John then tasted the sharpness as He knew God was going to take back the earth which was legitimately His, and be lifted up, respected and celebrated as He merited. John understood the ghastly discipline that was going to be given to unrepentant unbelievers and that brought about the sweet taste to swing to severity.

10:11 And he said unto me, Thou must prediction again before numerous people groups, and countries, and tongues, and rulers.

****This verse is a key to the order of the Book of Revelation. John is advised to forecast again concerning numerous people groups, and countries, and tongues, and lords. The seal and trumpet judgments have conveyed the sequence near the end of the Tribulation period and to the arrival of Christ to the earth (Rev. 11-15). ********

Presently John must prediction through the period a second time, focusing this time on the significant personages and developments of the tribulation (e.g., Satan, the brutes, the mistress or Babylonian framework). This copied prescience starts in part 12 and finishes in the vial (dish) judgments, the annihilation of the monster, and the arrival of Christ.

CHAPTER 11

The Outer Court,
Trials And Tribulations

11:1 And there was given me a reed like unto a pole: and the holy messenger stood, saying, Rise, and measure the sanctuary of God, and the holy place, and them that love in that.

This heavenly attendant is advising John to take an estimation of the sanctuary and the general population. We read in Ezekiel 40:5, that this reed is nine feet long (six cubits). This is by all accounts a comparable message in Ezekiel to the one here in Revelation.

The appalling thing in the greater part of this is among the external court (the unsaved) are numerous ostensible Christians, who trust that they will be spared. This is by all accounts just requested that of John make him mindful of the large number of genuine adherents who will be in the very vicinity of God. It is, likewise, to help him to remember those purported Christians that have brought trade off and satisfying of the substance into God's congregation.

The external court for the Gentiles implies only this, the devotee who is a Christian in name just, not in deed. The fickle segment of the congregation that we read about in second Timothy 3 verse 5 "has a type of purity however denies the power". This external court is not the spot for adherents to be.

This announcement about the "sanctuary and them that love in that" is discussing the genuine devotee's who by and large make up the sanctuary (assemblage of Christ).

11:2 But the court which is without the sanctuary forget, and measure it not; for it is given unto the Gentiles: and the blessed city should they tread on the ground forty [and] two months.

I might want to say again here that the Bible (and particularly Revelation) must be comprehended by its signs and images through the soul and can't be seen truly. As any fantasy or vision must be translated, so does Revelation.

The external court speaks to the control of Jerusalem and Israel by Gentiles amid the last 50% of the Tribulation period. As it were it is too common for God. He is stating (toss them out) they are not part of the choose. They are not part of the group of Christ. The inward court makes up the assortment of devotees.

We see here in this forty-two month that the heavenly city is trodden down; that the adherents to Jesus "sacred city" will experience 3-1/2 years of hardships. All through Revelation, the "sacred city" is typical of the assortment of devotees.

The heavenly city is the natural Jerusalem (Dan. 9:24; Zech. 13:8, 9; 14:2). The forty and two months demonstrate that Jerusalem will be under Gentile control for three-and-a-half years, presumably the last 50% of the seven-year Tribulation period (Dan. 9:24-27, where the time of the Tribulation is seen as the Seventieth Week, or seven-year period in God's postexilic project for Israel. Tribulation

Next "A Powerful Proclamation to the World" - Christ is unquestionably not saying that this gospel must be lectured each individual. Millions have as of now passed on without listening to it. Maybe it must be declared in; "in all the world for a witness to all countries." That expression sounds as if the day is coming when people as well as every one of the countries of the world will be capably faced by the gospel and the outcomes of dismissing it. John appears to have been demonstrated such a period in his vision in (Rev. 11 v.3-6).

11:3-6 "And I will give [power] unto my two witnesses, and they might forecast a thousand two hundred [and] threescore days, dressed in sackcloth." "These are the two olive trees, and the two candles remaining before the God of the earth." "And if any man will hurt them, fire proceedeth out of their mouth, and devoureth their adversaries: and if any man will hurt them, he should in this way be killed." "These have energy to close paradise, that it downpour not in the times of their prediction: and have control over waters to swing them to blood, and to destroy the earth with all infections, as frequently as they will".

The two witnesses of Revelation 11 will have amazing power and effect, together with the 144,000 witnesses, in delivering the gigantic soul harvest of the initial forty two months of the Tribulation depicted in Rev. 7. They will give the a huge number of Jews in the Holy Land a philosophical and profound scaffold to the Christian gospel. A hefty portion of the souls collected at that the reality of the situation will become obvious eventually the children and little girls of Abraham.

What a dynamic and convincing message from God these two stunning witnesses will convey to "all countries!" No one can discount them as crazies, for they show mind blowing otherworldly powers and oppose the Antichrist and his subordinates to stop them. Undoubtedly they will be seen day by day on universal TV in each edge of the earth as they caution humanity of God's coming judgment.

The world police and even the military will be feeble to hush them. Any individual who endeavors to prevent them from lecturing is in a flash wrecked. Indeed, even Antichrist's otherworldly powers are no match for these two daring and God enabled ministers of truth. There can be probably these two witnesses will have the consideration of the whole world! Their message will be an assertion to every one of the countries on this planet to atone and to recognize that Jesus Christ is the world's legitimate ruler.

The 3-1/2 years of their convincing lecturing would appear to concur with the primary portion of Daniel's 70th week. Numerous will trust the gospel they declare and will from that point decline to love the Antichrist or to take his imprint, and will be martyred for their confidence.

Who Are They - Some attempt to distinguish one of the witnesses with Enoch (in light of the fact that he never kicked the bucket, Gen. 5 v.24) and the other with either Elijah (who likewise never passed on, (2 Kings 2 v.11-12) or Moses. For three reasons Tim LaHaye is slanted to think they are Moses and Elijah.

Moses and Elijah are the two most persuasive men ever. Moses acquainted God's composed law with Israel and composed the initial five books of the Old Testament. Elijah was the first of the written work prophets and began the school of the prophets. At whatever point the Jews said, "Moses and Elijah," they generally signified "the law and the prophets."

Moses and Elijah went with Jesus and the 3 followers when He was "transfigured before them" on the mount and where He talked about His looming penance on the cross (Mat. 17). The 3-1/2 years of their convincing lecturing would appear to correspond with the principal portion of Daniel's 70th week. Numerous will trust the gospel they declare and will from that point decline to love the Antichrist or to take his imprint, and will be martyred for their confidence.

The 2 witnesses are said to replicate the very wonders that Moses and Elijah performed while on this planet. John said of them, "And on the off chance that anybody needs to damage them, fire continues from their mouth and eats up their foes. These have energy to close paradise, so that no downpour falls in the times of their prescience; and they have control over waters to swing them to blood, and to hit the earth with all diseases, as frequently as they longing." (Rev. 11 v.5-6)

Elijah is celebrated for calling down flame from paradise. The most acclaimed case happens in 1 Kings 18 v.36-38) in the record of the challenge between the prophets of Baal and Elijah. The Lord sent flame on Elijah's holy place on Mt. Carmel in light of his basic request to God: "Ruler God of Abraham, Isaac, and Israel, let it be known this day that You are God in Israel, and that I am Your worker, and that I have done every one of these things at Your Word. Hear me, O Lord, hear me, this individuals might realize that You are the Lord God, and that You have turned their hearts back to You once more."

Elijah is associated with incredibly brought about dry season and also to judgments of flame. Truth be told, the first occasion when he is specified in the Scriptures he is heard saying to fiendish King Ahab, "As the Lord God of Israel lives, before whom I remain, there should not be dew nor downpour these years, except at my word." (1 Kings 17 v.1) And there wasn't; God honored the prophet's word.

Moses, obviously, is personally associated with the ten torment that struck Egypt just before the (Exodus 7-12) In the main sickness God transformed the waters of Egypt into blood - including the Nile, all streams, waterways, lakes, pools, and even the water in cans of wood and stone. The water swung to blood, slaughtered the area's fish and brought on the water to stink, and conditions did not come back to ordinary for a week.

How fitting that Moses and Elijah would come back to Jerusalem to start these most recent 7 years of the Tribulation to "witness, affirm and forecast."

11:7 And when they might have completed their affirmation, the mammoth that ascended out of the endless pit should make war against them, and should overcome them, and murder them.

"The monster that surfaces from the Abyss" alludes to the mammoth depicted in Rev. 13 v.1 to 7" and is an expression utilized here surprisingly. The way that he will come up out of the Abyss is a reference until the very end and revival of the Antichrist. However let me interpose something here. Satan really indwelled two individuals in the book of scriptures. Who can let me know who they were? In the event that you said Judas and the Antichrist you are right. Antichrist

The Antichrist will kick the bucket and be revived. Rev. 17 v.8 states that "the mammoth, which you saw, once was, currently is not, and will leave the Abyss and go to his decimation." at the end of the day, the Antichrist will kick the bucket amidst the Tribulation. Since Satan will be thrown out of paradise, mindful that his time is short, he will indwell the Antichrist and copy the revival. Starting there on, indwelled by Satan himself, Antichrist will have energy to perform "fake supernatural occurrences, signs and ponders" (2 Thess. 2 v.9-12) and can conceivably mislead "the individuals who are dying." Satan

The brute or Antichrist, the man of sin, will loathe the two witnesses, make war against them, and slaughter them. In any case, take note of that he will have no control over them until "they have completed their confirmation." at the end of the day, they will be "interminable until their work is done", which can be said of every one of God's hirelings who stroll in acquiescence to His will.

The totally decline and cruel qualities of individuals living amid the Tribulation period is found in Rev. 11 v.8, which advises us that the assemblages of the two witnesses will be left open in the avenues of Jerusalem.

The Holy City will be so decline profoundly that she will be called Sodom and Egypt Sodom being an image of shamelessness and Egypt an image of realism. The lives of the general population backpedaling to possess the Holy Land today are definitely not Holy. They at times even go to synagogues on the Sabbath.

11:8-10 "And their dead bodies [shall lie] in the road of the immense city, which profoundly is called Sodom and Egypt, where likewise our Lord was killed." "And they of the general population and kindreds and tongues and countries should see their dead bodies three days and a half, and might not endure their dead bodies to be placed in graves." "And they that abide upon the earth might cheer over them, and make joyful, and might send endowments one to another; in light of the fact that these two prophets tormented them that harped on the earth".

And afterward the unsaved individuals of the world that loathe the witnesses so much will remark an inconceivably underhanded deed. They reject them a tolerable entombment, leaving their dead bodies to rot in the boulevards of Jerusalem. They even make a Christmas like festival out of their homicides by sending and getting presents "in honor" of the event. At that point a much more mind-boggling thing happens. John forecasts that "those from the people groups, tribes, tongues, and countries will see their dead bodies three and a half days" (Rev. 11 v.9). How could the entire world see their dead bodies? Very few years prior it was difficult to satisfy that prescience, yet today it could happen at any minute. We are the original ever to have that broadcasting capacity through Satellite transmission innovation!

The most extraordinary occasion of those times will be broadcast in a split second far and wide - "to the general population, tribes, tongues, and countries." Among different things, this will be an adoring motion by God Almighty, not just to restore and take to paradise His two prophets, additionally to make known His presence and force the world over. We have doubtlessly a great many souls to whom the 144,000 Jewish witnesses will be talking and whom the Holy Spirit will be indicting will see this exhibition of the perfect and react to the Savior.

God is an adoring Father who is "not willing that any ought to die but rather that all ought to come to atonement" (2 Peter 3 v.9). That "all" methods those left behind after the Rapture and additionally the individuals who have the benefit of reacting in confidence before it happens. What's more, the two witnesses are a major a portion of God's methods in the primary portion of the Tribulation to see that numerous men and ladies do, truth be told, apologize and go into unceasing life.

These are the same individuals who "cheer," "make joyful," and "send blessings to each other" over the killings of God's two witnesses at the midpoint of the Tribulation (Rev. 11 v.10);

the same individuals who "reviled the name of God who has control over these sicknesses; and they didn't atone and give Him brilliance" (Rev. 16 v.9); the same individuals who "cursed the God of paradise as a result of their torments and their wounds, and did not apologize of their deeds:" (Rev. 16 v.11) the same individuals who "reviled God due to the disease of the hail" (Rev. 16 v.21); and the same individuals whose "transgressions have come to paradise", who are blameworthy of "the blood of prophets and holy people, and of all who were killed on the earth". (Rev. 18 v.5, 24)

11:11-12 "And following three days and a large portion of the Spirit of life from God went into them, and they remained upon their feet; and incredible trepidation fell upon them which saw them." "And they heard an awesome voice from paradise saying unto them, Come up here. Also, they climbed up to paradise in a cloud; and their foes viewed them."

The Witnesses Resurrected - But after the three and a half days a breath of life from God entered them, and they remained on their feet, and fear struck the individuals who saw them. At that point they heard an uproarious voice from paradise saying to them, "Come up here." And they went up to paradise in a cloud.

As our Lord was killed, covered, and in three days became alive once again, these men, subsequent to being killed and presented to the eyes of the world, will hear the voice of God restoring them. A cloud will get them beyond anyone's ability to see even with their adversaries. It is no big surprise that "fear struck the individuals who saw them." The restoration of these men will be the last affirmation that they were men of God, another delineation that God does not overlook His own.

11:13 And that hour arrived an incredible quake, and the tenth part of the city fell, and in the tremor were killed of men seven thousand: and the remainder were alarmed, and offered greatness to the God of paradise.

God loses no time managing the individuals who have rejected the Lord or even the individuals who have said, I will fix up later. There is no later. It is presently. We see here that one tenth of the general population lose their life in this seismic tremor.

11:14-15 "The second misfortune is past; [and], view, the third burden cometh rapidly." "And the seventh holy messenger sounded; and there were extraordinary voices in paradise, saying, The kingdoms of this world are ended up [the kingdoms] of our Lord, and of his Christ; and he should rule for ever and ever".

The Seventh Trumpet - Loud Voices in Heaven - The third "misfortune,". The blowing of the seventh trumpet is similar to the softening of the seventh seal up that it presents the following arrangement of celestial judgments. The seventh trumpet is not in itself a judgment yet rather demonstrates all paradise cheering at the impending culminated triumph of Christ over the Antichrist. John records that "boisterous voices" in paradise yelled, "The kingdoms of the world have turned into the kingdoms of our Lord and of His Christ, and He should rule always and ever!" (v.15) Great celebrating and uproarious worship fill heaven, and on earth many lightning's, noise, thundering, hail, and an earthquake announce the approaching end.

The seventh trumpet results in the establishment of the millennial kingdom of Christ. The seven vials or bowls (16:1) are probably contained in the judgment of the seventh trumpet. They will occur in a very brief period of time at the end of the Great Tribulation.

The second happening to Christ, while an incredible gift for adherents, will be God's most serious judgment of the earth. The kingdoms of this world will be totally toppled by the coming kingdom of earth. The kingdoms of this world will be totally toppled by the coming kingdom of Christ (19:11-21; Dan 2:34,35,44), who will rule for ever and ever (Dan 7: verses 13, 14 and 27).

11:16-17 "And the four and twenty senior citizens, which sat before God on their seats, fell upon their countenances, and adored God," "Saying, We give thee much obliged, O Lord God Almighty, which workmanship, and wast, and craftsmanship to come; since thou hast taken to thee thy awesome force, and hast ruled.

These you recollect, spoke to the greater part of the adherents. They have something to applaud about, seeing that they were saved the anger of God. It was an ideal opportunity to fall on their countenances altogether love to God.

God is worshiped by the senior citizens since what He guaranteed is currently expert. Their appreciation is for the foundation of the millennial kingdom (1 Cor. 15:24). (Kingdom) The Gentile countries will be oppressed (Ps 2:1, 2). The anger of God will take retribution on His adversaries (Ps 2:5; 2 Thess. 1:7,8). The dead of all ages will be judged at the future Great White Throne Judgment (Rev. 20:11-15). (Great White Throne Judgment) Old Testament and Tribulation holy people who have passed on will be raised and compensated (Is. 26:19, 20; Dan 12:2; Matt. 25). The individuals who have attempted to obliterate the earth will themselves be devastated by God (Rev. 19:20,21). The ark of his confirmation (pledge) is an image of the vicinity of God and of His steadfastness in satisfying His contract guarantees.

God implied this world to be a rich wellspring of gift to humankind, however Satan, the Antichrist, and a large number of their false prophets have driven humankind to defy God, creating this world to be a position of awesome enduring. The older folks in paradise celebrate in light of the fact that the season of God's judgment and correction for goodness' sake is just three and one-half years away.

We see here that Jesus took power. The setting up of His kingdom conveys last triumph to the Christian. The thanks truly go to Jesus here; the adherents have not set up the kingdom, Jesus did. Everything we can do is to commend him for setting up the Kingdom. It was not done through our energy and might, but rather by His (Lord-Supreme Authority, Divinity, Almighty-Omnipotent). You see from this; He is all of it. His power is beyond reproach. His reign is forever and ever. He has no beginning and no end. He alone is worthy of our praise.

11:18 And the nations were angry, and thy wrath is come, and the time of the dead, that they should be judged, and that thou shouldest give reward unto thy servants the prophets, and to the saints, and them that fear thy name, small and great; and shouldest destroy them which destroy the earth.

The countries, (common people} had a feed day mistreating the adherents. They were irate and extremely unfavorable to those with confidence. Presently the tables are turned. These extremely ones, whom they aggrieved, will run over them. Here we see discipline for the individuals who did not acknowledge the endowment of salvation and extraordinary prizes given to the individuals who did acknowledge and live for Jesus. These, who will be annihilated, are really the reason for the earth being devastated. The fierceness of God pulverized them, as well as harmed the earth also.

11:19 And the sanctuary of God was opened in paradise, and there was found in his sanctuary the ark of his confirmation: and there were lightnings, and voices, and thunderings, and a quake, and incredible hail.

We see here the home of God in all its amazingness. There was an ark of the contract in the sanctuary in the wild. There is much hypothesis about where that natural ark is today. Some trust that it is underneath the city of Jerusalem; some trust it is in Rome. The odd thing is that it is insignificant where it is.

At the point when the offspring of Israel made a trip to the guaranteed land, It was a noticeable consolation that God was with them and would keep His agreement with them.

The one that is truly vital to devotees, we see here at the throne of God. We are consoled that God's agreement with us will never fall flat. We see God's energy and might in every one of these signs, for example, these seismic tremors. We should recall ceaselessly, that Revelation is not in sequential request. God does not let us know just precisely when every thing happens. We simply know they will happen. These quakes and so on., simply demonstrate God's managing man.

CHAPTER 12

The Birth of Jesus and
of Christianity

12:1 And there showed up an awesome marvel in paradise; a lady dressed with the sun, and the moon under her feet, and upon her head a crown of twelve stars:

The lady speaks to Israel, and her tyke is Christ; the Messiah (12:5; Isaiah 7:14; 9:6; 66:7.8; Micah 5:2; Romans. 9:4,5)

The lady is not the congregation, since the congregation did not deliver Christ, But rather He delivered the congregation.

The sun reflects reclaimed Israel's exceptional superbness, splendor and nobility on account of her delighted status and demonstrates her as God's picked country.

The moon under her feet implies God's guarantee of domain, and the crown of twelve stars pictures sovereignty and identifies with the 12 tribes of Israel. Go to Genesis 37 verses 9 - 11 and read about the fantasy Joseph had about the sun, moon and 11 stars which were bowing down to Joseph. (who was the twelfth)

In this look toward paradise by John, we are taken to an alternate part of the fight that has gone ahead through all ages in the middle of Jesus and Satan. In the event that Jesus is in fighting with Satan, then His kin are in fight also.

12:2 And she being pregnant cried, travailing in conception, and tormented to be conveyed.

Ladies, who have had youngsters, realize that there is torment included in conception. This Scripture is profoundly talking about the conception of Jesus and of Christianity.

The conception torments allude to the period before the conception of Christ when Israel was sitting tight for reclamation by the Messiah (Rom. 8:22, 23).

12:3 And there seemed another miracle in paradise; and see an extraordinary red mythical beast, having seven heads and ten horns, and seven crowns upon his heads.

We see here this "red dragon". This is the devil, and he is shown red all over to show his murderous and destructive personality. This is the only place in the New Testament that dragon is used. Here it is not a literal "dragon", but a figure of Satan. (Satan)

These seven are heads of evil governments. This world power, through these earthly kingdoms, comes from Satan himself. The seven crowned heads mean universal rule, and the ten horns mean world power to the utmost.

Five rulers had traveled every which way by the Apostle John's chance; one ruled amid his time; and the seventh speaks to the Antichrist to come. We will get into additional on this in a later part about the 6 realms that have come which is generally fascinating.

His ten horns demonstrate Satan's association with the fourth brute of Daniel 7 (verses 7 and 24) and with the Beast from the ocean in Chapter 13 of Rev.

12:4 And his tail drew the third part of the stars of paradise, and did cast them to the earth: and the mythical beast remained before the lady which was prepared to be conveyed, for to eat up her kid when it was conceived.

At the point when John lets us know that the fallen angels' tail drew 33% of the stars of paradise and tossed them to earth, he is portraying the first satanic uprising against God.

Satan by one means or another figured out how to persuade 33% of every one of God's holy messengers to go along with him in his insubordination; these creatures we now call "evil presences" or "fallen blessed messengers." They serve Satan and assume an essential part in the judgments of the Tribulation.

We see here, likewise, the lady going to conception, and this is the conception of Jesus the Christ.

Satan utilized Herod to attempt to execute Jesus the minute He was conceived. That was not God's arrangement, so Jesus was ensured until the season of the cross. This additionally shows here the conception of the congregation, which the villain has attempted to eat up each way he could.

12:5 And she delivered a man tyke, who was to run all countries with a pole of iron: and her tyke was gotten up to speed unto God, and [to] his throne.

This is discussing Jesus Christ. Jesus was gotten up to speed unto God to set on the right hand of God at the revival and is setting at the right hand of God. When He returns, Jesus will lead all countries as Lord of rulers and King of rulers.

Amid Jesus' natural, thousand years kingdom, this guideline is a breaking, and shattering work of judgment.

An iron pole is one that can't be broken and talks about the determination of Christ's standard. He will quickly and promptly judge all transgression and put down any disobedience.

12:6 And the lady fled into the wild, where she hath a spot arranged of God, that they ought to sustain her there a thousand two hundred [and] threescore days.

The wild speaks to anyplace outside Palestine. Amid the last 50% of the Tribulation period (1260 days is three and one half years), Israel will take shelter among the Gentile countries, where God will administer to her. (Maybe through the Gentile adherents) (Tribulation) God will disappoint Satan's endeavor to annihilate Israel amid the Tribulation and will conceal His kin pretty much as Jesus expressed in Matthew section 24 verses 15 - 21.

12:7-8 "And there was war in paradise: Michael and his blessed messengers battled against the monster; and the winged serpent battled and his holy messengers," "And won not; nor was their place found any more in paradise."

The vision of war in paradise expects Satan's avoidance from "paradise" and his confinement to the earth amid the last 50% of the Tribulation. Michael the chief heavenly messenger is the pioneer of God's sacred blessed messengers (Dan 10:13,21; 12:1; Jude 9).

Sooner or later of the Tribulation period, God will enable Michael and his powers to cast Satan and his powers out of access to paradise, with the goal that Satan should from there on limit his exercises to the natural circle.

I accept there is a request of order in paradise as there arrives on the earth. We see here, that not just the congregation of the Lord Jesus Christ is being assaulted here on the earth, yet that there is war in paradise also. Here we see annihilation of Satan to such a degree, to the point that he is not permitted in paradise anymore, not even to charge the devotees.

His annihilation on the earth is finished too. His fate was fixed when Jesus passed on the cross and was revived.

12:9 And the colossal mythical beast was thrown out, that old serpent, called the Devil, and Satan, which deceiveth the entire world: he was thrown out into the earth, and his holy messengers were thrown out with him.

The abhorrent one is given four assignments:

(1) Dragon pictures his tremendous character as the foe of God; (2) Serpent interfaces him with the cunning duplicity of Eve in Genesis 3; (3) Devil signifies "slanderer" (v. 10); (4) Satan signifies "Enemy" (1 Pet. 5:8). He likewise deceiveth the whole world.

Notice we are told here, that the serpent that deceived Eve was the fallen angel too. You can call him by any name you need to. On the off chance that whatever you call him is malicious, it is the fallen angel or his craftsmanship.

Here we see that he deceiveth (is persistently beguiling) the entire world. The fallen angel hurries forward and backward all through the earth looking for whom he might eat up. The fiend does not by any means trouble the lost by any stretch of the imagination. He as of now has them. He is after the adherent.

He comes to chapel routinely, attempting to urge you away. He brings false tenet and strife in the congregation. Check everybody and all that they say by the Word of God. The liar will come wearing sheep's attire, Matt. 7:15 He plants uncertainty and trepidation wherever he goes.

The villain is the extremely one who gets the "vibe great" religion. Be careful, he is a destroyer, he spoke to Eve's fragile living creature and annihilated her. The tissue is at war with the Spirit. Try not to LISTEN TO THE FLESH.

12:10 And I heard an uproarious voice saying in paradise, Now is come salvation, and quality, and the kingdom of our God, and the force of his Christ: for the informer of our brethren is thrown down, which blamed them before our God day and night.

The words salvation, quality (Greek dunamis, "power"), kingdom, and force (Gr. exousia, "power") all allude to the happening to the millennial kingdom of Christ. Kingdom

He (the demon) is hurled out for the last time. His day is over. The last 50% of the Tribulation will be a period of horrendous inconvenience on earth (Jer. 30:7; Dan 9:27; 12:1; Zeph. 1:15; Matt 24:15-22). It will be Satan's last endeavor to keep the arrival and the rule of Christ. He has just a brief span to attempt to keep the foundation of Christ's kingdom so his rage escalates of his abuse of Israel, God's picked country.

12:11 And they overcame him by the blood of the Lamb, and by the expression of their affirmation; and they adored not their lives unto the passing.

Triumph is Theirs - Thank God that His Word does not leave the tale of the Tribulation holy people with their natural destruction, however noisily broadcasts their definitive triumph through the blood of the Lamb. The "they" here are the Christians. At the point when Jesus shed his blood on Calvary and turned into the ideal Lamb give up once for unsurpassed, Satan was crushed.

You can see here the expression of our confirmation is the point at which we open our mouths and pronounce that we trust Jesus Christ is Lord, furthermore trust He became alive once again; we will be spared. We should announce this, regardless of the possibility that we know it will mean our life. We are not to respect life here on this planet as exceptionally important. The life that is imperative is in paradise. This world is not the Christian's home. We are just passing through.

12:12 Therefore celebrate, [ye] sky, and ye that abide in them. Burden to the inhabiters of the earth and of the ocean! for the villain is descended unto you, having awesome anger, since he knoweth that he hath however a brief span.

Here we Christians are advised to turn upward and cheer when we see horrendous things happening, on the grounds that our reclamation draweth near. The fallen angel, even now, is in a hard and fast push to devastate the congregation as it used to be fifty years back. He understands his time is running out, and he is taking a shot at the adherents, attempting to change over them to his way. His plan is to let us know not to be a radical Christian. He is attempting to make us not consider God genuine important. He wouldn't fret going to most holy places, since he hears almost no unadulterated Word of God and no sermons on the blood. Diluting Jesus is one of his most loved apparatuses to decimate the congregation.

It will be Satan's last endeavor to keep the arrival and the rule of Christ. He has just a brief span to attempt to keep the foundation of Christ's kingdom. In this way he has extraordinary fury and strengthens his mistreatment of Israel, God's picked country, which setting up his own particular fake kingdom through the Beast, the false savior.

12:13 And when the winged serpent saw that he was thrown unto the earth, he abused the lady which delivered the man [child].

Satan's oppression of Israel is evidently an endeavor to eliminate God's picked individuals, in this manner keeping the satisfaction of God's guarantees to Abraham and David in the messianic from abuse.

12:14 And to the lady were given two wings of an extraordinary falcon, that she may fly into the wild, into her place, where she is supported for a period, and times, and a large portion of a period, from the substance of the serpent.

The wings of an extraordinary falcon speak to quick escape from mistreatment. The falcon in numerous examples in the

Bible is typical of God. I trust, it implies that God will ensure us amidst the issues. This I accept is the thing that the "fixing of the adherents" is about.

That expression originates from Dan. 12 verse 11. This alludes to the second 50% of the Tribulation which starts by the evil entity of devastation. In Matt. 24 verse 15 Jesus said "When ye subsequently might see the plague of devastation, discussed by Daniel the prophet, stand in the blessed spot, (whoso readeth, let him comprehend)." Abomination of Desolation

Amid this time, God shields Israel from the Satan who might know where the Jews are stowing away, yet will be not able get at them due to God's celestial security.

12:15 And the serpent cast out of his mouth water as a surge after the lady, that he may make her be diverted of the surge.

The surge symbolizes overpowering abhorrence and mistreatment.

This symbolism symbolizes inconvenience as a rule. Satan's strengths will clear towards the Jew's concealing spot like an awesome surge in order to be suffocate, slaughtered or devoured by them.

12:16-17 "And the earth helped the lady, and the earth opened her mouth, and gobbled up the surge which the mythical beast cast out of his mouth." "And the winged serpent was wroth with the lady, and went to make war with the remainder of her seed, which keep the charges of God, and have the affirmation of Jesus Christ."

This is compare to the armed force of Pharaoh's the point at which the greater part of his chariots were decimated in Exodus 15. Verse 12 states: You extended Your right Hand, the earth gulped them."

This truly enrages Satan. He can't get to Jesus, as we said some time recently, so he is venting his indignation on the adherents of Jesus. Notice here that there is just a remainder left that has not fallen for the demons false tenet. A remainder means a little parcel that is cleared out.

You see here, this little divide (leftover) of Christians are as yet keeping God's commandants, and despite the fact that the restriction has been extraordinary, regardless they have given the confirmation of Jesus Christ. These two names (Jesus, Christ) together mean The Savior, the Anointed One.

The leftover might be a reference either to

(1) Jewish devotees, who have declined to love Satan and his Beast or (2) Gentile Believers, who are the seed of Abraham through Christ.

CHAPTER 13

The Antichrist and
The False Prophet

"1 And I remained upon the sand of the ocean, and saw a brute ascent up out of the ocean, having seven heads and ten horns, and upon his horns ten crowns, and upon his heads the name of profanation."

The New Testament word "antichrist" originates from the Greek antichristos, which means contrary to Christ or in substitution for Christ; and, is discovered just in the epistles of the Apostle John, e.g., "Little kids, it is the Last Time: and as ye have heard that Antichrist might come, even now arrive numerous antichrists; whereby we realize that it is the Last Time" (1John 2:18). Here, in a prophetically calamitous vision, John remains "upon the sand of the ocean" (13:1), where the "ocean" portrays the Gentile countries, i.e., the "isles of the Gentiles" (Genesis 10:5). "Sing unto the LORD another melody, and His acclaim from the end of the Earth, ye that go down to the ocean, and all that is in that; the isles, and the occupants thereof" (Isaiah 42:10). The "brute" that ascents up "out of the ocean" (13:1) has been generally comprehended to be the Antichrist. Victorinus (around third fourth century) commented about the "mammoth" (13:1): "This implies the kingdom of that season of Antichrist, and the general population blended with the assortment of countries" (from Victorinus' "Editorial on the Apocalypse").

The Antichrist or the Beast is portrayed as "having seven heads and ten horns" (13:1)- - bringing to brain Daniel's depiction of the Roman Empire, that at last delivers the "Man of Sin" (2Thessalonians 2:3) from its resuscitated structure. "7 After this I found in the night dreams, and observe a fourth brute [the Roman Empire], loathsome and repulsive, and solid exceedingly; and it had incredible iron teeth: it ate up and brake in pieces, and stamped the deposit with the feet of it: and it was differing from every one of the mammoths that were before it; and it had ten horns. 8 I considered the horns, and, observe, there came up among them another Little Horn [the Antichrist], before whom there were three of the primary horns culled up by the roots: and, see, in this horn were eyes like the eyes of man, and a mouth talking incredible things" (Daniel 7:7-8). The "seven heads" (13:1) speak to seven progressive periods of legislative history (cp. Disclosure 17:10-12), while the "ten horns" (13:1) connote ten at the same time ruling rulers, who will be counterparts with the Antichrist (cp. 17:12). In the Book of Revelation, both the "horns" and "crowns" (13:1) are images of legislative power; and in this occasion, they are utilized to impiously supplant or usurp the genuine power of the KING of Kings, and LORD of Lords, i.e., "and upon his heads the name of sacrilege" (13:1). Despite the fact that human government was organized by God "to execute fury upon him that doeth abhorrent" (Romans 13:4), it will at last be distorted to revile and war against the arrival of the LORD Jesus Christ, "Who is the Blessed and Only Potentate" (1Timothy 6:15), to set up His natural Kingdom "wherein dwelleth [good and] honorability" (2Peter 3:13).

Seven progressive phases of Gentile politically influential nation - out of which the Antichrist will come- - are spoken to by the "seven heads and ten horns" (13:1). The trouble of understanding is the genuine predisposition of every pundit, who is awed that he is one "upon whom the finishes of the world are come" (1Corinthians 10:11). As we approach the finish of the matter, the Infallible Commentator, which is the Holy Spirit, will drop the scales from our eyes to show us the awesome mystery of His dependable translation. "For the froward is evil entity to the LORD: however His mystery is with the upright" (Proverbs 3:32). Of the seven phases of Gentile force to be reckoned with, six are chronicled, and the seventh is a restored type of the 6th (the Roman Empire):

(1) Egypt (1600-1200 BC),

(2) Assyria (900-600 BC),

(3) Babylon (606-536 BC),

(4) Medo-Persia (536-330 BC),

(5) Greece (330-146 BC),

(6) Rome (200 BC-400 AD), and

(7) the Revived Roman Empire, which is by all accounts the European Union, that was framed from the more seasoned European Economic Community (1957-1958) through the Treaty on European Union (Maastricht Treaty), which was ordered on November first, 1993 (Stewart. 2016).

How would we land at recognizing the Beast "out of the ocean" (13:1) with the Roman Empire? To answer that question, we should read the predictions of the second part of Daniel. There, we are given a portrayal of Nebuchadnezzar's fantasy of an "extraordinary picture" (Daniel 2:31), whose "head was of fine gold [Babylon], his bosom and his arms of silver [Medo-Persia], his midsection and his thighs of metal [Greece], 33 His legs of iron [Rome], his feet some portion of iron and a portion of dirt [the Revived Roman Empire]" (2:32-33). The Almighty gave Nebuchadnezzar's fantasy and its translation to Daniel in light of trusting petition to God, i.e., they sought "leniencies of the God of Heaven concerning this mystery... At that point was the mystery uncovered" (Daniel 2:18, 19). "Thou, O lord [Nebuchadnezzar]... craftsmanship this head of gold [the Babylonian Empire]" (2:37-38). As it was with Daniel, so it is valid with the Saints all through time, divinely uncovered prescience is simply history in its yet to be satisfied structure. "39 And after thee [Nebuchadnezzar] might emerge another kingdom [the Medo-Persian Empire of Darius and Cyrus] mediocre compared to thee, and another third kingdom [the Greek Empire of Alexander the Great] of metal, which should bear guideline over all the Earth. 40 And the fourth kingdom [the Roman Empire] should be solid as iron" (2:39-40)(Stewart. 2016).

"2 And the monster which I saw was similar to unto a panther, and his feet were as the feet of a bear, and his mouth as the mouth of a lion: and the winged serpent gave him his energy, and his seat, and awesome power."

John the Beloved Apostle depicts his vision of the "mammoth" as "like unto a panther, and his feet were as the feet of a bear, and his mouth as the mouth of a lion" (13:2). Thus, the Old Testament prophet Daniel was given a dream of "four extraordinary brutes [of prey, which] came up from the ocean" (Daniel 7:3). Daniel depicted the Babylonian Empire as a "lion, [that] had hawk's wings" (7:4). A second kingdom, the Medo-Persian Realm, was spoken to as a bear, i.e., "And observe another mammoth, a second, as to a hold up under, and it raised up itself on one side, and it had three ribs [i.e., overwhelming Media, Persia, Babylonia] in the mouth of it between the teeth of it: and they said subsequently unto it, Arise, eat up much tissue [i.e., repressing Lydia, Egypt, etc.]" (7:5).

A third world domain, Greece, was delineated as a panther, which discusses the quickness of Alexander the Great's triumphs, i.e., "After this I viewed, and lo another, similar to a panther, which had upon the back of it four wings of a fowl; the brute had additionally four heads; and territory was given to it" (7:6). At long last, the Roman Empire was compared to a horrendous brute with ten horns, i.e., "After this I found in the night dreams, and see a fourth mammoth, repulsive and unpleasant, and solid exceedingly; and it had extraordinary iron teeth: it ate up and brake in pieces, and stamped the buildup with the feet of it: and it was assorted from every one of the monsters that were before it; and it had ten horns"

(7:7). As, Nebuchadnezzar's fantasy of an "extraordinary picture" (2:31) concurs with both Daniel's vision of "four awesome mammoths"

(7:3) and John's vision of the "brute which... was similar to unto a panther... a bear... [and] a lion" (Revelation 13:2).

It is said that the "monster [Satan] gave him [the Antichrist] his energy, and his seat, and incredible power" (13:2). Be that as it may, how could the demon give legislative force and power to the Antichrist, when God never put them in Satan's grasp? "Furthermore, Jesus came and spoke unto them, saying, All force is given unto Me in Heaven and in Earth" (Matthew 28:18). Tragically, in any case, when the offspring of this world offer acquiescence to the fallen angel, then they recognize his illicit seizure of that power. "Know ye not, that to whom ye yield yourselves workers to comply, his hirelings ye are to whom ye comply; whether of sin unto demise, or of submission unto honorability?" (Romans 6:16). Satan is the "ruler of the force of the air" (Ephesians 2:2) and the "divine force of this world" (2Corinthians 4:4) simply because he has been delegated in that capacity through the adamant surrender of dutifulness of any and each ethical operators, when they exhibit themselves to be "significant others of their own selves" (2Timothy 3:2) and not of God. Antichrist will be the human embodiment of the self esteem advanced by Lucifer, when he endeavored to grab the eminent throne of the High and Lofty One That Inhabiteth Eternity (Isaiah 57:15). "13 For thou [Lucifer] hast said in thine heart, I will rise into Heaven, I will lift up my throne over the stars of God: I will sit likewise upon the mount of the gathering, in the sides of the north: 14 I will rise over the statures of the mists; I will be similar to the most High" (Isaiah 14:13-14).

"3 And I saw one of his heads so to speak injured to death; and his savage injury was mended: and all the world pondered after the brute."

Understanding that the Beast with "seven heads" (13:1) speaks to Gentile force to be reckoned with, the Apostle John "saw one of [the Beast's] heads so to speak injured to death" (13:3). This alluded to the possible breakdown of the Roman Empire in the fifth century, when the Vandals ravaged the city of Rome (455 AD) and the last Roman sovereign, Romulus Augustulus, surrendered (476 AD). The Beast's "savage injury was recuperated"

(13:3) shows that the Lamb of the Revelation expected Satan's endeavor to resuscitate the force of the Roman Empire. "I [Christ, the Lamb of God] am Alpha and Omega, the Beginning and the End, the First and the Last" (22:13). What is known as the Holy Roman Empire- - initially including what is currently Germany, Austria, the Czech Republic, Switzerland, eastern France, the Low Countries, and parts of northern and focal Italy- - was the endeavor of the papacy to develop its energy through the control of common governments, starting with the crowning ceremony of Charlemagne, lord of the Franks, in 800 AD by Pope Leo III, to the leaving of the magnificent title of Holy Roman head by Francis II, ruler of Austria, in 1806. "For we wrestle not against fragile living creature and blood, but rather against realms, against forces, against the leaders of the obscurity of this world, against otherworldly fiendishness in high places" (Ephesians 6:12).

The majestic title of Holy Roman ruler was for all intents and purposes genetic to the Austrian House of Habsburg, starting in the fifteenth century. "Thou shalt not take after a huge number to do detestable; neither shalt thou talk in a cause to decay after numerous to wrest judgment" (Exodus 23:2). Insinuating Otto von Bismarck's German Empire (1871-1918)- - where the reciprocals of caesar and realm are the German, kaiser and reich, individually - as the Second Holy Roman Empire (or, Second Reich), Adolph Hitler alluded to Nazi Germany as the Third Reich. "Despite the fact that hand join close by, the shrewd should not be unpunished: but rather the seed of the honorable might be conveyed" (Proverbs 11:21). Every endeavor to resuscitate the force of the Roman Empire has fizzled - until (perhaps) now, with the blossoming political and financial quality of the advanced European Union (2000). In any case, "God hath talked once; twice have I heard this; that Power belongeth unto God" (Psalm 62:11). Subsequent to the Beast "out of the ocean"

(13:1) is both a framework, i.e., Gentile force to be reckoned with as a Revived Roman Empire, and a man that is known as the Antichrist, who leaves that framework, then the "fatal injury" (13:3), in all probability will likewise allude to a real twisted to Antichrist's head. The Greek word for "wound" (13:3) is plege, which is additionally interpreted as disease. Pretty much as the LORD Jesus Christ seemed to be "injured for our transgressions" (Isaiah 53:5) and "by His stripes we are mended" (53:5), the Antichrist will erroneously recreate a restoration from what seems, by all accounts, to be a mortal head wound. "For there might emerge false Christs, and false prophets, and should shew awesome signs and ponders; insomuch that, on the off chance that it were conceivable, they should misdirect the exceptionally Elect" (Matthew 24:24). Since the ability to make life or revive from the dead have a place just to the Living God, i.e., "Jesus said unto her, I am the Resurrection, and the Life: he that believeth in Me, however he were dead, yet should he live" (John 11:25), Antichrist's restoration may be a "lying wonder". "8 And then should that Wicked [the Antichrist] be uncovered, whom the LORD might devour with the Spirit of His mouth, and might pulverize with the shine of His coming: 9 Even him [the Antichrist], whose coming is after the working of Satan with all force and signs and lying ponders" (2Thessalonians 2:8-9).

"4 And they venerated the winged serpent which gave power unto the mammoth: and they adored the monster, saying, Who is similar to unto the brute? why should capable make war with him?"

Love is coordinated to the Father by the Son. "21 Jesus saith unto her, Woman, accept Me, the hour cometh, when ye might neither in this mountain, nor yet at Jerusalem, venerate the Father. 23 But the hour cometh, and now is, the point at which the genuine admirers might adore the Father in Spirit and in Truth: for the Father seeketh such to love Him" (John 4:21, 23). In a bogus impersonation of the relationship of Christ to the Father of Mercies (2Corinthians 1:3), the Antichrist will be instrumental in guiding love to Satan, i.e., "And they loved the winged serpent [Satan] which gave power unto the brute [Antichrist]" (13:4).

Satan would have no enthusiasm for offering energy to the Antichrist, on the off chance that it would not some way or another return to him in love. "What's more, [Satan] saith unto Him [the LORD Jesus Christ], All these things will I give Thee, if Thou shrivel tumble down and adore me" (Matthew 4:9). What the LORD Jesus cannot, Antichrist will happily get. "Once more, the fallen angel taketh Him [Jesus] up into a surpassing high mountain, and sheweth Him every one of the kingdoms of the world, and the magnificence of them; 10 Then saith Jesus unto him, Get thee thus, Satan: for it is composed, Thou shalt love the LORD thy God, and Him just shalt thou serve" (4:8,10).

Who "adored the mythical serpent... what's more, the brute" (13:4)? "All the world" (13:3), who "pondered after the brute" (13:3), are the "they" of verse four, who are swindled into adoring Satan and the Antichrist. Before cutting edge times, when worldwide correspondences and the Internet have now personally connected the furthest reaches of the planet, it would have been troublesome for any man or fallen angel to have accomplished the deed of picking up the love and reverence of not just a country or mainland, but rather of "all the world" (13:3). "They are of the world: in this manner talk they of the world, and the world heareth them" (1John 4:5). This is the climactic demonstration of the world framework, to venerate the fallen angel and his false Christ. "15 Love not the world [system], neither the things that are on the planet. On the off chance that any man love the world, the adoration for the Father is not in him. 16 For all that is on the planet, the desire of the substance, and the desire of the eyes, and the pride of life, is not of the Father, but rather is of the world. 17 And the world passeth away, and the desire thereof: however he that doeth the will of God abideth for ever" (2:15-17).

"Who is similar to unto the brute? why should capable make war with him?" (13:4) will be the hero worship of the world for the Antichrist.

The quality of human government is measured by how its strength keeps up principle inside of its fringes, and how it effectively shields against remote adversaries. "For he [human government, as expected by God] is the clergyman of God to thee for good. In any case, if thou do what is underhanded, be apprehensive; for he beareth not the sword futile: for he is the pastor of God, a revenger to execute rage upon him that doeth insidious" (Romans 13:4). forty and two months."

Blasphemia is the Greek word for profanation, which implies fiendish talking, particularly in the feeling of talking underhandedness of God. "Furthermore, men were seared with extraordinary warmth, and reviled the name of God, which hath control over these diseases: and they apologized not to give Him superbness" (16:9). Any individual who might dishonestly claim to be the Son of God, talks disrespect; and, incidentally, the LORD Jesus was assaulted as a blasphemer since He really said that He was the Son of God. "33 The Jews addressed Him, saying, For a decent work we stone Thee not; but rather for irreverence; and in light of the fact that that Thou, being a Man, makest thyself God... 36 Say ye of Him, Whom the Father hath purified, and sent into the world, Thou blasphemest; in light of the fact that I said, I am the Son of God?" (John 10:33, 36). Yet, the very reality that the Antichrist (prophetically) "sitteth in the sanctuary of God, In keeping with Antichrist's applause, i.e., "why should capable make war with him?" (13:4), Antichrist will take care of business of military and political force, for he will be in charge of the "contract with numerous" (Daniel 9:27) that happens toward the start of the Seventieth Week of Daniel. This usurper will be a priest of Satan against the Saints for shrewdness, who will be known for his execution of fury in the affliction of the Godly, who rehearse exemplary nature.

"What's more, he [Antichrist] might talk awesome words against the most High, and should wear out the Saints of the

Most High, and think to change times and laws: and they might be given into his hand until a period and times and the partitioning of time" (Daniel 7:25).

"5 And there was given unto him a mouth talking extraordinary things and lewdnesses; and force was given unto him to keep shewing himself that he is God" (2Thessalonians 2:4) is a definitive profanation. "Also, there was given unto him [Antichrist] a mouth talking awesome things and obscenities" (13:5).

It might be at first interesting to the psyches of the Godly that "power was given unto" (13:5) Antichrist by Jehovah to return disrespect against Jehovah; however, God permits Antichrist and the unelect "to top off their wrongdoings" (1Thessalonians 2:16) through this reviling, which legitimizes the Almighty's conceding of their free good organization and their consequent "endless perdition [Greek, krisis, or judgment]" (Mark 3:29). "4 For if God saved not the blessed messengers that trespassed, but rather cast them down to hellfire, and conveyed them into chains of dimness, to be saved unto judgment... 9 [then] The LORD knoweth how to convey the Godly out of allurements, and to save the unreasonable unto the day of judgment to be rebuffed" (2Peter 2:4, 9). Furthermore, Antichrist's "energy"

(13:5) or freedom to "proceed" (13:5) sitting in the reproduced Jerusalem Temple "as God" (2Thessalonians 2:4) is for "forty and two months" (13:5)- - or, 3 1/2 prophetic years, which is 1,260 days. This period will start at the Middle of the Tribulation Week, which is the "Anathema of Desolation, discussed by Daniel the prophet" (Matthew 24:15). The forty-two month period, which takes after the Abomination of Desolation, is ordinarily known as the Great Tribulation. "For then should be Great Tribulation, for example, was not subsequent to the start of the world to this time, no, nor ever might be" (24:21). [See our article, "The Seventy Weeks of Daniel" -New Window which diagrams "The Wisdom of God in All of the Seventy Weeks".] (Stewart. 2016).

"6 And he opened his mouth in sacrilege against God, to swear His name, and His sanctuary, and them that stay in Heaven."

Once more, the sign of Antichrist's short vocation is his lewdness of every one of that worries the Living God, i.e., "he opened his mouth in impiety against God, to swear His Name, and His Tabernacle, and them that stay in Heaven" (13:6). The base utilization of the Name of God to damn whoever and whatever, is basic to humankind; and, it is this free however unreasonable discourse that qualifies as lewdness. "1 This know likewise, that in the Last Days unsafe times should come. 2 For men might be beaus of their own selves, greedy, boasters, glad, blasphemers, insubordinate to folks, unthankful, unholy" (2Timothy 3:12). We, in this end Laodicean Age of Church History, have seen a more prominent than any time in recent memory degeneration of fiendishness talking, that will come full circle in the Antichrist's sacrilege (Stewart. 2016).

"In any case, detestable men and tempters might wax more terrible and more awful, misdirecting, and being bamboozled" (3:13). Consider the accompanying, to benchmark the amount of more regrettable the present profanation has ended up. Amid the Philadelphian Age of the Church (eighteenth and nineteenth hundreds of years), when the Church was still portrayed as having "a little quality" (Revelation 3:8), the evangelist Charles G. Finney (1792-1875) depicted the sacrilege he experienced in the minimal New York town of Antwerp of the mid 1800's (Stewart. 2016).

"In going around the town I heard an immense measure of irreverence. I thought I had never heard such a great amount in wherever that I had ever gone to. It appeared as though the men, in taking care of business upon the green, and in each business put that I ventured into, were all reviling and swearing and accursing one another. I felt as though I had landed upon the fringes of hellfire. I had a sort of horrendous feeling, I remember, as I went around the town on Saturday. The very environment appeared to me to be toxic substance; and a sort of dread took ownership of me.

I offered myself to supplication to God on Saturday, lastly encouraged my appeal till this answer came: 'Be not anxious, but rather talk, and hold not thy peace; for I am with thee, and no man should set on thee to hurt thee. For I have much individuals in this city' [Acts 18:910]" (from Chapter 8, "Recovery at Antwerp", of "An Autobiography" - New Window by Charles G. Finney).

"7 And it was given unto him to make war with the Saints, and to overcome them: and force was given him over all kindreds, and tongues, and countries."

John Bunyan's "The Pilgrim's Progress" - New Window portrays CHRISTIAN's way to deal with the Palace Beautiful, where he experiences two lions on either side of the slender way to deal with the royal residence. While rethinking his need to enter the castle, WATCHFUL, the doorman of the royal residence, shouts to Christian, "Is thy quality so little? dread not the lions; for they are binded, and are set there for trial of confidence where it is; and for disclosure of those that have none: keep amidst the way, and no harmed might come unto thee!" "And [Jesus] said unto them, Why are ye so frightful? how is it that ye have no confidence?" (Mark 4:40). In spite of the fact that the Almighty has made us eternal until our work on Earth is done, "If there is no more work for you to accomplish for your Master, it can't trouble you that He is going to take you Home [through martyrdom] and put you where you will be past the span of enemies" (from C. H. Spurgeon's "Confidence's Checkbook" - New Window April eighth section, "Protected to Work's End") (Stewart. 2016).

What's more, the night taking after the LORD remained by him, and said, Be of positivity, Paul: for as thou hast affirmed of Me in Jerusalem, so should thou take the stand at Rome" (Acts 23:11). However, the All Wise God has picked that some of His Saints will give a definitive admission and witness of their confidence in the LORD Jesus Christ through their affliction, i.e., "And it was given unto [Antichrist] to make war with the Saints, and to overcome them" (13:7). "Jesus replied, Thou [Pontius Pilate] couldest have no force at all against Me, aside from it were given thee from Above" (John 19:11). Also, energy to hurt the Saints, shows that the Antichrist has had the limitation evacuated to give him power "over all kindreds, and tongues, and countries" (13:7). "For the Mystery of Iniquity doth as of now work: just He [the Holy Spirit indwelling the Saints] Who now letteth [i.e., limits Satan and sin] will let [continue to restrain], until He [the Holy Spirit] be taken off the beaten path [at the Pre-Tribulational Rapture]" (2Thessalonians 2:7). [See our article, "Affliction: They Loved Not Their Lives Unto the Death" -New Window, to investigate further the idea of Christian martyrdom.]

"8 And all that stay upon the Earth should venerate him, whose names are not composed in the Book of Life of the Lamb killed from the establishment of the world."

The individuals who are not Heavenly minded, are portrayed as "all [those] that stay upon the Earth" (13:8), i.e., Earth inhabitants. "He that cometh from Above will be most importantly [i.e., Jesus Christ]: he that is of the Earth is natural, and speaketh of the Earth [i.e., Antichrist, and his followers]" (John 3:31). Sacred text lets us know that "all that abide upon the Earth might adore" (13:8) the Antichrist; be that as it may, later in this section, we will discover the purpose behind this widespread love, i.e., pressure based upon the risk of death. "Furthermore, he [the False Prophet] had energy to give life unto the picture of the brute [image of the Antichrist], that the picture of the monster ought to both talk, and cause that the same number of as would not love the picture of the mammoth ought to be executed" (13:15). These Earth occupants, "whose names are not composed in the Book of Life of the Lamb killed from the establishment of the world" (13:8), are the unelect, who never will atone (Stewart. 2016).

In any case, take note of that a charge to leave Babylon the Great, i.e., "And I heard another voice from Heaven, saying, Come out of her, My kin, that ye be not partakers of her wrongdoings, and that ye get not of her infections" (18:4), comes towards the End of the Tribulation Week, demonstrating that a percentage of the Earth inhabitants probably apologized. "View, I have graven thee upon the palms of My hands; thy dividers are consistently before Me" (Isaiah 49:16). Hence, it creates the impression that some that venerated the Beast, will apologize; at the same time, Scripture gives nobody the scarcest possibility of Heaven, who thinks to protect himself through aforethought and intention to bow down to the Beast. "He that saith, I know Him, and keepeth not His Commandments, is a liar, and the Truth is not in him" (1John 2:4). Furthermore, the "dreadful, and unbelieving, and the loathsome, and killers, and whoremongers, and magicians, and misguided worshipers, and all liars, might have their part in the lake which burneth with flame and brimstone: which is the Second Death" (Revelation 21:8).

"9 If any man have an ear, let him listen."

The voice of the Holy Spirit is just to the individuals who "have an ear" (13:9). With regards to the Creator's unique arrangement of a "flawless man" who measures up unto the "stature of the fulness of Christ" (Ephesians 4:13), the Spirit of Christ is always looking for any man "whose heart is immaculate toward Him" (2Chronicles 16:9). That flawlessness happens the minute a man atones of sin, for it is the flawlessness of goal (where opportunity permits) that dependably shows itself in the "organic products meet for [literally, commendable of] apology" (Matthew 3:8). "22 But the product of the Spirit is affection, bliss, peace, forgiving, tenderness, goodness, confidence, 23 Meekness, moderation: against such there is no law" (Galatians 5:22-23).

Who will this Antichrist be? Occasionally, every era has had its own particular Antiochus Epiphanes, Caligula, Pontifex Maximus, Hitler, or Mussolini that should be the Antichrist. Be that as it may, why? The presence of the Antichrist will go before the Second Advent of the LORD Jesus Christ for the fake to appropriately work its trickery. "Give no man a chance to deceive you by any methods: for that day might not come, with the exception of there come a falling without end to start with, and that man of sin be uncovered, the child of destruction" (2Thessalonians 2:3).

The way that the LORD Jesus educated His kin that He would return, must be a vast part of the explanation behind the Saints' suspicion that "Antichrist should come" (1John 2:18). [See our article, "Antichrist Shall Come" - New Window, for an advancement of the Scripture concerning the Antichrist.] "2 In My Father's home are numerous chateaus: in the event that it were not really, I would have let you know. I go to set up a spot for you. 3 And in the event that I go and set up a spot for you, I will come back once more, and get you unto Myself; that where I am, there ye might be likewise" (John 14:2-3).

Combined with the Savior's Promise that He would return, is His certification that He would return expediently. Assuredly, this has aroused the Saints' yearning for His arrival and their flight. "See, I come immediately: honored is he that keepeth the platitudes of the prediction of this book" (Revelation 22:7). [See our publication, "Observe, I Come Quickly" -New Window, to survey the benefits of this Promise.] Remembering that the Restraining Influence, which is the Holy Spirit abiding in His Saints, should first "be taken off the beaten path" (2Thessalonians 2:7), just "then might that Wicked [the Antichrist] be uncovered" (2:8). Along these lines, the Pre-Tribulational Rapture will uproot the Watching and Waiting Saints before the disclosure of the "man of sin" (2:3). [See our article, "Must There Be a Pre-Tribulational Rapture?" - New Window, for a brief work of 2Thessalonians 2.]

The Protestant Reformation, which set apart by an arrival from a reliable pope to the power and dependability of the Scriptures and the simultaneous right and need that each man ought to be his own cleric, regularly saw the Roman pontiff as the Antichrist. "However, ye are a picked era, an imperial brotherhood, a heavenly country, an unconventional individuals; that ye ought to shew forward the gestures of recognition of Him who hath got you out of haziness into His wonderful Light" (1 Peter 2:9). Indeed, even before Martin Luther (1520) kept in touch with, "I realize that the Papacy is none other than the kingdom of Babylon, and the viciousness of Nimrod the forceful seeker"; John Milicius (1294-1374), Archdeacon and Canon of the Archiepiscopal Cathedral of the Hradschin, Prague, was so stunned at the ethical embarrassments of the Rome that he served, that on his visit to the Pontifical city, "he composed over the entryway of one of the cardinals, 'Antichrist is currently come, and sitteth in the Church,' and [then] withdrew" (from James A. Wylie's "The History of Protestantism", Volume 1, Book 3 - New Window) (Stewart. 2016).

Sacred text gives numerous signs to the personality of the Antichrist:

(1) He will emerge from the Revived Roman Empire. "I considered the horns, and, observe, there came up among them another Little Horn [the Antichrist], before whom there were three of the principal horns culled up by the roots: and, view, in this horn were eyes like the eyes of man, and a mouth talking extraordinary things" (Daniel 7:8). [See our remarks on Revelation 13:1 for an advancement of Daniel 7:8.] Also, "26 And following threescore and two weeks should Messiah be cut off, however not for Himself: and the general population of the sovereign that might come might demolish the city and the asylum [which was expert by the Roman general Titus in 70 AD]; and the end thereof should be with a surge, and unto the end of the war destructions are resolved. 27 And he [Antichrist, who should emerge from the 'general population of the ruler that might come' (v. 26)] might affirm the contract with numerous for one week: and amidst the week he should bring about the penance and the oblation to stop, and for the overspreading of horrifying presences he might make it barren, even until the culmination, and that decided should be poured upon the ruined" (Daniel 9:26-27).

(2) He will fake himself as the True Christ, sitting "in the sanctuary of God, shewing himself that he is God" (2Thessalonians 2:4); accordingly, he might show a significant number of the attributes of the LORD Jesus Christ. For instance, similar to Jesus, he might be around thirty years of age, when he starts his brief profession, i.e., "Jesus Himself started to be around thirty years old" (Luke 3:23).

(3) He will be very much associated with the force structure of the world framework, i.e., the religious, monetary, political, military force of the world. "What's more, they venerated the winged serpent which gave power unto the monster: and they adored the mammoth, saying, Who is similar to unto the brute? why should capable make war with him?" (Revelation 13:4).

(4) He will be instrumental in building up a contract or arrangement "with numerous" (Daniel 9:27), including Israel, toward the Beginning of the Tribulation Week; in this way, he might as of now be working as a government official or force dealer at the season of the Pre-Tribulational Rapture. Be that as it may,

(5) He won't be permitted to be uncovered "as God [sitting] in the sanctuary" (2Thessalonians 2:4) until the Middle of the Tribulation Week; along these lines, Antichrist won't be clear as Antichrist until he is requesting the love of the world to himself as God, on punishment of death. "What's more, [the False Prophet] had energy to give life unto the picture of the mammoth, that the picture of the brute ought to both talk, and cause that the same number of as would not love the picture of the monster ought to be executed" (Revelation 13:15).

"10 He that leadeth into bondage should go into imprisonment: he that killeth with the sword must be murdered with the sword. Here is the persistence and the confidence of the Saints."

This verse starts with a Promise of Divine retaliation, i.e., "He that leadeth into imprisonment should go into bondage" (13:10). "Also, thine eye should not feel sorry for; but rather life might go forever, eye for eye, tooth for tooth, hand for hand, foot for foot" (Deuteronomy 19:21). The gravity of God's Divine Law requires an equity that "he that killeth with the sword must be murdered with the sword" (13:10). "Retribution is mine; I will reimburse, saith the LORD" (Romans 12:19). Indeed, even in these Gospel times, God is still an "equitable God and a Savior" (Isaiah 45:21); and, the Godly still cheer that the Almighty performs His judgments, when the remorseless spot themselves past His absolution. "1 And after these things I heard an awesome voice of much individuals in Heaven, saying, Alleluia; Salvation, and heavenliness, and respect, and power, unto the LORD our God: 2 For genuine and noble are His judgments: for He hath judged the Great Whore, which did degenerate the Earth with her sex, and hath retaliated for the blood of His workers at her hand. 3 And again they said, Alleluia. Also, her smoke ascended for ever and ever" (Revelation 19:1-3).

Why does this verse of Divine retaliation talk about the "persistence and the confidence of the Saints" (13:10)? Since "it was given unto [Antichrist] to make war with the Saints, and to overcome them" (13:7) just beforehand, this Promise of requital, most certainly, is to those whom the Almighty asks to set out their lives in witness of His vicinity, prevalence, and Truth (Stewart. 2016).

"What's more, they overcame him [Satan] by the blood of the Lamb, and by the expression of their affirmation; and they cherished not their lives unto the passing" (12:11). This Promise- - "confidence" (13:10)- - urges the Tribulation Martyrs to stay their course to the end- - "persistence" (13:10)- - in light of the fact that the individuals who will never atone, will be judged with the same conviction that the Penitent will be overlooked. "In the event that we admit our transgressions, He is reliable and just to overlook us our wrongdoings, and to purify us from all wickedness" (1John 1:9). Also, the Penitent, God will laud. "However, as it is composed, Eye hath not seen, nor ear listened, neither have gone into the heart of man, the things which God hath arranged for them that affection Him" (1Corinthians 2:9).

"11 And I viewed another mammoth coming up out of the Earth; and he had two horns like a sheep, and he spake as a mythical serpent."

The Greek word therion is deciphered as monster in both verse one and this verse; and, another originates from the Greek word allos, which implies one more of the same kind, i.e., "And I observed another mammoth" (13:11).

Since verse one alludes to the Antichrist, then verse eleven must be depicting another savage animal of the same kind. "By their organic products ye should know them" (Matthew 7:20). This Beast comes "up out of the Earth" (13:11), showing that he is an animal of the Earth and not of Heaven. "This shrewdness descendeth not from above, but rather is natural, sexy, fiendish" (James 3:15). One component of this Beast is that "he had two horns like a sheep" (13:11), implying that he had the outward qualities of a submissive and mellow sheep. This infers this Beast will endeavor to seem such as the LORD Jesus Christ, who is really the "Sheep of God, which taketh away the wrongdoing of the world" (John 1:29). In any case, the genuine way of this Beast is sold out by the way that "he spake as a winged serpent" (13:11).

"Also, he [the great angel] laid hang on the monster, that old serpent, which is the Devil, and Satan, and bound him a thousand years" (Revelation 20:2). In this way, we can be guaranteed that the Beast "out of the Earth" (13:11) must be another savage animal like the Antichrist, who endeavors to shield his fierce character with a sheep such as veil. "What's more, He [Jesus] said, Take regard that ye be not misled: for some should come in My name, saying, I am Christ; and the time draweth close: go ye not in this manner after them" (Luke 21:8).

"12 And he exerciseth all the force of the main mammoth before him, and causeth the Earth and them which abide in that to revere the primary monster, whose destructive injury was recuperated."

Potentially, the Godly have mixed up this Beast "out of the Earth" (13:11) as the Antichrist; at the same time, this Beast is unmistakably another personage than the Antichrist. "What's more, he exerciseth all the force of the primary monster before him" (13:12). Subsequent to the Beast "out of the Earth" (13:11) is equivalent in force and power to the Beast "out of the ocean" (13:1), it must be by shared assent this second Beast makes the "Earth and them which stay in that to venerate the main brute" (13:12). A sign of recognition for the Antichrist will be that his "fatal [head] wound was recuperated" (13:12 cp. 13:3). Numerous reporters, including this one, trust that this Beast "out of the Earth" (13:11) depicts the Endtime identity that is regularly alluded to as the False Prophet, i.e., he "causeth the Earth and them which abide in that to revere the principal brute" (13:12). The love that the False Prophet coordinates toward the Antichrist will eventually be gotten by Satan, i.e, "And they revered the mythical serpent which gave power unto the [Antichrist]: and they loved the [Antichrist], saying, Who is similar to unto the monster? why should capable make war with him?" (13:4). Also, Satan is willing to exchange the wealth and influence of the world to purchase himself the love that he doesn't merit. "Also, [Satan] saith unto Him [Jesus], All these things will I give Thee, if thou shrink tumble down and venerate me" (Matthew 4:9).

"13 And he doeth awesome marvels, so that he maketh fire descend from paradise on the Earth in seeing men,"

Both Antichrist and his False Prophet are liars, similar to their "dad the fallen angel" (John 8:44). All things considered, the main sort of "awesome marvels" (13:13) that they perform, are untruths. "Indeed, even him [Antichrist], whose coming is after the working of Satan with all force and signs and lying ponders [performed by the False Prophet]" (2Thessalonians 2:9).

We should backtrack to the Old Testament to review that even a false prophet can make forecasts that happen, pretty much as some have imagined that the visionary quatrains of Nostradamus (1503-1566) precisely anticipated certain points of interest of the French Revolution of the eighteenth century. "1 If there emerge among you a prophet, or a visionary of dreams, and giveth thee a sign or a marvel, 2 And the sign or the miracle happen, whereof he spake unto thee, saying, Let us follow different divine beings, which thou hast not known, and let us serve them; 3 Thou shalt not notice unto the expressions of that prophet, or that visionary of dreams: for the LORD your God proveth you, to know whether ye love the LORD your God with everything that is in you and with your entire existence" (Deuteronomy 13:1-3). [See our article, "How to Identify a False Prophet" -New Window, for a Scriptural study of how to distinguish any false prophet.]

Mystical performers and illusionists perform their deeds for stimulation or preoccupation. Be that as it may, when are their traps and illusions really "lying ponders" (2Thessalonians 2:9) disguising "as just a trap"? At the point when the conjuring of their mystical demonstration looks to draw men far from the Living God, i.e., "And the sign or the miracle happen, whereof he spake unto thee, saying, Let us follow different divine beings, which thou hast not known, and let us serve them" (Deuteronomy 13:2), then they are performing "lying ponders". Generally, men, for example, Simon the Sorcerer utilized their specialty to swindle individuals into trusting that they had the force of God, and were, hence, His delegates. "9 But there was a sure man, called Simon, which before time in the same city utilized magic, and charmed the general population of Samaria, giving out that himself was some awesome one: 10 To whom they all gave notice, from the slightest to the best, saying, This man is the considerable force of God" (Acts 8:9-10). In spite of the fact that enchantment regularly utilizes mechanical props to trap the psyche, the otherworldly force of Satan might be unlawfully utilized to permit the prestidigitator to go past the negligible "slight of hand" to perform what science can't clarify. "9

When Pharaoh should talk unto you, saying, Shew a supernatural occurrence for you: then thou shalt say unto Aaron, Take thy pole, and cast it before Pharaoh, and it might turn into a serpent. 10 And Moses and Aaron went in unto Pharaoh, and they did as such as the LORD had ordered: and Aaron cast down his bar before Pharaoh, and before his workers, and it turned into a serpent.

11 Then Pharaoh likewise called the astute men and the alchemists: now the mystical performers of Egypt, they additionally did in like way with their charms. 12 For they cast down each man his pole, and they got to be serpents: however Aaron's bar gobbled up their poles" (Exodus 7:9-12).

At the point when the False Prophet makes "fire [to] descend from paradise on the Earth in seeing men" (13:13), he might have the intrigue of a percentage of the best experimental personalities to help him in inspiring the considerable mass of humankind; at the same time, paying little mind to any help from man, the False Prophet will have the powerful guide of Lucifer the fallen heavenly attendant. "What's more, the Beast [Antichrist] was taken, and with him the False Prophet that fashioned supernatural occurrences before him, with which he swindled them that had gotten the Mark of the Beast, and them that loved his picture.

These both were thrown alive into a Lake of Fire smoldering with brimstone" (19:20). Satan's energy is more prominent than any man. "4 What is man, that thou craftsmanship aware of him? also, the child of man, that thou visitest him? 5 For thou hast made him somewhat lower than the heavenly attendants, and hast delegated him with wonderfulness and honor" (Psalm 8:45). Be that as it may, keeping in mind that the Saints ought to wind up exceedingly inspired or scared with the force of the Satanic trinity- - Satan, the Antichrist, and the False Prophet- - God is more noteworthy. "3 And each soul that confesseth not that Jesus Christ is come in the substance is not of God: and this is soul of antichrist, whereof ye have heard that it ought to come; and even now as of now is it on the planet. 4 Ye are of God, little kids, and have overcome them [Antichrist, etc.]: on the grounds that more noteworthy is He that is in you [the Holy Spirit], than he [Satan] that is on the planet" (1John 4:3-4).

"14 And deceiveth them that harp on the Earth by the method for those supernatural occurrences which he had energy to do in seeing the monster; saying to them that harp on the Earth, that they ought to make a picture to the brute, which had the injury by a sword, and did live."

Pretty much as disrespect is the sign of Antichrist's profession -talking "profanation against God" (13:6)- - double dealing is the fundamental element of the False Prophet's service, i.e., he "deceiveth them that harp on the Earth" (13:14). All things considered, without the False Prophet's trickiness, who might care to love the Antichrist, on the off chance that they genuinely trusted that because of their love, God would damn them until the end of time?

"9 And the third heavenly attendant tailed them, saying with a boisterous voice, If any man revere the monster and his picture, and get his imprint in his temple, or in his grasp, 10 The same should beverage of the wine of the rage of God, which is emptied out without blend into the measure of His resentment; and he might be tormented with flame and brimstone in the vicinity of the blessed holy messengers, and in the vicinity of the Lamb: 11 And the smoke of their torment ascendeth up for ever and ever: and they have no rest day nor night, who adore the brute and his picture, and whosoever receiveth the characteristic of his name" (14:9-11).

It will be troublesome for those "that harp on the Earth" (13:14) not to be hoodwinked by the False Prophet's supernatural occurrences, "which he had energy to do in seeing the mammoth" (13:14). Why? To the unelect, the wonders will talk more boisterously than any beforehand rejected Scriptures. God will send them "solid hallucination" (2Thessalonians 2:11), particularly, on the grounds that "they got not the adoration for the Truth, that they may be spared" (2:10). What's more, the choose yet at the same time lost won't yet have any establishment upon the Scripture of Truth (Daniel 10:21)- - however they might be uneasy about the False Prophet's wonders - to oppose the double dealing. It is just by the "shield of confidence" that we can "extinguish all the red hot darts of the underhanded [one]" (Ephesians 6:16). The charlatanism of the False Prophet will make the pitch to the world that "they ought to make a picture to the monster, which had the injury by a sword, and did live" (13:14). At the end of the day, the False Prophet will persuade the world that they ought to make the "picture of the brute" (13:14); or, at any rate, it ought to be worked by prevalent interest. "9 They that make a graven picture are every one of them vanity; and their delicious things should not benefit; and they are their own witnesses; they see not, nor know; that they might be embarrassed. 17 And the deposit thereof he maketh a divine being, even his graven picture: he falleth down unto it, and worshippeth it, and prayeth unto it, and saith, Deliver me; for thou craftsmanship my god" (Isaiah 44:9, 17).

"15 And he had energy to give life unto the picture of the brute, that the picture of the monster ought to both talk, and cause that the same number of as would not adore the picture of the mammoth ought to be executed."

The False Prophet will be particularly acclaimed for two supernatural occurrences or miracles:

(1) calling fire down from paradise, i.e., "he maketh fire descend from paradise on the Earth in seeing men" (13:13), and

(2) giving "life unto the picture of the monster" (13:15).

He will "cause that the same number of as would not venerate the picture of the monster ought to be executed" (13:15). Also, this should help us to remember what Jesus said amid His natural service, i.e., "4 And I say unto you My companions, Be not anxious of them that slaughter the body, and after that have no more that they can do. 5 But I will caution you whom ye might fear: Fear Him, which after He hath executed hath energy to cast into damnation; yea, I say unto you, Fear Him" (Luke 12:4-5).

Pneuma is the Greek word that the Authorized Version (KJV) has deciphered as "life" (13:15); at the same time, it is all the more regularly interpreted as soul or apparition, and even as wind, i.e., "The wind [Greek, pneuma] bloweth where it listeth, and thou hearest the sound thereof, however canst not tell whence it cometh, and whither it goeth: so is each one that is conceived of the Spirit [Greek, pneuma]" (John 3:8). "Nor is venerated with men's hands, just as He required anything, seeing He giveth to all life [Greek, zoe], and breath, and all things" (Acts 17:25). Along these lines, the "life [Greek, pneuma]" (13:15) that the False Prophet provides for the "picture of the monster" (13:15) won't be the same sort of "life [Greek, zoe]" (Acts 17:25) that just the Almighty presents.

Does the Scripture provide us any insight into the character of this False Prophet? Yes. By investigation, if the Beast "out of the Earth"

(13:11) is the False Prophet, and the Great Whore

(17:1) is the Church of Rome, then the Pope would be the False Prophet. We are informed that the Great Whore sits "upon numerous waters" (17:1), i.e., upon numerous countries, generally as the Antichrist ascends "up out of the ocean" (13:1).

BABYLON THE GREAT is the name of the Great Whore, "with whom the lords of the Earth have submitted sex [Greek, porneia]" (17:2). "17 And upon her temple was a name composed, MYSTERY, BABYLON THE GREAT, THE MOTHER OF HARLOTS AND ABOMINATIONS OF THE EARTH. 18 And the lady which thou sawest is that incredible city [papal Rome], which reigneth over the lords of the Earth" (17:5-18).

The profound sex of the Church of Rome famously qualifies her as the otherworldly posterity of MYSTERY BABYLON, making her the core of harlotry, and fittingly, "THE MOTHER OF HARLOTS AND ABOMINATIONS OF THE EARTH" (17:17).

Despite the fact that the Protestant Reformers most generally alluded to the Roman pontiff as the Antichrist, all the more precisely, he is best qualified to be the False Prophet, since he "exerciseth all the force of the primary mammoth [the Antichrist] before him" (13:12). Church history entered the Worldly Church period of the Thyatiran Age (2:18-29) after the fall of Rome, and proceeded in it through the Dark Ages and the Middle Ages until the Protestant Reformation, for almost a thousand years (500-1500 AD). This time of world and Church history was ruled by the vicinity of the Bishop of Rome and the force of the Roman Catholic Church. "Despite I have a couple of things against thee, in light of the fact that thou sufferest that lady Jezebel [the harlotry of Rome], which calleth herself a prophetess, to instruct and to entice My workers to submit sex, and to eat things yielded unto symbols" (Revelation 2:20). In the blink of an eye, we have yet to see when or whether the Pope will pronounce himself positive or accessible to such endeavors as the United Religions (2000), the official religious partner of the United Nations; be that as it may, the United Religions (without further ado) has all the earmarks of being the most practical vehicle for the False Prophet. "Escape out of the middle of Babylon, and convey each man his spirit: be not cut off in her injustice; for this is the season of the LORD'S retaliation; He will render unto her a recompence" (Jeremiah 51:6). [See our arrangement, "Babylon the Great" - New Window, for the historical backdrop of Babylon, the Church of Rome, and ecumenism. Likewise, encourage investigation of the United Religions might be found in our publication, "United Religions (2000): A Tower Unto Heaven" - New Window.]

"16 And he causeth all, both little and extraordinary, rich and poor, free and bond, to get an imprint in their right hand, or in their brows:"

Verse sixteen is the main notice of the Mark of the Beast, which even the ostensibly astute might in the blink of an eye hate."

Furthermore, it happened in those days, that there went out an announcement from Caesar Augustus, that all the world ought to be exhausted [literally, enlisted or selected, i.e., in the general population records, the names surprisingly, with the end goal of burdened their domains or property]" (Luke 2:1). Notice that the False Prophet instrumentally "causeth all" to "get an imprint" (13:16), implying that, the False Prophet, not the Antichrist, is the boss promoter of the Mark of the Beast. On the off chance that the Antichrist were to exclusively advance the gathering of the Mark of the Beast, it would be by crude power, i.e., "And in the last time of their kingdom, when the transgressors are gone to the full, a lord of wild face, and comprehension dull sentences, might stand up" (Daniel 8:23). However, in the event that the False Prophet is the prime promoter for the gathering of the Mark of the Beast- - which he will- - then it will be expert by misleadingly bringing on the world to craving to get it. "[The False Prophet] deceiveth them that harp on the Earth by the method for those supernatural occurrences which he had energy to do" (13:14). Adversely, refusal to adore the Antichrist will be deserving of death (13:15), while then again, the capacity to live, i.e., "purchase or offer" (13:17), will be controlled by the eagerness to "get an imprint" (13:16).

Three sets are counted for the Mark of the Beast, demonstrating the totality of those checked:

(1) "little and extraordinary" (13:16), alludes to perceived status in the public eye,

(2) "rich and poor" (13:16), alludes to total assets of belonging, and

(3) "free and bond" (13:16), alludes to level of freedom for human activity.

As opposed to the Mark of the Beast, the LORD denote His own. "4 And the LORD said unto him, Go through the middle of the city, through the middle of Jerusalem, and set an imprint upon the temples of the men that moan and that weep for every one of the evil entities that be done in the middle thereof. 5 And to the others He said in mine listening ability, Go ye after him through the city, and destroy: let not your eye extra, neither have ye pity: 6 Slay absolutely old and youthful, both servants, and little youngsters, and ladies: yet come not close to any man upon whom is the imprint; and start at My asylum.

At that point they started at the old men which were before the house" (Ezekiel 9:4-6). On the whole, no section of the world will be avoided from getting the Mark of the Beast, for it will be Satan's image upon his belonging, as much as cows are marked by farmers, i.e., "his workers ye are to whom ye comply; whether of sin unto demise, or of submission unto exemplary nature" (Romans 6:16).

Much prophetic exchange encompasses the innovation of the Mark of the Beast, i.e., the "imprint in their right hand, or in their temples" (13:16). The utilization of the Social Security Number (SSN)- - utilized in some structure by most present day nations as an enrollment of its nationals, to give a societal wellbeing net to disorder, incapacity, retirement, and so forth.--is regularly fundamental for livelihood, and the installment of salary assessments.

"15 And when cash fizzled in the place that is known for Egypt, and in the place that is known for Canaan, all the Egyptians came unto Joseph, and said, Give us bread: for why would it be a good idea for us to bite the dust in thy vicinity? for the cash faileth... 18 When that year was finished, they came unto him the second year, and said unto him, We won't conceal it from my master, how that our cash is spent; my ruler likewise hath our groups of cows; there is not should left in seeing my ruler, yet our bodies, and our properties: 19 Wherefore might we kick the bucket before thine eyes, both we and our territory? purchase us and our property for bread, and we and our territory will be hirelings unto Pharaoh: and give us seed, that we might live, and not kick the bucket, that the area be not forsaken. 20 And Joseph purchased all the place where there is Egypt for Pharaoh; for the Egyptians sold each man his field, on the grounds that the starvation beat them: so the area got to be Pharaoh's" (Genesis 47:15, 19-20).

The multiplication of PCs, databases, credit and check cards, scannable standardized tags((UPC), and remote satellite Internet, information, and information transfers - they all encourage the following of the developments and movement of a great part of the created world, notwithstanding the bunch of records customarily kept by all legislatures. "Be that as it may, thou, O Daniel, quiets down the Words, and seal the Book, even to the season of the end: numerous should raced back and forth, and information might be expanded" (Daniel 12:4).

Perhaps, all that would remain, would be the livelihood of a sort of programmable, scannable "brilliant chip" that would be embedded under the skin of "their right hand, or in their temples" (13:16)- - as has been finished with pets and domesticated animals - that would empower a cashless society, and additionally for recognizable proof and following, i.e., therapeutic data, military status, movement records, criminal records, and so on. "He which testifieth these things saith, Surely I come rapidly. So be it. Indeed, even in this way, come [quickly], LORD Jesus" (22:20). So be it, and Amen.

"17 And that no man may purchase or offer, spare he that had the imprint, or the name of the monster, or the quantity of his name."

Regardless of the possibility that one were to avoid capital punishment for not revering the Antichrist, still, he would not have the capacity to "purchase or offer, spare that he had the imprint" (13:17). The Almighty will at long last permit Satan the utilization of this imprint to compel the issue with every one of the occupants of the world- - "Who is on the LORD'S side?" (Exodus 32:26). As at last round of a chess match, the LORD of the Harvest (Luke 10:2) should skillfully position His diversion pieces to reap all the Elect, while precisely rebuffing just the devilish. "Whose fan is in His grasp, and He will thoroughly cleanse His floor, and accumulate His wheat into the collect; however He will consume the debris with insatiable flame" (Matthew 3:12). At the point when the LORD Jesus Christ returns at His Second Coming, and "each eye should see Him" (Revelation 1:7), He will painstakingly isolate for judgment and punishment (cp. 14:9-11), the "tares", which are the beneficiaries of the Mark of the Beast. "28 He said unto them, An adversary hath done this. The workers said unto Him, Wilt Thou then that we go and accumulate them up? 29 But He said, Nay; keeping in mind that while ye get together the tares [a sort of darnel, which is a toxic grass], ye root up likewise the wheat with them. 30 Let both become together until the harvest: and in the season of harvest I will say to the collectors, Gather ye together first the tares, and tie them in groups to blaze them: however accumulate the wheat into My horse shelter" (Matthew 13:28-30). Along these lines, the Almighty's utilization of the "anger of man" (Psalm 76:10) as the Mark of the Beast, will "laud" (76:10) Himself, when He isolates for judgment the shrewd, and jam all the staying Righteous ones. "[Jesus implored instantly before the Garden of Gethsemane:] While I was with them on the planet, I kept them in Thy Name: those that Thou gavest Me I have kept, and none of them is lost, yet the child of condemnation; that the Scripture may be satisfied" (John 17:12).

The "imprint [Greek, charagma, or imprint], or the name of the brute, or the quantity of his name" (13:17) interfaces the imprint with the name and the quantity of the Beast. In the event that the Mark of the Beast is at first sold to the world as an accommodating or advantageous identifier of the beneficiary, then the Scriptures uncover the genuine inspiration for the gadget -to mark each individual as the individual property of the demon. "Ye are of your dad the fallen angel, and the desires of your dad ye will do" (John 8:44). At the end of the day, the Antichrist's name will be digitally communicated and encoded into the imprint, which will likewise extraordinarily recognize and control the beneficiary. "Jesus addressed them, Verily, verily, I say unto you, Whosoever committeth sin is the hireling of sin" (8:34).

"18 Here is shrewdness. Let him that hath understanding check the quantity of the brute: for it is the quantity of a man; and his number is Six hundred threescore and six."

Some have clarified the "Six hundred threescore and six [666]" (13:18) as an including of the numerical reciprocals of the Hebrew, Greek, or Latin letters of the Antichrist's name. Case in point, it is said that Caesar Nero is spelled Kaisar Neron, if composed with Hebrew endings. As needs be, the total of the letters that would be Hebrew consonants, would add up to 666, i.e., K rises to 100, S approaches 60, R breaks even with 200, N meets 50, R measures up to 200, O parallels 6, and N squares with 50. Be that as it may, the verse starts with the expression, "Here is insight" (13:18); and, intelligence or "learning is simple unto him that understandeth" (Proverbs 14:6). Scriptural numerics are suitable for the Saints to concentrate; be that as it may, similar to every single legal try, Biblical numerics must be appropriately comprehended when they are submitted to the direction of the Spirit of God through His God Breathed Word.

"16 All Scripture is given by motivation of God, and is productive for regulation, for denunciation, for rectification, for guideline in honorability: 17 That the man of God might be impeccable, thoroughly outfitted unto every great work" (2Timothy 3:16-17).

This author has discovered fulfillment with the understanding that the number 666 speaks to the "quantity of a man" (13:18). Since man was made on the 6th day (Genesis 1:26-31), the number six speaks to man (Stewart. 2016).

When it is rehashed three times, it is the LORD earnestly expressing that the Antichrist is not God, but rather just a man... a man... a man. Nebuchadnezzar, who at long last went to the "learning of the Truth" (1Timothy 2:4), would without a doubt vouch for the position that the Antichrist is only an insignificant man. He endured the mortification of being dealt with as a mammoth, in light of his pride and haughtiness. "32 And they might drive thee from men, and thy staying should be with the brutes of the field: they might make thee to eat grass as bulls, and seven times should ignore thee, until thou realize that the Most High ruleth in the kingdom of men, and giveth it to whomsoever He will... 34 And toward the end of the days I Nebuchadnezzar lifted up mine eyes unto Heaven, and mine comprehension returned unto me, and I favored the Most High, and I lauded and regarded Him that liveth forever, whose domain is an everlasting territory, and His kingdom is from era to era: 35 And every one of the occupants of the Earth are presumed as nothing: and He doeth as indicated by His will in the armed force of Heaven, and among the tenants of the Earth: and none can stay His hand, or say unto Him, What doest Thou? 36 in the meantime my reason returned unto me; and for the greatness of my kingdom, mine honor and brilliance returned unto me; and my advisors and my rulers looked for unto me; and I was built up in my kingdom, and fantastic superbness was included unto me. 37 Now I Nebuchadnezzar commend and laud and respect the King of Heaven, every one of whose works are Truth, and His ways judgment: and those that stroll in pride He can dishonor" (Daniel 4:32, 34-37).

CHAPTER 14

The Grapes of Fury Are Smashed

The past part was enlightening about occasions that happen on earth when Satan is thrown out of paradise. This section gives us data about the immense harvest of souls on earth that happens as a consequence of the considerable tribulation that Satan brings on the earth.

1 And I saw, and see, the Lamb remaining on the mount Zion, and with him a hundred and forty and four thousand, having his name, and the name of his Father, composed on their temples.

Some say that this 144,000 are diverse individuals than the 144,000 in part seven however that view is not established on any sacred text and is not intelligent. This is the same 144,000 that were fixed on the earth. They have the name of the Father and the Son composed on their brows since they dropped from Israel and are followers of Jesus. The Lamb remains on Mount Zion with the 144,000 siblings who stroll in His strides. Jesus is in the Holy City called Mt Zion (Psa 48:2). There is a Mt Zion on earth too however the following entry makes it clear that they are in the Holy City. These brethren might have been executed or God might have powerfully expelled them from the earth. Sacred writing gives no answer as to the destiny of their mortal bodies (Koerig, 2016).

2 And I heard a voice from paradise, as the voice of numerous waters, and as the voice of an awesome thunder: and the voice which I heard was as the voice of harpers harping with their harps:

3 and they sing figuratively speaking another tune before the throne, and before the four living animals and the older folks: and no man could take in the melody spare the hundred and forty and four thousand, even they that had been obtained out of the earth.

4 These are they that were not contaminated with ladies; for they are virgins. These are they that take after the Lamb whithersoever he goeth. These were bought from among men, to be the first fruits unto God and unto the Lamb.

5 And in their mouth was found no untruth: they are without flaw.

John hears the voice of Jesus as the sound of "numerous waters". The voice of incredible thunder is likely the Father's voice proclaiming judgment on the earth. The thunder could contain the seven thunders that we were told about in part ten, yet what the thunders contain is fixed until the named time. John additionally hears great ambient sounds for the melody that the 144,000 sing before all the host of paradise. Just the 144,000 obtained Jewish brethren who have been reclaimed by the blood of Christ can realize this new tune. These men have followed in the strides of Jesus for 3 ½ years of service on earth. They have announced the good news of the kingdom as a witness to the entire world (Koerig, 2016).

These are called first natural products unto God and the Lamb, so before these men touch base in the Holy City the prizes couldn't have been given to the Church and the marriage couldn't have occurred in paradise.

These men have never hitched and God considers them to be as a rule profoundly unadulterated. These 144,000 are the best of the yield and they are hand picked before the general harvest happens. These brethren run with Jesus wherever He goes, so they are the same ones remaining with Jesus when He accumulates the countries before Him at the sheep and goat judgment portrayed in Matthew part 25. How the survivors of the tribulation treated these 144,000 Jewish brethren will figure out if they will go into the kingdom on earth or be assembled to be smashed in the colossal winepress of God (Koerig, 2016).

6 And I saw another holy messenger flying in mid paradise, having everlasting great greetings to broadcast unto them that harp on the earth, and unto each country and tribe and tongue and individuals;

Prior to the blessed messengers do the judgment of Father God, God will send a heavenly attendant to fly in the environment and give the everlasting uplifting news to all that harp on the earth. Nobody on the earth will have any reason for not listening to the message of salvation in Jesus Christ (Koerig, 2016).

7 and he saith with an awesome voice, Fear God, and give him eminence; for the hour of his judgment is come: and love him that made the paradise and the earth and ocean and wellsprings of waters.

This blessed messenger flying in the air has an awesome voice and he will be listened! The message of the heavenly attendant will be that the hour of God's judgment has come. As it were, the time has come to pick sides: Either fear God and love the God that really made the paradise and the earth, or apprehension and love the Beast on earth who cases to be God.

8 And an additional, a second heavenly attendant, took after, saying, Fallen, fallen is Babylon the colossal, that hath made every one of the countries to drink of the wine of the rage of her sex.

After the message of salvation is given by a heavenly attendant flying in the environment, a second holy messenger will come to tell the world that Babylon (the Beast fake Kingdom of God) has been judged by God and is currently going to experience God's fierceness. A great deal more will be told about the fall of Babylon in chapter18. This is just the declaration of her coming judgment. Babylon is not really crushed at this claim; this will turn out to be more clear when we read whatever is left of the section (Koerig, 2016).

9 And another heavenly attendant, a third, tailed them, saying with an incredible voice, If any man worshippeth the brute and his picture, and receiveth a blemish on his temple, or upon his hand,

Taking after the second heavenly attendant will be a third. This holy messenger will tell the world how their decision will be made. There will be no mischances or anybody asserting that they were gullible. He says, any individual who loves the Beast, his picture or takes his imprint have settled on their decision against the God of paradise.

10 he likewise might drink of the wine of the fierceness of God, which is readied unmixed in the measure of his displeasure; and he should be tormented with flame and brimstone in the vicinity of the blessed holy messengers, and in the vicinity of the Lamb:

11 and the smoke of their torment goeth up for ever and ever; and they have no rest day and night, they that love the monster and his picture, and whoso receiveth the characteristic of his name.

Those that apprehension the Beast more than the God of paradise have a dreary future. The smoke of their torment goes up for eternity. Their fate is the Lake of Fire! This is the place all individuals will run who side with the Beast by taking his 666 sign of faithfulness and turning out to be a piece of his kingdom. The individuals who by apprehension or unwaveringness try to spare their lives in the substance by making the Beast their God will lose their spirit (Koerig, 2016).

12 Here is the tolerance of the holy people, they that keep the charges of God, and the confidence of Jesus.

13 And I heard the voice from paradise saying, Write, Blessed are the dead beyond words the Lord from hereafter: yea, saith the Spirit, that they might rest from their works; for their works take after with them.

Numerous will take to heart the message of the 144,000 and the messages given by holy messengers and they will put their trust in Jesus. Those that continue to the end will be spared and the individuals who lose their lives for Jesus purpose will spare their souls for time everlasting. Their works take after with them in light of the fact that their prize depends on what they did amid this period. On the off chance that they pass on they will rest from their works until the delegated time for Jesus to come (Koerig, 2016).

14 And I saw, and see, a white cloud; and on the cloud I saw one sitting like unto a child of man, having on his head a brilliant crown, and in his grasp sharp sickle.

15 And another holy messenger turned out from the sanctuary, crying with an extraordinary voice to him that sat on the cloud, Send forward thy sickle, and procure: for the hour to harvest is come; for the harvest of the earth is ready.

16 And he that sat on the cloud provide reason to feel ambiguous about his sickle the earth; and the earth was harvested.

This entry is around a harvesting on the earth of grain and a get-together of the grapes to be smashed in the winepress. This entry discusses the harvesting done by the Son of Man (Jesus). The procuring is the thing that Jesus was discussing when He said to leave the wheat and tares to develop until the end of the age. The tares are the individuals who develop among the wheat and from all appearances look like wheat. Tares are weeds that take food from the dirt and trick the development of the genuine wheat. They are the children of Satan taking on the appearance of children of light.

Mat 13:30 Let both become together until the harvest: and in the season of harvest I will say to the collectors, Gather ye together first the tares, and tie them in packs to blaze them: however assemble the wheat into my animal dwelling place

This entry in Matthew says the tares would first be accumulated in groups to be blazed. Some may think the entry in Matthew says the tares are harvested before the wheat. That appears to be inconceivable; tares are fake wheat that develop in the same field -they should be procured together. What the section is inferring is that amid the considerable tribulation the tares are initially uprooted and accumulated in packs to be blazed and after that the wheat is sifted to evacuate polluting influences before it is assembled into the stable.

The harvesting and sifting is the season of the considerable tribulation. Matthew shows that the season of the smoldering of the tares put in packs (areas) on the earth starts things out. This happens when the Beast smolders the whore lady (all sorted out religion) toward the start of the immense tribulation of 3 ½ years (see part 17). The sifting that happens instantly after that amid the considerable tribulation uproots everything except the wheat portion before the bit is put into God's horse shelter (the book of life). The sifting of the wheat happens when the Beast abuses all on earth that hold the confirmation of Jesus and keep his precepts.

This wheat harvest is over only before the last judgment amid the immense tribulation. The grapes really will be smashed after the seventh vial judgment at the sheep and goat judgment of the countries. This happens just before the post-harvest marriage feast for the Son of the field proprietor (God - the proprietor of the earth).

The harvest is great to the point that John said that the quantity of spared that leave it is more prominent than any man could number. Those living in this period will be sifted and numerous will kick the bucket in the substance instead of take the sign of the Beast. Billions of souls will be spared in the colossal tribulation when the wheat stalks that tie individuals to this world are uprooted in the sifting of the immense tribulation.

A touch of the wheat on earth will in any case be in the field after the harvest. These are the gleanings that by mosaic law are required to be left in the fields after the general harvest. These are left to repopulate the earth amid the thousand years however sacred writing says that men will get to be rarer than gold after the colossal tribulation.

17 Another blessed messenger turned out from the sanctuary which is in paradise, he likewise having a sharp sickle.

18 And another blessed messenger turned out from the holy place, he that hath control over flame; and he called with an extraordinary voice to him that had the sharp sickle, saying, Send forward thy sharp sickle, and accumulate the groups of the vine of the earth; for her grapes are completely ready.

19 And the heavenly attendant cast his sickle into the earth, and accumulated the vintage of the earth, and cast it into the winepress, the considerable winepress, of the fierceness of God.

20 And the winepress was trodden without the city, and there turned-out blood from the winepress, even unto the harnesses of the stallions, to the extent a thousand and six hundred furlongs.

This is a totally distinctive harvest of a completely diverse product than was the procuring of the tares and wheat. This procuring is not about wheat or even tares, it is the collecting of aging acrid grapes. This judgment comes after the wheat is collected and sifted amid the colossal tribulation. Those in this get-together make no mystery that they are adversaries of the God of paradise. The tares were assembled in groups (diverse areas on earth) and smoldered yet these are accumulated the entire length of Israel (1600 furlongs – 185 miles) to be squashed.

What really happens here is that Satan and his holy messengers will accumulate every one of the adversaries of the God of paradise the whole length of Israel in the valley of Jehoshaphat. Jesus alone will pulverize them and their blood will blend with water that makes up their bodies and run like streams in the desert. The blood might be blended with spring water, downpour or the as yet dissolving hailstones of the seventh vial judgment since this entry pronounces their blood will course through this valley to the stallions' harnesses. We will read more about these occasions in part 19.

Isa 63:1 Who is this that cometh from Edom, with colored pieces of clothing from Bozrah? this that is heavenly in his clothing, going in the enormity of his quality? I that talk in honorability, forceful to spare.

2 Wherefore craftsmanship thou red in thine attire, and thy pieces of clothing such as him that treadeth in the wine fat?

3 I have trodden the winepress alone; and of the general population there was none with me: for I will tread them in mine outrage and trample them in my fierceness; and their blood should be sprinkled upon my articles of clothing, and I will recolor all my attire.

4 For the day of retribution is in mine heart, and the year of my reclaimed is come.

5 And I looked, and there was none to help; and I pondered that there was none to maintain: hence mine own arm brought salvation unto me; and my anger, it maintained me.

6 And I will tread down the general population in mine resentment, and make them tanked in my fierceness, and I will cut down their their strength to the earth.

CHAPTER 15

Holy Messengers Get Ready To Convey Last Torment

The data from the little book is finished. John in this section sees the last arrangement that happens in paradise before the overflowing of the seven vial judgments from Father God. The vials are poured out on a world that rejected the benevolence He gave through His Son. They would not have His Son spare them from the cycle of sin and passing on the earth and this cycle can't proceed without bringing keeping enduring on the pure. This section is the prologue to these judgments to scrub the world from criminals so that a kingdom of honesty can be built up on the earth. The judgments themselves are portrayed in the following part (Koerig, 2016).

1 And I saw another sign in paradise, extraordinary and wonderful, seven heavenly attendants having the seven last torment; for in them is topped off the fury of God.

John sees another incredible sign in paradise he sees seven heavenly attendants with the seven last torment that finish the anger of God. After these sicknesses, Jesus will come, vanquish the Beast and set up the Kingdom of God on the earth. As holy messengers completed the rage of the Lamb in the trumpet judgments heavenly attendants will likewise do the rage of the Father on all who won't acknowledge God's Son to govern over the earth (Koerig, 2016).

2 And I saw so to speak an ocean of glass blended with flame: and them that had gotten the triumph over the monster, and over his picture, and over his imprint, and over the quantity of his name, stand on the ocean of glass, having the harps of God.

The individuals who had gotten triumph over the Beast stand on what looks to John such as an ocean of glass. The ocean of glass John sees is really an ocean of individuals. This is a photo of the Church made flawless resting at the throne of God. The flame seen inside of this ocean is the Holy Spirit that abides in their middle. Those now remaining on the establishment made unadulterated are the holy people who passed on amid the immense tribulation. They got triumph over the Beast by biting the dust for their confidence in Jesus. They demonstrated this confidence by not bowing to the picture of the Beast or accepting his imprint or his number. Since the tribulation holy people are in paradise, the spouse is finished (Koerig, 2016).

3 And they sing the melody of Moses the hireling of God, and the tune of the Lamb, saying, Great and wonderful are thy works, Lord God Almighty; just and genuine are thy ways, thou King of holy people.

4 Who should not fear thee, O Lord, and laud thy name? for thou just craftsmanship sacred: for all countries should come and love before thee; for thy judgments are made show.

These that left the immense tribulation sing the melody of Moses and the tune of the Lamb. The King of the Saints is Jesus. The expressions of the melody that they sing are somewhat given in the verse. The melody is one of triumph such as the tune Moses composed telling about Israel's deliverance from Pharaoh's armed force at the Red Sea (Pharaoh was a sort or hint of the Beast). God extraordinarily conveyed Israel and after that obliterated Pharaoh and his armed force in the red ocean. This was an anticipate of the pulverization of the Beast and the throwing of the Beast alive into the Lake of Fire (a Red Sea) (Koerig, 2016).

They likewise sing a melody of endless recovery through the blood of the Lamb. In their melody they broadcast the sacredness of God and sing that all countries might come and love before Jesus after the last judgments are poured out.

5 And after that I looked, and, view, the sanctuary of the sanctuary of the affirmation in paradise was opened:

6 And the seven blessed messengers left the sanctuary, having the seven sicknesses, dressed in immaculate and white cloth, and having their bosoms braced with brilliant supports.

After the full measure of tribulation holy people are in paradise and singing tunes of triumph, the sanctuary of the sanctuary of the confirmation is opened in paradise. This is the Holy of Holies. The sanctuary made on earth was only a duplicate of what Moses was told was in paradise. The sanctuary of the confirmation contained the "Ark of the Covenant". The natural duplicate contained the Ten Commandments, sustenance, and Aaron's pole. The Ark found in paradise will be a witness against the world in light of the fact that the world has now dismisses everything in it. They dismisses the contract in paradise that contains the Word of God (Jesus), the genuine bread of life (Jesus) and God's decision for consecrated cleric (Jesus) (Koerig, 2016).

Out of the sanctuary come the seven holy messengers that have the errand to bring the seven last torment that will go ahead every one of the individuals who dismiss the God of paradise and who venerate the Beast. The white cloth that the heavenly attendants wear demonstrates that these blessed messengers are upright and stand in the vicinity of God. Their brilliant supports show that these seven blessed messengers are clerics in the wonderful sanctuary and have full power from God to do His orders (Koerig, 2016).

7 And one of the four mammoths gave unto the seven blessed messengers seven brilliant vials loaded with the rage of God, who liveth for ever and ever.

8 And the sanctuary was loaded with smoke from the brilliance of God, and from his energy; and no man could go into the sanctuary, till the seven diseases of the seven heavenly attendants were satisfied.

The seven brilliant vials loaded with the anger of God are given to the seven incredible holy messengers by one of the four living Beasts that encompass the throne of God. The chain of importance in paradise stays steady. After this is done the sanctuary is loaded with smoke from the eminence of God and nobody can go into the sanctuary until the seven maladies are satisfied. This is showing that the judgment is firm and there will be no mediation before God to defer or intervene against these judgments. Since those on earth show rejected God's leniency (Jesus) the main thing they have left to get is God's anger (Koerig, 2016).

CHAPTER 16

Seven Last Torment Poured Out

John now depicts the vial judgments that originate from Father God on a world that is worshiping Satan as God. As abnormal as the judgments show up, these are genuine occasions that happen on the earth only before the arrival of Jesus to set up the Kingdom of God on earth. These vial judgments likely start around 6 months before His coming. I trust the judgments traverse the most recent 6 months or so in light of the fact that their portrayals make it sure that every vial influences the world for some period of time. The social affair of all the world armed forces to Armageddon after the 6th vial would seem to take some time even with the assistance of Satan's blessed messengers. The judgments are sure to happen in the last part of the 3 ½ years on the grounds that The Beast has had room schedule-wise to set up his fake kingdom by driving individuals to take his 666 imprint (Koerig, 2016).

1 And I heard an incredible voice out of the sanctuary saying to the seven holy messengers, Go your ways, and pour out the vials of the fierceness of God upon the earth.

The immense voice out of the sanctuary is the voice of Jesus serving as esteemed minister in the sanctuary. He advises the seven heavenly attendants to go in the request they were allotted to pour out the fierceness of God upon the earth.

2 And the first went, and poured out his vial upon the earth; and there fell a pernicious and offensive sore upon the men which had the characteristic of the monster, and upon them which worshiped his picture.

The principal vial is poured out and loathsome injuries happen upon all who have taken the characteristic of the Beast and on the individuals who have worshiped his picture. The bruises are ulcers or bubbles.

They are similar to what Egypt experienced in old days when God passed judgment on her (Exodus). The bruises will caution individuals who have not worshiped Satan to swing to approach the God of paradise. It will likewise be a motivator for wickedness individuals who need Satan to be God, to discover motivation to abhor the God of paradise and to try to battle against God (Koerig, 2016).

3 And the second heavenly attendant poured out his vial upon the ocean; and it got to be as the blood of a dead man: and each living soul passed on in the ocean.

In the past trumpet judgments, there was a comparable judgment on 33% of the earth. Presently we see these things are occurring all in all earth. These judgments can't happen until the heavenly attendant pours out the vial, so these are particular judgments and are not only extensions of the trumpet judgments like a few essayists have hypothesized. At the point when the second heavenly attendant pours out his vial the ocean will get to be similar to the blood of a dead man and everything in it will bite the dust. This is not dull red/chestnut nourishment shading; it is an exceptionally foul dangerous substance that executes each living thing with a spirit in the ocean (Koerig, 2016).

4 And the third holy messenger poured out his vial upon the waterways and wellsprings of waters; and they got to be blood.

5 And I heard the holy messenger of the waters say, Thou workmanship honorable, O Lord, which craftsmanship, and

wast, and shalt be, on account of thou hast judged along these lines.

6 For they have shed the blood of holy people and prophets, and thou hast given them blood to drink; for they are commendable.

7 And I listened to one more of the sacrificial stone say, Even in this way, Lord God Almighty, genuine and honorable are thy judgments.

At the point when the third holy messenger pours out his vial all the crisp water on the earth will likewise be swung to blood. God is giving them blood to drink since they have butchered His holy people and prophets. These judgments are reimbursement for those that were butchered for their confidence because of "Babylon the Great" (section 18). The heavenly attendant that held these martyred souls under the holy place affirms that God's judgments on these individuals on earth are meriting and just (Koerig, 2016).

8 And the fourth blessed messenger poured out his vial upon the sun; and power was given unto him to burn men with flame.

9 And men were burned with awesome warmth, and reviled the name of God, which hath control over these diseases: and they apologized not to give him heavenliness.

This fourth judgment ought to make it clear that these judgments are worldwide basically. I have perused a great deal of hypothesis about what might bring the warmth and it ranges from atomic fighting to drained ozone in the environment. Nonetheless, the content evidently says that the vial will be poured out on the sun and not on the earth. No country will get away from the warmth of the sun when it goes into a nova and sears all humanity with incredible warmth. This is the genuine future an Earth-wide temperature boost that man ought to stress over (Koerig, 2016).

With this, regardless they won't concede that the God of paradise is Almighty. They will revile His name for these judgments and most likely call Him the Devil. Those that love the Beast on earth truly need Satan to be God, as do his fallen blessed messengers. Accepting or wishing an untruth is genuine does not make it genuine. There is one and only Creator God and He is the one that abides in paradise (Koerig, 2016).

10 And the fifth blessed messenger poured out his vial upon the seat of the brute; and his kingdom was loaded with murkiness; and they chewed their tongues for agony,

11 And cursed the God of paradise as a result of their agonies and their bruises, and atoned not of their deeds

At the point when the fifth vial is poured out the kingdom of the Beast will be brimming with murkiness. It will be an obscurity that can be felt and they will bite their tongues for agony. There will be no light in the kingdom of the Beast since God will demonstrate the world that the Beast controlling the earth has no light in himself. An illustration of this kind of dimness can be found in Exodus when God judged Egypt.

In Egypt, the haziness endured three days; we are not told to what extent this dimness will last. The general population in the Beast's kingdom living with injuries, warmth, thirst and haziness won't atone of taking after Satan as God, or of their transgressions. They will rather swear the God of paradise.

With this disease of dimness God is graphically exhibiting to the general population on the earth who have not yet worshiped the Beast or taken his imprint what damnation will be similar to for time everlasting on the off chance that they do. They should by their own particular unrestrained choice approach the God of paradise for kindness and salvation and acknowledge Jesus to be spared from Satan.

On the off chance that they did, God would have his heavenly attendants shield them from the sicknesses yet to come.

Yet, most left on earth will keep on trusting the falsehood that Satan is God.

12 And the 6th heavenly attendant poured out his vial upon the immense stream Euphrates; and the water thereof was become scarce, that the method for the lords of the east may be arranged.

13 And I saw three unclean spirits like frogs leave the mouth of the mythical serpent, and out of the mouth of the mammoth, and out of the mouth of the false prophet.

14 For they are the spirits of fallen angels, working supernatural occurrences, which go forward unto the rulers of the earth and of the entire world, to accumulate them to the skirmish of that awesome day of God Almighty.

At the point when the 6th vial is poured out on the waterway Euphrates every one of the armed forces of the world are assembled by the sinister trinity (Dragon, Beast, False Prophet) to the arranging ground of Megiddo in Israel (Armageddon). The Euphrates River that isolates East from West will be become scarce so that the armed forces of the east can stroll to Israel. At the point when every one of the armed forces of the world are accumulated to the valley of choice, they will be judged in the winepress of God. Amid the following couple of months, the accompanying sacred writing will be totally satisfied (Koerig, 2016).

Joe 3:9 Proclaim ye this among the Gentiles; Prepare war, wake up the relentless men, let every one of the men of war draw close; let them come up:

10 Beat your plowshares into swords, and your pruninghooks into lances: let the frail say, I am solid.

11 Assemble yourselves, and come, all ye rapscallion, and accumulate yourselves together indirect: thither cause thy relentless ones to descend, O LORD.

12 Let the pagan be wakened, and come up to the valley of Jehoshaphat: for there will I sit to judge all the barbarian indirect.

13 Put ye in the sickle, for the harvest is ready: come, get you down; for the press is full, the fats flood; for their naughtiness is awesome.

14 Multitudes, hoards in the valley of choice: for the day of the LORD is close in the valley of choice.

15 The sun and the moon might be obscured, and the stars should pull back their sparkling.

16 The LORD likewise might thunder out of Zion, and utter his voice from Jerusalem; and the sky and the earth should shake: yet the LORD will be the trust of his kin, and the quality of the offspring of Israel.

17 So might ye realize that I am the LORD your God abiding in Zion, my sacred mountain: then should Jerusalem be heavenly, and there should no outsiders go through her anymore.

Evil holy messengers will utilize lying signs and ponders to mislead and to assemble each one of the individuals who wish to battle against the God of paradise. They will procure the results of such an absurd and pointless endeavor to war against the genuine Creator.

15 Behold, I come as a hoodlum. Favored is he that watcheth, and keepeth his pieces of clothing, for fear that he walk exposed, and they see his disgrace

This is an incidental entry between the 6th and seventh vial that says that Jesus will come as a cheat. Some think it is alluding back to the season of the pre-tribulation euphoria however I don't. Prior to the last fight happens keeping in mind the Beast is social affair his strengths, God will send his blessed messengers to accumulate each one of the individuals who are searching for

Him before the last vial is poured out. This is by all accounts the get-together discussed in Matthew and Luke (Koerig, 2016)

Mt 24:40 Then should two be in the field; the one might be taken, and the other left.

Mt 24:41 Two ladies should be pounding at the plant; the one might be taken, and the other left.

Lu 17:35 Two ladies might be pounding together; the one should be taken, and the other left.

Lu 17:36 Two men might be in the field; the one should be taken, and the other left.

These here have no white robes so it is not those found in paradise who left the colossal tribulation (Rev 7:14). They are wearing the articles of clothing of their acts of kindness and tolerance in the tribulation. Those said to be "strolling" bare likely either had no benevolent acts or quit doing acts of kindness. Some will be embarrassed before whatever remains of them however they will at present go. This social event might possibly incorporate the regular relatives of Israel who did not take the imprint. Maybe right now, a few relatives of Israel on the planet still don't have a clue about that Jesus is Jehovah. Whatever the case, Isaiah discusses the arrival of characteristic Israel in the most recent days in the accompanying section: (Koerig, 2016).

Isa 11:16 And there should be an expressway for the remainder of his kin, which might be left, from Assyria; such as it was to Israel in the day that he came up out of the place where there is Egypt.

2 Behold, God is my salvation; I will trust, and not be apprehensive: for the LORD JEHOVAH is my quality and my tune; he likewise is turned into my salvation.

3 Therefore with satisfaction should ye coax water out of the wells of salvation.

4 And in that day might ye say, Praise the LORD, call upon his name, announce his doings among the general population, make say that his name is lifted up.

5 Sing unto the LORD; for he hath done brilliant things: this is known in all the earth.

6 Cry out and yell, thou occupant of Zion: for incredible is the Holy One of Israel amidst thee.

Isa 35: 8 And a thruway should be there, and a way, and it might be known as The method for blessedness; the unclean should not ignore it; but rather it should be for those: the wayfaring men, however tricks, might not blunder in that.

9 No lion might be there, nor any avaricious mammoth should go up subsequently, it should not be found there; but rather the reclaimed should stroll there:

10 And the delivered of the LORD might return, and come to Zion with tunes and everlasting delight upon their heads: they should get happiness and energy, and distress and moaning might escape away.

16 And he accumulated them together into a spot brought in the Hebrew tongue Armageddon.

Joe 3:2 I will likewise accumulate all countries, and will bring them down into the valley of Jehoshaphat, and will beg them there for my kin and for my legacy Israel, whom they have scattered among the countries, and separated my property.

Armageddon is Megiddo in northern Israel; Megiddo will be the organizing territory for the armed forces of the Beast however this is not where the armed forces will be obliterated.

At the point when Jesus crushes these armed forces, the blood of the armed forces will stream in this valley of

Jehoshaphat (Rev 14:20). The valley of Jehoshaphat will be an extraordinary crack valley that keeps running for around 185 miles on the east side of Israel. A lot of it was made by the seismic tremor that opened this valley for the respectful in Jerusalem to escape to the mountains for awesome assurance.

The God of paradise will solicit the rulers from the earth and their armed forces to permit all relatives of regular Israel to come back to the area that He named for them. The countries will agree on the grounds that they will fear judgment or will see a chance to murder every one of the Jews on earth at one area. In any case, as Egypt did in antiquated days, after they let the children of Israel go; they will solidify their hearts and follow them to kill them.

God will judge all the world's armed forces that come against Israel in this valley. They will get all out obliteration, as did the armed forces of Pharaoh who came against Israel. The genuine decimation of this armed force is portrayed in section 19 after John first tells about the deeds and devastation of "Riddle Babylon" in part 17 and "Babylon the Great" in part 18 (Koerig, 2016).

Notice the verse in Joel says they separated the place where there is God. This procedure of separating the place that is known for God guaranteed to the relatives of Israel is the center in the Middle-East peace handle even today.

17 And the seventh holy messenger emptied out his vial into the air; and there came an incredible voice out of the sanctuary of paradise, from the throne, saying, It is finished.

18 And there were voices, and thunders, and lightnings; and there was an extraordinary seismic tremor, for example, was not since men were upon the earth, so forceful a quake, thus incredible.

19 And the considerable city was partitioned into three sections, and the urban areas of the countries fell: and extraordinary Babylon came in recognition before God, to give unto her the measure of the wine of the wildness of his anger.

20 And each island fled away, and the mountains were not found.

21 And there fell upon men an extraordinary hail out of paradise, each stone about the heaviness of an ability: and men reviled God in light of the disease of the hail; for the sickness thereof was surpassing awesome.

At the point when the seventh heavenly attendant pours out his vial in the climate the best seismic tremor that ever was or that ever will happen on earth will happen. Every one of the urban areas of the world will fall. All high mountain extents will break down and all islands will be moved or disappear. Jerusalem will be isolated into three sections around then. The heap of the Lord will be raised as the most noteworthy point in the region or conceivably the world.

This aggregate changing of the world's outside layer will permit satisfaction of the predictions that talk about the desert area being watered and being rich amid the millennial rule. Most betrays are brought about by high mountain ranges. At the point when the mountain reaches are broken up the majority of the world will get to be fruitful. This change of the covering will dispense with issue lines. There will be no real seismic tremors amid the thousand years. There will likewise be more delicate wind designs without the mountain ranges, which means less serious tempests. The earth will turn into a heaven (Koerig, 2016).

Isa 2:2 And it should happen in the most recent days, that the pile of the LORD'S house might be set up in the highest point of the mountains, and should be magnified over the slopes; and all countries might stream unto it.

The heaviness of the hailstones is around an ability. An ability was 3000 shekels - these hailstones weigh around 100 pounds each. The hailstones will pour down everywhere throughout the earth amid this last torment before the second happening to Jesus. This change on earth occurs by a stone made without hands hitting the earth at Babylon. Daniel talks about this stone. These sections in Daniel have a double satisfaction. They discuss the Rock (Jesus) wrecking the works of the Devil they likewise talk about the kingdom of the Beast (Babylon) being crushed by a stone. More will be said in regards to the demolition of the Beast kingdom in part 18.

Dan 2:34 Thou sawest till that a stone was removed without hands, which destroyed the picture upon his feet that were of iron and mud, and brake them to pieces.

Dan 2:45 Forasmuch as thou sawest that the stone was removed of the mountain without hands, and that it brake in pieces the iron, the metal, the mud, the silver, and the gold; the considerable God hath made known not lord what should happen in the future: and the fantasy is sure, and the translation thereof beyond any doubt.

1 And I heard an extraordinary voice out of the sanctuary saying to the seven heavenly attendants, Go your ways, and pour out the vials of the fury of God upon the earth.

The considerable voice out of the sanctuary is the voice of Jesus serving as devout cleric in the sanctuary. He advises the seven heavenly attendants to go in the request they were appointed to pour out the anger of God upon the earth.

2 And the first went, and poured out his vial upon the earth; and there fell a dangerous and deplorable sore upon the men which had the characteristic of the monster, and upon them which worshiped his picture.

The main vial is poured out and horrible bruises happen upon all who have taken the characteristic of the Beast and on the individuals who have worshiped his picture. The injuries are ulcers or bubbles. They are similar to what Egypt experienced in old days when God passed judgment on her (Exodus). The bruises will caution individuals who have not worshiped Satan to swing to approach the God of paradise. It will likewise be a motivating force for abhorrence individuals who need Satan to be God, to discover motivation to despise the God of paradise and to look to battle against God (Koerig, 2016).

3 And the second blessed messenger poured out his vial upon the ocean; and it got to be as the blood of a dead man: and each living soul passed on in the ocean.

In the past trumpet judgments, there was a comparative judgment on 33% of the earth. Presently we see these things are occurring all in all earth. These judgments can't happen until the blessed messenger pours out the vial, so these are independent judgments and are not only extensions of the trumpet judgments like a few essayists have guessed. At the point when the second holy messenger pours out his vial the ocean will get to be similar to the blood of a dead man and everything in it will bite the dust. This is not dim red/chestnut nourishment shading; it is an exceptionally foul dangerous substance that slaughters each living thing with a spirit in the ocean (Koerig, 2016).

4 And the third holy messenger poured out his vial upon the streams and wellsprings of waters; and they got to be blood.

5 And I heard the heavenly attendant of the waters say, Thou craftsmanship upright, O Lord, which workmanship, and wast, and shalt be, on the grounds that thou hast judged hence.

6 For they have shed the blood of holy people and prophets, and thou hast given them blood to drink; for they are commendable.

7 And I listened to one more of the sacrificial table say, Even thus, Lord God Almighty, genuine and upright are thy judgments.

At the point when the third heavenly attendant pours out his vial all the new water on the earth will likewise be swung to blood. God is giving them blood to drink since they have butchered His holy people and prophets. These judgments are reimbursement for those that were butchered for their confidence because of "Babylon the Great" (part 18). The holy messenger that held these martyred souls under the sacred place affirms that God's judgments on these individuals on earth are meriting and just (Koerig, 2016).

8 And the fourth blessed messenger poured out his vial upon the sun; and power was given unto him to singe men with flame.

9 And men were seared with incredible warmth, and cursed the name of God, which hath control over these diseases: and they atoned not to give him wonderfulness.

This fourth judgment ought to make it clear that these judgments are worldwide basically. I have perused a ton of theory about what might bring the warmth and it ranges from atomic fighting to drained ozone in the air. Be that as it may, the content clearly says that the vial will be poured out on the sun and not on the earth. No country will get away from the warmth of the sun when it goes into a nova and sears all humankind with awesome warmth. This is the genuine future an Earth-wide temperature boost that man ought to stress over (Koerig, 2016).

With this, regardless they won't concede that the God of paradise is Almighty. They will curse His name for these judgments and presumably call Him the Devil. Those that love the Beast on earth truly need Satan to be God, as do his fallen holy messengers. Accepting or wishing a falsehood is genuine does not make it genuine. There is one and only Creator God and He is the one that abides in paradise (Koerig, 2016).

10 And the fifth holy messenger poured out his vial upon the seat of the monster; and his kingdom was brimming with haziness; and they chewed their tongues for torment,

11 And reviled the God of paradise due to their torments and their injuries, and apologized not of their deeds

At the point when the fifth vial is poured out the kingdom of the Beast will be loaded with dimness. It will be a dimness that can be felt and they will chew their tongues for torment. There will be no light in the kingdom of the Beast since God will demonstrate the world that the Beast managing the earth has no light in himself. A sample of this kind of haziness can be found in Exodus when God judged Egypt.

In Egypt, the obscurity kept going three days; we are not told to what extent this murkiness will last. The general population in the Beast's kingdom living with bruises, warmth, thirst and murkiness won't atone of taking after Satan as God, or of their transgressions. They will rather revile the God of paradise (Koerig, 2016).

With this sickness of dimness God is graphically exhibiting to the general population on the earth who have not yet worshiped the Beast or taken his imprint what hellfire will be similar to for endlessness on the off chance that they do. They should by their own through and through freedom approach the God of paradise for leniency and salvation and acknowledge Jesus to be spared from Satan. On the off chance that they did, God would have his holy messengers shield them from the maladies yet to come. Yet, most left on earth will keep on trusting the falsehood that Satan is God.

12 And the 6th holy messenger poured out his vial upon the immense stream Euphrates; and the water thereof was become scarce, that the method for the lords of the east may be arranged.

13 And I saw three unclean spirits like frogs leave the mouth of the mythical serpent, and out of the mouth of the mammoth, and out of the mouth of the false prophet.

14 For they are the spirits of fallen angels, working supernatural occurrences, which go forward unto the rulers

of the earth and of the entire world, to assemble them to the skirmish of that awesome day of God Almighty.

At the point when the 6th vial is poured out on the stream Euphrates every one of the armed forces of the world are assembled by the sinister trinity (Dragon, Beast, False Prophet) to the arranging ground of Megiddo in Israel (Armageddon). The Euphrates River that isolates East from West will be gone away so that the armed forces of the east can stroll to Israel. At the point when every one of the armed forces of the world are accumulated to the valley of choice, they will be judged in the winepress of God. Amid the following couple of months, the accompanying sacred writing will be totally satisfied.

Joe 3:9 Proclaim ye this among the Gentiles; Prepare war, wake up the strong men, let every one of the men of war draw close; let them come up:

10 Beat your plowshares into swords, and your pruninghooks into lances: let the feeble say, I am solid.

11 Assemble yourselves, and come, all ye rapscallion, and accumulate yourselves together circuitous: thither cause thy strong ones to descend, O LORD.

12 Let the barbarian be wakened, and come up to the valley of Jehoshaphat: for there will I sit to judge all the rapscallion indirect.

13 Put ye in the sickle, for the harvest is ready: come, get you down; for the press is full, the fats flood; for their insidiousness is extraordinary.

14 Multitudes, hoards in the valley of choice: for the day of the LORD is close in the valley of choice.

15 The sun and the moon might be obscured, and the stars should pull back their sparkling.

16 The LORD likewise should thunder out of Zion, and utter his voice from Jerusalem; and the sky and the earth might shake: yet the LORD will be the trust of his kin, and the quality of the offspring of Israel.

17 So might ye realize that I am the LORD your God staying in Zion, my heavenly mountain: then should Jerusalem be sacred, and there should no outsiders go through her any more.

Satanic angels will utilize lying signs and ponders to swindle and to accumulate every one of the individuals who wish to battle against the God of paradise. They will harvest the results of such a silly and worthless endeavor to war against the genuine Creator.

15 Behold, I come as a hoodlum. Favored is he that watcheth, and keepeth his articles of clothing, for fear that he walk stripped, and they see his disgrace

This is an incidental entry between the 6th and seventh vial that says that Jesus will come as a cheat. Some think it is alluding back to the season of the pre-tribulation happiness yet I don't. Prior to the last fight happens keeping in mind the Beast is social occasion his powers, God will send his heavenly attendants to accumulate each one of the individuals who are searching for Him before the last vial is poured out. This is by all accounts the social affair talked about in Matthew and Luke.

Mt 24:40 Then should two be in the field; the one might be taken, and the other left.

Mt 24:41 Two ladies might be granulating at the factory; the one should be taken, and the other left.

Lu 17:35 Two ladies might be granulating together; the one should be taken, and the other left.

Lu 17:36 Two men might be in the field; the one should be taken, and the other left.

These here have no white robes so it is not those found in paradise who left the considerable tribulation (Rev 7:14). They are wearing the pieces of clothing of their acts of kindness and persistence in the tribulation. Those said to be "strolling" exposed most likely either had no acts of kindness or quit doing acts of kindness. Some will be embarrassed before whatever is left of them however they will in any case go. This social affair could possibly incorporate the common relatives of Israel who did not take the imprint. Maybe as of right now, a few relatives of Israel on the planet still don't have the foggiest idea about that Jesus is Jehovah. Whatever the case, Isaiah talks about the arrival of normal Israel in the most recent days in the accompanying section:

Isa 11:16 And there might be an expressway for the remainder of his kin, which should be left, from Assyria; such as it was to Israel in the day that he came up out of the place where there is Egypt.

2 Behold, God is my salvation; I will trust, and not be anxious: for the LORD JEHOVAH is my quality and my melody; he likewise is turned into my salvation.

3 Therefore with delight might ye coax water out of the wells of salvation.

4 And in that day should ye say, Praise the LORD, call upon his name, proclaim his doings among the general population, make say that his name is lifted up.

5 Sing unto the LORD; for he hath done great things: this is known in all the earth.

6 Cry out and yell, thou tenant of Zion: for awesome is the Holy One of Israel amidst thee.

Isa 35: 8 And a roadway might be there, and a way, and it should be known as The method for sacredness; the unclean might not disregard it; but rather it might be for those: the wayfaring men, however tricks, should not blunder in that.

9 No lion should be there, nor any avaricious brute might go up subsequently, it might not be found there; but rather the reclaimed might stroll there:

10 And the emancipated of the LORD should return, and come to Zion with melodies and everlasting happiness upon their heads: they might acquire euphoria and energy, and distress and murmuring should escape away.

16 And he assembled them together into a spot brought in the Hebrew tongue Armageddon.

Joe 3:2 I will likewise assemble all countries, and will bring them down into the valley of Jehoshaphat, and will beg them there for my kin and for my legacy Israel, whom they have scattered among the countries, and separated my territory.

Armageddon is Megiddo in northern Israel; Megiddo will be the organizing zone for the armed forces of the Beast yet this is not where the armed forces will be obliterated. At the point when Jesus decimates these armed forces, the blood of the armed forces will stream in this valley of Jehoshaphat (Rev 14:20). The valley of Jehoshaphat will be an extraordinary fracture valley that keeps running for around 185 miles on the east side of Israel. A lot of it was made by the tremor that opened this valley for the faithful in Jerusalem to escape to the mountains for heavenly security (Koerig, 2016).

The God of paradise will solicit the lords from the earth and their armed forces to permit all relatives of normal Israel to come back to the area that He named for them. The countries will consent since they will fear judgment or will see a chance to execute every one of the Jews on earth at one area. In any case, as Egypt did in antiquated days, after they let the children of Israel go; they will solidify their hearts and follow them to kill them. (Koerig, 2016).

God will judge all the world's armed forces that come against Israel in this valley. They will get downright demolition, as did the armed forces of Pharaoh who came against Israel. The real decimation of this armed force is depicted in part 19 after John first tells about the deeds and pulverization of "Puzzle Babylon" in section 17 and "Babylon the Great" in part 18 (Koerig, 2016).

Notice the verse in Joel says they separated the place where there is God. This procedure of separating the place that is known for God guaranteed to the relatives of Israel is the center in the Middle-East peace prepare even today.

17 And the seventh holy messenger emptied out his vial into the air; and there came an extraordinary voice out of the sanctuary of paradise, from the throne, saying, It is finished.

18 And there were voices, and thunders, and lightnings; and there was an incredible seismic tremor, for example, was not since men were upon the earth, so powerful a quake, thus awesome.

19 And the immense city was partitioned into three sections, and the urban communities of the countries fell: and awesome Babylon came in recognition before God, to give unto her the measure of the wine of the furiousness of his anger.

20 And each island fled away, and the mountains were not found.

21 And there fell upon men an awesome hail out of paradise, each stone about the heaviness of an ability: and men reviled God in view of the disease of the hail; for the maladie thereof was surpassing extraordinary.

At the point when the seventh blessed messenger pours out his vial in the air the best quake that ever was or that ever will happen on earth will happen. Every one of the urban communities of the world will fall. All high mountain extents will disintegrate and all islands will be moved or disappear. Jerusalem will be partitioned into three sections around then. The pile of the Lord will be raised as the most elevated point in the region or conceivably the world.

This aggregate changing of the world's outside layer will permit satisfaction of the predictions that talk about the desert area being watered and being rich amid the millennial rule. Most leaves are created by high mountain ranges. At the point when the mountain extents are disintegrated the vast majority of the world will get to be ripe. This change of the covering will wipe out flaw lines. There will be no significant seismic tremors amid the thousand years. There will likewise be more tender wind designs without the mountain ranges, which means less extreme tempests. The earth will turn into a heaven (Koerig, 2016).

Isa 2:2 And it should happen in the most recent days, that the heap of the LORD'S house might be built up in the highest point of the mountains, and might be commended over the slopes; and all countries might stream unto it.

The heaviness of the hailstones is around an ability. An ability was 3000 shekels - these hailstones weigh around 100 pounds each. The hailstones will pour down everywhere throughout the earth amid this last torment before the second happening to Jesus. This change on earth happens by a stone made without hands hitting the earth at Babylon. Daniel talks about this stone. These sections in Daniel have a double satisfaction. They discuss the Rock (Jesus) decimating the works of the Devil they additionally talk about the kingdom of the Beast (Babylon) being obliterated by a stone. More will be said in regards to the pulverization of the Beast kingdom in part 18 (Koerig, 2016).

Dan 2:34 Thou sawest till that a stone was removed without hands, which destroyed the picture upon his feet that were of iron and dirt, and brake them to pieces.

Dan 2:45 Forasmuch as thou sawest that the stone was removed of the mountain without hands, and that it brake in pieces the iron, the metal, the dirt, the silver, and the gold; the colossal God hath made known not ruler what should happen in the future: and the fantasy is sure, and the translation thereof beyond any doubt.

John now depicts the vial judgments that originate from Father God on a world that is worshiping Satan as God. As odd as the judgments show up, these are genuine occasions that happen on the earth only before the arrival of Jesus to set up the Kingdom of God on earth. These vial judgments presumably start around 6 months before His coming. I trust the judgments traverse the most recent 6 months or so in light of the fact that their portrayals make it sure that every vial influences the world for some period of time. The social affair of all the world armed forces to Armageddon after the 6th vial would seem to take some time even with the assistance of Satan's blessed messengers. The judgments are sure to happen in the last part of the 3 ½ years in light of the fact that The Beast has had sufficient energy to set up his fake kingdom by driving individuals to take his 666 imprint.

1 And I heard an extraordinary voice out of the sanctuary saying to the seven heavenly attendants, Go your ways, and pour out the vials of the fierceness of God upon the earth.

The considerable voice out of the sanctuary is the voice of Jesus serving as devout minister in the sanctuary. He advises the seven holy messengers to go in the request they were allocated to pour out the rage of God upon the earth.

2 And the first went, and poured out his vial upon the earth; and there fell a baneful and horrifying sore upon the men which had the sign of the brute, and upon them which worshiped his picture.

The primary vial is poured out and unpleasant bruises happen upon all who have taken the sign of the Beast and on the individuals who have worshiped his picture. The bruises are ulcers or bubbles. They are similar to what Egypt experienced in old days when God passed judgment on her (Exodus). The wounds will caution individuals who have not worshiped Satan to swing to approach the God of paradise. It will likewise be a motivation for wickedness individuals who need Satan to be God, to discover motivation to abhor the God of paradise and to try to battle against God.

3 And the second heavenly attendant poured out his vial upon the ocean; and it got to be as the blood of a dead man: and each living soul kicked the bucket in the ocean.

In the past trumpet judgments, there was a comparable judgment on 33% of the earth. Presently we see these things are occurring in general earth. These judgments can't happen until the heavenly attendant pours out the vial, so these are particular judgments and are not only extensions of the trumpet judgments like a few scholars have conjectured. At the point when the second heavenly attendant pours out his vial the ocean will get to be similar to the blood of a dead man and everything in it will bite the dust. This is not dull red/chestnut sustenance shading; it is an exceptionally foul lethal substance that slaughters each living thing with a spirit in the ocean.

4 And the third holy messenger poured out his vial upon the streams and wellsprings of waters; and they got to be blood.

5 And I heard the holy messenger of the waters say, Thou craftsmanship exemplary, O Lord, which workmanship, and wast, and shalt be, on account of thou hast judged along these lines.

6 For they have shed the blood of holy people and prophets, and thou hast given them blood to drink; for they are commendable.

7 And I listened to one more of the sacrificial stone say, Even in this way, Lord God Almighty, genuine and equitable are thy judgments.

At the point when the third holy messenger pours out his vial all the crisp water on the earth will likewise be swung to blood. God is giving them blood to drink since they have butchered His holy people and prophets. These judgments are reimbursement for those that were butchered for their confidence on account of "Babylon the Great" (part 18). The blessed messenger that held these martyred souls under the sacred place affirms that God's judgments on these individuals on earth are meriting and just.

8 And the fourth blessed messenger poured out his vial upon the sun; and power was given unto him to singe men with flame.

9 And men were seared with incredible warmth, and reviled the name of God, which hath control over these maladies: and they atoned not to give him heavenliness.

This fourth judgment ought to make it clear that these judgments are worldwide basically. I have perused a great deal of theory about what might bring the warmth and it ranges from atomic fighting to drained ozone in the environment. Notwithstanding, the content evidently says that the vial will be poured out on the sun and not on the earth. No country will get away from the warmth of the sun when it goes into a nova and singes all humankind with incredible warmth. This is the genuine future a worldwide temperature alteration that man ought to stress over.

With this, regardless they won't concede that the God of paradise is Almighty. They will revile His name for these judgments and most likely call Him the Devil. Those that love the Beast on earth truly need Satan to be God, as do his fallen blessed messengers. Accepting or wishing an untruth is genuine does not make it genuine. There is stand out Creator God and He is the one that stays in paradise (Koerig, 2016).

10 And the fifth blessed messenger poured out his vial upon the seat of the mammoth; and his kingdom was loaded with murkiness; and they chewed their tongues for agony,

11 And cursed the God of paradise as a result of their agonies and their bruises, and atoned not of their deeds

At the point when the fifth vial is poured out the kingdom of the Beast will be brimming with murkiness. It will be an obscurity that can be felt and they will bite their tongues for agony. There will be no light in the kingdom of the Beast since God will demonstrate the world that the Beast controlling the earth has no light in himself. An illustration of this sort of murkiness can be found in Exodus when God judged Egypt.

In Egypt, the haziness endured three days; we are not told to what extent this murkiness will last. The general population in the Beast's kingdom living with injuries, warmth, thirst and haziness won't apologize of taking after Satan as God, or of their wrongdoings. They will rather curse the God of paradise.

With this disease of murkiness God is graphically exhibiting to the general population on the earth who have not yet worshiped the Beast or taken his imprint what damnation will be similar to for time everlasting on the off chance that they do. They should by their own unrestrained choice approach the God of paradise for leniency and salvation and acknowledge Jesus to be spared from Satan. In the event that they did, God would have his holy messengers shield them from the diseases yet to come. Yet, most left on earth will keep on trusting the untruth that Satan is God.

12 And the 6th heavenly attendant poured out his vial upon the immense waterway Euphrates; and the water thereof was become scarce, that the method for the lords of the east may be arranged.

13 And I saw three unclean spirits like frogs leave the mouth of the mythical serpent, and out of the mouth of the monster, and out of the mouth of the false prophet.

14 For they are the spirits of fallen angels, working marvels, which go forward unto the rulers of the earth and of the entire world, to accumulate them to the skirmish of that incredible day of God Almighty.

At the point when the 6th vial is poured out on the waterway Euphrates every one of the armed forces of the world are assembled by the evil trinity (Dragon, Beast, False Prophet) to the arranging ground of Megiddo in Israel (Armageddon). The Euphrates River that isolates East from West will be become scarce so that the armed forces of the east can stroll to Israel. At the point when every one of the armed forces of the world are accumulated to the valley of choice, they will be judged in the winepress of God. Amid the following couple of months, the accompanying sacred text will be totally satisfied.

Joe 3:9 Proclaim ye this among the Gentiles; Prepare war, wake up the relentless men, let every one of the men of war draw close; let them come up:

10 Beat your plowshares into swords, and your pruninghooks into lances: let the frail say, I am solid.

11 Assemble yourselves, and come, all ye barbarian, and accumulate yourselves together circuitous: thither cause thy powerful ones to descend, O LORD.

12 Let the rapscallion be wakened, and come up to the valley of Jehoshaphat: for there will I sit to judge all the barbarian indirect.

13 Put ye in the sickle, for the harvest is ready: come, get you down; for the press is full, the fats flood; for their insidiousness is incredible.

14 Multitudes, hoards in the valley of choice: for the day of the LORD is close in the valley of choice.

15 The sun and the moon might be obscured, and the stars should pull back their sparkling.

16 The LORD likewise should thunder out of Zion, and utter his voice from Jerusalem; and the sky and the earth might shake: however the LORD will be the trust of his kin, and the quality of the offspring of Israel.

17 So might ye realize that I am the LORD your God staying in Zion, my heavenly mountain: then should Jerusalem be sacred, and there should no outsiders go through her any more.

Sinister blessed messengers will utilize lying signs and ponders to beguile and to assemble every one of the individuals who wish to battle against the God of paradise. They will procure the results of such a stupid and worthless endeavor to war against the genuine Creator.

15 Behold, I come as a criminal. Favored is he that watcheth, and keepeth his pieces of clothing, or he walk stripped, and they see his disgrace

This is an incidental entry between the 6th and seventh vial that says that Jesus will come as a hoodlum. Some think it is alluding back to the season of the pre-tribulation euphoria yet I don't. Prior to the last fight happens keeping in mind the Beast is social affair his powers, God will send his blessed messengers to assemble every one of the individuals who are searching for Him before the last vial is poured out. This is by all accounts the get-together talked about in Matthew and Luke.

Mt 24:40 Then should two be in the field; the one might be taken, and the other left.

Mt 24:41 Two ladies should be crushing at the plant; the one might be taken, and the other left.

Lu 17:35 Two ladies should be crushing together; the one might be taken, and the other left.

Lu 17:36 Two men should be in the field; the one might be taken, and the other left.

These here have no white robes so it is not those found in paradise who left the immense tribulation (Rev 7:14). They are wearing the articles of clothing of their acts of kindness and tolerance in the tribulation. Those said to be "strolling" exposed presumably either had no acts of kindness or quit doing acts of kindness.

Some will be embarrassed before whatever remains of them yet they will in any case go. This get-together could conceivably incorporate the regular relatives of Israel who did not take the imprint. Maybe right now, a few relatives of Israel on the planet still don't have the foggiest idea about that Jesus is Jehovah. Whatever the case, Isaiah talks about the arrival of common Israel in the most recent days

Isa 11:16 And there should be a roadway for the leftover of his kin, which might be left, from Assyria; such as it was to Israel in the day that he came up out of the place where there is Egypt.

2 Behold, God is my salvation; I will trust, and not be perplexed: for the LORD JEHOVAH is my quality and my tune; he additionally is turned into my salvation.

3 Therefore with happiness should ye coax water out of the wells of salvation.

4 And in that day might ye say, Praise the LORD, call upon his name, proclaim his doings among the general population, make say that his name is lifted up.

5 Sing unto the LORD; for he hath done magnificent things: this is known in all the earth.

6 Cry out and yell, thou occupant of Zion: for awesome is the Holy One of Israel amidst thee.

Isa 35: 8 And an interstate might be there, and a way, and it should be known as The method for blessedness; the unclean should not ignore it; but rather it should be for those: the wayfaring men, however tricks, might not fail in that.

9 No lion should be there, nor any eager mammoth might go up subsequently, it should not be found there; but rather the recovered should stroll there:

10 And the delivered of the LORD might return, and come to Zion with melodies and everlasting bliss upon their heads: they should get euphoria and happiness, and distress and murmuring should escape away.

16 And he accumulated them together into a spot brought in the Hebrew tongue Armageddon.

Joe 3:2 I will likewise accumulate all countries, and will bring them down into the valley of Jehoshaphat, and will beg them there for my kin and for my legacy Israel, whom they have scattered among the countries, and separated my territory.

Armageddon is Megiddo in northern Israel; Megiddo will be the organizing territory for the armed forces of the Beast however this is not where the armed forces will be devastated. At the point when Jesus demolishes these armed forces, the blood of the armed forces will stream in this valley of Jehoshaphat (Rev 14:20). The valley of Jehoshaphat will be an incredible fracture valley that keeps running for around 185 miles on the east side of Israel. A lot of it was made by the seismic tremor that opened this valley for the faithful in Jerusalem to escape to the mountains for heavenly assurance.

The God of paradise will solicit the rulers from the earth and their armed forces to permit all relatives of regular Israel to come back to the area that He named for them. The countries will consent since they will fear judgment or will see a chance to slaughter every one of the Jews on earth at one area. Be that as it may, as Egypt did in old days, after they let the children of Israel go; they will solidify their hearts and follow them to kill them.

God will judge all the world's armed forces that come against Israel in this valley. They will get complete obliteration, as did the armed forces of Pharaoh who came against Israel. The real devastation of this armed force is portrayed in section 19 after John first tells about the deeds and demolition of "Puzzle Babylon" in part 17 and "Babylon the Great" in part 18.

Notice the verse in Joel says they separated the place where there is God. This procedure of separating the place that is known for God guaranteed to the relatives of Israel is the center in the Middle-East peace handle even today.

17 And the seventh blessed messenger emptied out his vial into the air; and there came an incredible voice out of the sanctuary of paradise, from the throne, saying, It is finished.

18 And there were voices, and thunders, and lightnings; and there was an extraordinary tremor, for example, was not since men were upon the earth, so strong a seismic tremor, thus incredible.

19 And the considerable city was separated into three sections, and the urban communities of the countries fell: and incredible Babylon came in recognition before God, to give unto her the measure of the wine of the wildness of his rage.

20 And each island fled away, and the mountains were not found.

21 And there fell upon men an extraordinary hail out of paradise, each stone about the heaviness of an ability: and men reviled God on account of the disease of the hail; for the sickness thereof was surpassing incredible.

At the point when the seventh heavenly attendant pours out his vial in the air the best seismic tremor that ever was or that ever will happen on earth will happen. Every one of the urban areas of the world will fall. All high mountain reaches will break up and all islands will be moved or disappear. Jerusalem will be isolated into three sections around then. The heap of the Lord will be raised as the most astounding point in the zone or conceivably the world.

This aggregate changing of the world's outside layer will permit satisfaction of the predictions that talk about the desert area being watered and being rich amid the millennial rule. Most forsakes are created by high mountain ranges. At the point when the mountain reaches are broken up the greater part of the world will get to be rich. This change of the hull will kill flaw lines. There will be no significant tremors amid the thousand years. There will likewise be more delicate wind designs without the mountain ranges, which means less extreme tempests. The earth will turn into a heaven.

Isa 2:2 And it should happen in the most recent days, that the pile of the LORD'S house might be built up in the highest point of the mountains, and might be commended over the slopes; and all countries might stream unto it.

The heaviness of the hailstones is around an ability. An ability was 3000 shekels - these hailstones weigh around 100 pounds each. The hailstones will pour down everywhere throughout the earth amid this last torment before the second happening to Jesus.

This change on earth comes to fruition by a stone made without hands hitting the earth at Babylon. Daniel talks about this stone. These sections in Daniel have a double satisfaction. They discuss the Rock (Jesus) obliterating the works of the Devil they likewise talk about the kingdom of the Beast (Babylon) being pulverized by a stone. More will be said in regards to the devastation of the Beast kingdom in part 18. (Koerig, 2016).

Dan 2:34 Thou sawest till that a stone was removed without hands, which destroyed the picture upon his feet that were of iron and dirt, and brake them to pieces.

Dan 2:45 Forasmuch as thou sawest that the stone was removed of the mountain without hands, and that it brake in pieces the iron, the metal, the dirt, the silver, and the gold; the colossal God hath made known not lord what might happen from now on: and the fantasy is sure, and the translation thereof beyond any doubt.

1 And I heard an awesome voice out of the sanctuary saying to the seven blessed messengers, Go your ways, and pour out the vials of the rage of God upon the earth.

The colossal voice out of the sanctuary is the voice of Jesus serving as consecrated cleric in the sanctuary. He advises the seven blessed messengers to go in the request they were relegated to pour out the fury of God upon the earth.

2 And the first went, and poured out his vial upon the earth; and there fell a dangerous and terrible sore upon the men which had the sign of the monster, and upon them which worshiped his picture.

The main vial is poured out and shocking bruises happen upon all who have taken the sign of the Beast and on the individuals who have worshiped his picture. The injuries are ulcers or bubbles. They are similar to what Egypt experienced in old days when God passed judgment on her (Exodus).

The injuries will caution individuals who have not worshiped Satan to swing to approach the God of paradise. It will likewise be a motivating force for fiendishness individuals who need Satan to be God, to discover motivation to loathe the God of paradise and to look to battle against God.

3 And the second holy messenger poured out his vial upon the ocean; and it got to be as the blood of a dead man: and each living soul kicked the bucket in the ocean.

In the past trumpet judgments, there was a comparable judgment on 33% of the earth. Presently we see these things are occurring overall earth. These judgments can't happen until the blessed messenger pours out the vial, so these are partitioned judgments and are not only extensions of the trumpet judgments like a few authors have guessed. At the point when the second holy messenger pours out his vial the ocean will get to be similar to the blood of a dead man and everything in it will bite the dust. This is not dim red/chestnut sustenance shading; it is an extremely foul harmful substance that executes each living thing with a spirit in the ocean.

4 And the third heavenly attendant poured out his vial upon the waterways and wellsprings of waters; and they got to be blood.

5 And I heard the heavenly attendant of the waters say, Thou workmanship exemplary, O Lord, which craftsmanship, and wast, and shalt be, on the grounds that thou hast judged along these lines.

6 For they have shed the blood of holy people and prophets, and thou hast given them blood to drink; for they are commendable.

7 And I listened to one more of the holy place say, Even in this way, Lord God Almighty, genuine and exemplary are thy judgments.

At the point when the third heavenly attendant pours out his vial all the new water on the earth will likewise be swung to blood. God is giving them blood to drink since they have butchered His holy people and prophets. These judgments are reimbursement for those that were butchered for their confidence because of "Babylon the Great" (part 18). The blessed messenger that held these martyred souls under the sacred place affirms that God's judgments on these individuals on earth are meriting and just.

8 And the fourth blessed messenger poured out his vial upon the sun; and power was given unto him to sear men with flame.

9 And men were seared with awesome warmth, and reviled the name of God, which hath control over these diseases: and they atoned not to give him heavenliness.

This fourth judgment ought to make it clear that these judgments are worldwide as a result. I have perused a great deal of theory about what might bring the warmth and it ranges from atomic fighting to exhausted ozone in the climate. In any case, the content obviously says that the vial will be poured out on the sun and not on the earth. No country will get away from the warmth of the sun when it goes into a nova and burns all humankind with awesome warmth. This is the genuine future a worldwide temperature alteration that man ought to stress over.

With this, despite everything they won't concede that the God of paradise is Almighty. They will revile His name for these judgments and most likely call Him the Devil. Those that love the Beast on earth truly need Satan to be God, as do his fallen heavenly attendants. Accepting or wishing a falsehood is genuine does not make it genuine. There is one and only Creator God and He is the one that stays in paradise.

10 And the fifth heavenly attendant poured out his vial upon the seat of the brute; and his kingdom was loaded with obscurity; and they chewed their tongues for torment,

11 And reviled the God of paradise due to their torments and their wounds, and atoned not of their deeds

At the point when the fifth vial is poured out the kingdom of the Beast will be loaded with haziness. It will be a dimness that can be felt and they will bite their tongues for agony. There will be no light in the kingdom of the Beast since God will demonstrate the world that the Beast managing the earth has no light in himself. An illustration of this kind of obscurity can be found in Exodus when God judged Egypt.

In Egypt, the haziness kept going three days; we are not told to what extent this murkiness will last. The general population in the Beast's kingdom living with bruises, warmth, thirst and murkiness won't apologize of taking after Satan as God, or of their wrongdoings. They will rather revile the God of paradise.

With this infection of dimness God is graphically showing to the general population on the earth who have not yet worshiped the Beast or taken his imprint what hellfire will be similar to for time everlasting in the event that they do. They should by their own through and through freedom approach the God of paradise for benevolence and salvation and acknowledge Jesus to be spared from Satan. On the off chance that they did, God would have his holy messengers shield them from the sicknesses yet to come. Yet, most left on earth will keep on trusting the falsehood that Satan is God.

12 And the 6th heavenly attendant poured out his vial upon the colossal stream Euphrates; and the water thereof was gone away, that the method for the lords of the east may be arranged.

13 And I saw three unclean spirits like frogs leave the mouth of the winged serpent, and out of the mouth of the mammoth, and out of the mouth of the false prophet.

14 For they are the spirits of demons, working supernatural occurrences, which go forward unto the rulers of the earth and of the entire world, to accumulate them to the skirmish of that extraordinary day of God Almighty.

At the point when the 6th vial is poured out on the stream Euphrates every one of the armed forces of the world are assembled by the sinister trinity (Dragon, Beast, False Prophet) to the arranging ground of Megiddo in Israel (Armageddon).

The Euphrates River that isolates East from West will be gone away so that the armed forces of the east can stroll to Israel. At the point when every one of the armed forces of the world are accumulated to the valley of choice, they will be judged in the winepress of God. Amid the following couple of months, the accompanying sacred text will be totally satisfied.

Joe 3:9 Proclaim ye this among the Gentiles; Prepare war, wake up the strong men, let every one of the men of war draw close; let them come up:

10 Beat your plowshares into swords, and your pruninghooks into lances: let the powerless say, I am solid.

11 Assemble yourselves, and come, all ye pagan, and accumulate yourselves together indirect: thither cause thy relentless ones to descend, O LORD.

12 Let the barbarian be wakened, and come up to the valley of Jehoshaphat: for there will I sit to judge all the pagan circuitous.

13 Put ye in the sickle, for the harvest is ready: come, get you down; for the press is full, the fats flood; for their insidiousness is awesome.

14 Multitudes, hoards in the valley of choice: for the day of the LORD is close in the valley of choice.

15 The sun and the moon might be obscured, and the stars should pull back their sparkling.

16 The LORD likewise might thunder out of Zion, and utter his voice from Jerusalem; and the sky and the earth should shake: however the LORD will be the trust of his kin, and the quality of the offspring of Israel.

17 So might ye realize that I am the LORD your God staying in Zion, my sacred mountain: then should Jerusalem be blessed, and there might no outsiders go through her any more.

Otherworldly holy messengers will utilize lying signs and ponders to bamboozle and to assemble every one of the individuals who wish to battle against the God of paradise. They will harvest the results of such a stupid and useless endeavor to war against the real creator..

15 Behold, I come as a criminal. Favored is he that watcheth, and keepeth his articles of clothing, or he walk exposed, and they see his disgrace

This is an incidental entry between the 6th and seventh vial that says that Jesus will come as a cheat. Some think it is alluding back to the season of the pre-tribulation euphoria yet I don't. Prior to the last fight happens keeping in mind the Beast is social occasion his powers, God will send his holy messengers to accumulate each one of the individuals who are searching for Him before the last vial is poured out. This is by all accounts the social affair talked about in Matthew and Luke.

Mt 24:40 Then might two be in the field; the one should be taken, and the other left.

Mt 24:41 Two ladies might be granulating at the plant; the one should be taken, and the other left.

Lu 17:35 Two ladies might be granulating together; the one should be taken, and the other left.

Lu 17:36 Two men might be in the field; the one should be taken, and the other left.

These here have no white robes so it is not those found in paradise who left the considerable tribulation (Rev 7:14). They are wearing the articles of clothing of their acts of kindness and tolerance in the tribulation. Those said to be "strolling" exposed likely either had no acts of kindness or quit doing benevolent acts. Some will be embarrassed before whatever remains of them yet they will in any case go. This social affair could conceivably incorporate the regular relatives of Israel who did not take the imprint. Maybe as of right now, a few relatives of Israel on the planet still don't have the foggiest idea about that Jesus is Jehovah. Whatever the case, Isaiah talks about the arrival of characteristic Israel in the most recent days in the accompanying entry:

Isa 11:16 And there might be a thruway for the remainder of his kin, which should be left, from Assyria; such as it was to Israel in the day that he came up out of the place where there is Egypt.

2 Behold, God is my salvation; I will trust, and not be perplexed: for the LORD JEHOVAH is my quality and my tune; he additionally is turned into my salvation.

3 Therefore with satisfaction might ye coax water out of the wells of salvation.

4 And in that day should ye say, Praise the LORD, call upon his name, pronounce his doings among the general population, make say that his name is commended.

5 Sing unto the LORD; for he hath done great things: this is known in all the earth.

6 Cry out and yell, thou tenant of Zion: for extraordinary is the Holy One of Israel amidst thee.

Isa 35: 8 And a roadway might be there, and a way, and it should be known as The method for heavenliness; the unclean might not disregard it; but rather it might be for those: the wayfaring men, however tricks, might not fail in that.

9 No lion should be there, nor any insatiable mammoth might go up consequently, it might not be found there; but rather the reclaimed might stroll there:

10 And the emancipated of the LORD should return, and come to Zion with melodies and everlasting happiness upon their heads: they might acquire delight and energy, and distress and moaning shall flee away.

16 And he assembled them together into a spot brought in the Hebrew tongue Armageddon.

Joe 3:2 I will likewise assemble all countries, and will bring them down into the valley of Jehoshaphat, and will beg them there for my kin and for my legacy Israel, whom they have scattered among the countries, and separated my property.

Armageddon is Megiddo in northern Israel; Megiddo will be the arranging region for the armed forces of the Beast however this is not where the armed forces will be wrecked. At the point when Jesus pulverizes these armed forces, the blood of the armed forces will stream in this valley of Jehoshaphat (Rev 14:20). The valley of Jehoshaphat will be an incredible fracture valley that keeps running for around 185 miles on the east side of Israel. Quite a bit of it was made by the seismic tremor that opened this valley for the respectful in Jerusalem to escape to the mountains for celestial insurance.

The God of paradise will solicit the lords from the earth and their armed forces to permit all relatives of characteristic Israel to come back to the area that He named for them. The countries will go along in light of the fact that they will fear judgment or will see a chance to slaughter every one of the Jews on earth at one area. Nonetheless, as Egypt did in old days, after they let the children of Israel go; they will solidify their hearts and follow them to kill them.

God will judge all the world's armed forces that come against Israel in this valley. They will get all out annihilation, as did the armed forces of Pharaoh who came against Israel. The real devastation of this armed force is depicted in section 19 after John first tells about the deeds and decimation of "Puzzle Babylon" in part 17 and "Babylon the Great" in part 18.

Notice the verse in Joel says they separated the place that is known for God. This procedure of separating the place where there is God guaranteed to the relatives of Israel is the center in the Middle-East peace handle even today.

17 And the seventh blessed messenger emptied out his vial into the air; and there came an awesome voice out of the sanctuary of paradise, from the throne, saying, It is finished.

18 And there were voices, and thunders, and lightnings; and there was an awesome quake, for example, was not since men were upon the earth, so compelling a tremor, thus extraordinary.

19 And the colossal city was isolated into three sections, and the urban areas of the countries fell: and incredible Babylon came in recognition before God, to give unto her the measure of the wine of the savagery of his fury.

20 And each island fled away, and the mountains were not found.

21 And there fell upon men an awesome hail out of paradise, each stone about the heaviness of an ability: and men cursed God in light of the disease of the hail; for the plague thereof was exceeding great.

At the point when the seventh blessed messenger pours out his vial in the climate the best quake that ever was or that ever will happen on earth will happen. Every one of the urban areas of the world will fall. All high mountain extents will disintegrate and all islands will be moved or disappear. Jerusalem will be separated into three sections around then. The heap of the Lord will be raised as the most elevated point in the zone or perhaps the world.

This aggregate changing of the world's hull will permit satisfaction of the predictions that talk about the desert area being watered and being lavish amid the millennial rule. Most forsakes are brought on by high mountain ranges. At the point when the mountain reaches are disintegrated the vast majority of the world will get to be fruitful. This change of the hull will wipe out deficiency lines. There will be no significant seismic tremors amid the thousand years. There will likewise be more tender wind designs without the mountain ranges, which means less extreme tempests. The earth will turn into a heaven.

Isa 2:2 And it might happen in the most recent days, that the pile of the LORD'S house should be built up in the highest point of the mountains, and should be magnified over the slopes; and all countries might stream unto it.

The heaviness of the hailstones is around an ability. An ability was 3000 shekels - these hailstones weigh around 100 pounds each. The hailstones will pour down everywhere throughout the earth amid this last torment before the second happening to Jesus. This change on earth comes to fruition by a stone made without hands hitting the earth at Babylon. Daniel talks about this stone. These entries in Daniel have a double satisfaction. They talk about the Rock (Jesus) pulverizing the works of the Devil they likewise discuss the kingdom of the Beast (Babylon) being demolished by a stone. More will be said in regards to the decimation of the Beast kingdom in section 18.

Dan 2:34 Thou sawest till that a stone was removed without hands, which destroyed the picture upon his feet that were of iron and dirt, and brake them to pieces.

Dan 2:45 Forasmuch as thou sawest that the stone was removed of the mountain without hands, and that it brake in pieces the iron, the metal, the dirt, the silver, and the gold; the considerable God hath made known not ruler what should happen from this point forward: and the fantasy is sure, and the understanding thereof beyond any doubt.

CHAPTER 17

Mystery Babylon Clarified

In the past vial judgments, the Beast world framework is destroyed. In sections 17 and 18, John is taken to see a great deal more insight about the life, deeds and end destiny of the religious and political frameworks that had control over the world since the disobedience to God got to be formal at Babylon in the times of Nimrod. These two sections in Revelation are presumably the most hard to comprehend in the book of Revelation. A wide comprehension of prophetic sacred text is crucial to legitimately recognize what John is finding in these sections. The trouble is for the most part in deciding the characters of "Secret Babylon" of section 17 and "Babylon the Great" of part 18 and learning the contrasts between the two personalities. The timing of the occasions identified with them amid the tribulation likewise raises some debate.

1 And there came one of the seven heavenly attendants which had the seven vials, and chatted with me, saying unto me, Come here; I will shew unto thee the judgment of the colossal prostitute that sitteth upon numerous waters:

One of the seven holy messengers that has the vial or vials advises John to come and he will demonstrate to him the judgment of the colossal prostitute that sits upon numerous waters. The expression "sitting upon numerous waters" implies the prostitute sits over numerous countries or people groups of the earth. This is exceptionally characterized for us in verse 15.

2 With whom the lords of the earth have conferred sex, and the tenants of the earth have been made tanked with the wine of her sex.

The lords of the earth confer sex with this prostitute. In this manner, the prostitute herself is not liable to be one of the countries under the rulers. The individuals who occupy the earth get to be inebriated with the infidelity that this whore confers since they want to drink what she offers.

3 So he diverted me in the soul into the wild: and I saw a lady sit upon a red hued brute, brimming with names of irreverence, having seven heads and ten horns.

John was diverted in the soul into the wild where he saw the things depicted. Since he was conveyed into the wild the lady can't be whore Israel (as some think). The word for wild in Hebrew as a rule means an extensive field or tract of area and the Greek word implies practically the same thing. I accept here "wild" basically intends to be in conveyed to a vast area range some place other than in the place where there is Israel. The word wild could likewise mean a high mountain field and this could have been the place John was taken. I trust John was taken to see the restoration of the Holy Roman Empire (one of the names of obscenity).

John sees a lady in the wild that sits upon a red hued brute. This lady on the mammoth is clearly the prostitute that the blessed messenger said he was conveying John to see. The lady rides on a red shaded mammoth that has names of irreverence and the brute she rides has seven heads and ten horns. We have as of now found in section twelve that the Dragon (who is Satan) fits this depiction. In this manner, we can be sure that the lady on the red shaded brute is being conveyed along by Satan.

There have been seven world governments that have controlled the known humanized world. They were all under the managerial control of Satan. At the point when Jesus was appeared and offered every one of the kingdoms of the world by Satan and was informed that he had the power or energy to offer them to Him, Jesus did not repudiate his case (Mat 4:8). The seven world governments are the seven leaders of the brute yet we should likewise see that the seven heads additionally speak to seven slopes where the end time Beast home office is physically found. The ten horns speak to the pioneers who give their energy to the Beast in the last world kingdom that ascents just before Jesus comes to set up His kingdom on earth. These same ten horns are additionally talked about in Daniel Chapter 7. We are told the mistress lady rides these seven headed monsters, which means she has some control over the bearing of each of the seven world governments. There is one and only element that fits that depiction and that substance is "world religion". Man opposed the God of paradise when he began worshiping made creatures as opposed to the maker (Satan is the head of made creatures). This agnosticism turned into a formal puzzle religion at the tower of Babel under the principle of Nimrod. The vast majority of humankind stays affected by Babylonian agnostic practices today.

4 And the lady was showed in purple and red shading, and decked with gold and valuable stones and pearls, having a brilliant glass in her handful of cursed things and lack of sanitization of her sex:

5 And upon her temple was a name composed, MYSTERY, BABYLON THE GREAT, THE MOTHER OF HARLOTS AND ABOMINATIONS OF THE EARTH.

The lady has the name "Puzzle Babylon". Puzzle Babylon is not the same as the physical spot of Babylon in Iraq. Secret Babylon is the mother of whores and evil entities of the earth. She is a seen as a prostitute since she has an association with somebody other than God. She is the mother of all horrifying presences since she is playing the mistress with Satan who is the prime wellspring of all malevolence on the earth. The garments the lady wears and the riches she shows mirrors that she imagines that she is a ruler rather than a prostitute. The ministers of formal religions frequently wear comparative hues today. Large portions of them additionally utilize brilliant glasses for the act of their religious ceremonies. In her grasp is a container that is brimming with cursed things that originates from her sex with Satan.

Purple was the shade of Roman colonialism and red is the fundamental shading embraced by Roman Catholicism. The Vatican has been the boss element that represents religion on the earth and that is not only a fortuitous event. The Vatican is the main religious state and it has international safe havens in many countries of the world furthermore has a non-voting seat at the UN as an expert to this world body. In the final days, she will be the leader of the whore world religion when she and numerous different religions converge into a one-world religion with its base camp being at the Vatican in Rome.

6 And I saw the lady tipsy with the blood of the holy people, and with the blood of the saints of Jesus: and when I saw her, I pondered with awesome reverence.

The lady is tipsy with the blood of the holy people and with the saints of Jesus. The holy people are Old Testament individuals who were executed by the religious prostitute. They incorporate every one of the prophets and Old Testament adherents who were abused and executed by the religions framework (Judaism) that had sex with Babylonian devilish divine beings.

Most individuals from the initiative of Israel's religious framework were controlled by "their dad the Devil" as per Jesus (Joh 8:44). This demonstrates the mistress was in presence and was settled in Judaism even around then. These evil pioneers of Israel murdered the planters of the vineyard (the prophets) and even the Son of the proprietor of the vineyard (Jesus) with the goal that God would get nothing out of His field (Luk 20:13).

The saints of Jesus are the adherents of Jesus who kicked the bucket for their confidence in Him. Suffering of the genuine devotees of Jesus will keep on occurring under the hand of the prostitute until the day the considerable prostitute is eaten up by the Beast she rides. After Judaism, the greater part of suffering was by the hands of evil pioneers that rose to the highest point of Christian and later Islamic religion.

Later on, suffering will be by the hands of the World Church. At last, the prostitute herself will be eaten up and smoldered with flame by the Babylonian agnostic Beast that she undermined herself with.

Why did John wonder about her? John wondered in light of the fact that until the heavenly attendant discloses it to him, the lady and the brute she rides is a shrouded secret. Perhaps John likewise wondered on the grounds that God's arrangement that permits Satan to play God through the religions of the world is basically shocking. John more likely than not understood that through death, these saints really won triumph over the Devil and acquired everlasting life and superbness. In this way, the underhandedly motivated yearning of the whore to murder the offspring of the guarantee really conveyed the choose kids to unceasing salvation and prizes. The arrangement of God is a riddle essentially outside human ability to grasp.

7 And the blessed messenger said unto me, Wherefore didst thou wonder? I will tell thee the riddle of the lady, and of the mammoth that carrieth her, which hath the seven heads and ten horns.

Try not to take my statement for it - the heavenly attendant himself will plainly disclose to John and to us the puzzle of the lady, and the otherworldly Beast that she rides.

8 The monster that thou sawest was, and is not; and might rise out of the no-limit pit, and go into condemnation: and they that harp on the earth should wonder, whose names were not composed in the book of life from the establishment of the world, when they view the brute that was, and is not, but then is.

9 And here is the brain which hath knowledge. The seven heads are seven mountains, on which the lady sitteth.

10 And there are seven lords: five are fallen, and one is, and the other is not yet come; and when he cometh, he should proceed with a short space.

11 And the mammoth that was, and is not, even he is the eighth, and is of the seven, and goeth into condemnation.

Keep in mind in this vision the lady is not the monster that John saw the lady was sitting (riding) on the brute. The blessed messenger clarifies that this Beast is an element that rises out of the no-limit pit and that in the end goes to endless condemnation.

Since the blessed messenger clarified who the Beast is, he lets us know about the riddle of the "lady who rides the Beast". The blessed messenger tells John that the lady that rides the Beast will sit on seven (mountains, mounts or slopes). Rome sits on seven slopes. The whore lady that turns into the World Church will run from the Vatican.

I have seen photographs indicating Pope John Paul II entering a mosque and kissing the Koran. I have perused that he said eastern religions likewise give ways to God. One of Pope John Paul's dearest companions was the Dali Lama who is the world pioneer of eastern and "new age" agnosticism. This contact with unbelievers was continuous at the exceptionally same time that the Vatican assaulted crucial genuine Christianity in South America and somewhere else. This is average of the reasoning in a great part of the initiative of the Roman Catholic Church even at this point. There likewise is a significant parallel to the icon love of statues by "a few Catholics" and the symbol adore by Buddhists and Hindus.

It is not hard to perceive how all world religion will bind together on a focal topic once the impacts of the genuine Christians are evacuated in the Rapture. (There are genuine

Christians in the Roman Catholic Church however in somehow they will leave this Harlot.)

All religion is essentially the same at its center. Religions are approaches for man to develop to wind up like God, to assuage God and win brownie focuses by one's own particular acts of kindness, or to control God or a few "higher force power" into doing one's own particular will. There is dependably an inward hover of first class that set themselves up as being on a higher otherworldly plane and more like God or closer to God than the normal participation. The individuals who trust they are on this higher plane then make standards and customs to subjugate the masses to uphold what they accept are God's prerequisites for man.

Religion other than "genuine Christianity" (which truly is not a religion but rather is being naturally introduced to another creation through confidence and trust in God), is dependably a salvation by man's own works religious philosophy and dependably denies that salvation can be gained from confiding in the work of Jesus alone.

Jesus had minimal great to say in regards to the religious initiative over Israel and He will have minimal great to say in regards to the religious authority over Gentile religions in these last days. This incorporates the vast majority of the authority that relates to Christianity.

The sacred writings say there is yet one approach to God through His Son Jesus Christ and that He paid the cost for all humanity at the cross. To be spared one needs to trust that God cherished humanity enough to have arranged an arrangement of salvation and that He really has the ability to do it. This arrangement for recovering man is the thing that the Bible is about.

The colossal contrast between the lady of Christ and the prostitute is that the spouse knows she is made immaculate by the blood of Jesus yet the prostitute trusts she should get to be satisfactory to God by her own self exertion. She is perpetually attempting to discover approaches to assuage and please God. Since she rejects the genuine way of God, she has sex with each soiled soul in a self push to wind up like the God she trusts exists yet the God she supposes exists is really her dad the Devil. The individuals who say they adore God and who don't love or acknowledge His Son are hoodwinked or liars since Jesus is the express picture of God.

Heb 1:3 Who being the shine of his wonderfulness, and the express picture of his individual, and maintaining all things by the expression of his energy, when he had without anyone else's input cleansed our wrongdoings, sat down on the right hand of the Majesty on high;

Verse 11 of this entry lets us know the end time Beast that the lady rides will go into absolute decimation. The decimation of the Beast kingdom is portrayed in the following section.

12 And the ten horns which thou sawest are ten lords, which have gotten no kingdom so far; however get power as rulers one hour with the mammoth.

The ten horns are the ten world pioneers that will get a kingdom with the Beast. Whether they will be pioneers of ten countries on the earth, or 10 zones in the zone of the Old Roman Empire, or ten zones of the world is interested in theory. Both ten provincial zones in the region of the old Roman Empire and ten world local zones have been proposed by worldwide research organizations like the "Club of Rome". Both zone situations may be valid.

It may begin with ten zones in the range of the old Roman Empire and afterward the resuscitated Roman Empire turns into the head of ten world provincial zones. We are getting really near having ten local monetary unions around the world as of now. Regardless, the ten pioneers give their energy to the Beast. We are likewise informed that three of the world pioneers will be wiped out after the Beast/ Antichrist comes to control.

13 These have one personality and might give their energy and quality unto the monster.

The ten rulers will think alike. All their energy and quality will be utilized to do the wishes of the Beast Antichrist. It is really sheltered to accept by this announcement that these ten pioneers will be devilishly had.

14 These should make war with the Lamb, and the Lamb might overcome them: for he is Lord of rulers, and King of rulers: and they that are with him are called, and picked, and unwavering.

The Beast and the ten world pioneers will make war against Jesus. What complete trickiness needs to place for the rulers and individuals of the countries to believe that they can war against the same individual who made them!

15 And he saith unto me, The waters which thou sawest, where the prostitute sitteth, are people groups, and hoards, and countries, and tongues.

The blessed messenger clarifies what I said beforehand, that the waters where the prostitute sits really speaks to the general population she has impacted that originated from numerous countries and dialects. Just religion fills that part.

16 And the ten horns which thou sawest upon the mammoth, these might detest the prostitute, and should make her barren and bare, and should eat her tissue, and blaze her with flame.

At the point when the Satanic man shows up, the world will trust he is God and his administration won't endure any love other than worshiping him. They will assert that the Beast is God and pronounce the" Kingdom of God" is currently on earth. They will take every one of the belonging and all power far from every world religious associations that won't adore him. Numerous in the Harlot religious framework won't acknowledge the Beast as being "All-powerful God" or be swindled into trusting that the Beast Kingdom is the "Kingdom of God" and numerous will see the mistakes of their ways. At last, it will cost the majority of the individuals who won't revere the Beast their physical lives. In any case, by picking up the conviction that Jesus is the genuine Savior their souls will be spared. The ten world political pioneers will utilize their energy to wreck all that love any element other than the Beast.

Verse 16 portrays how and why the lady who rides the mammoth will be judged. She will be eaten by the Beast she rides and her structures will be blazed. She will have the same destiny as Jezebel in the Old Testament whose bones were eaten by canines.

17 For God hath put in their souls to satisfy his will, and to concur, and give their kingdom unto the brute, until the expressions of God might be satisfied.

God made Pharaoh and solidified his heart to realize the judgment of Egypt. These ten rulers' hearts are solidified by God to war against Jesus and to give their kingdoms to the Beast until this prediction is satisfied.

18 And the lady which thou sawest is that extraordinary city, which reigneth over the rulers of the earth.

This is a key entry that lets us know the character of the "lady that rides the brute". "Puzzle Babylon" is the considerable city that is administering over the earth. Rome was administering over the earth in the season of John and possesses all the necessary qualities yet Mystery Babylon couldn't be the city of Rome or the Roman Empire. "The lady rides the mammoth", so the lady couldn't in the meantime "be the monster". The lady couldn't be the congregation at Rome at the season of John on the grounds that the congregation was not administering over the earth around then. The religious framework ruling over the earth in the time John composed this was Babylonian agnosticism with Caesar revere.

The city in this entry is a city that rules over the earth. At the season of John, that city was Rome. The city might likewise be a city that rules over the earth toward the end time judgment of the "lady". That additionally is liable to be satisfied by Rome. Thus, the lady in this prescience must be recognized as a world religion that has additionally been penetrated by Babylonian agnosticism and that is situated at Rome.

With the goal that we can make certain of the genuine character of the lady we will analyze this somewhat closer. We are told the lady sits on a seven hilled city (Rome) and is tipsy with the blood of the martyred holy people and from that we can discover that "Riddle Babylon" is a religious framework that claims to love God yet has joined Babylonian religious practices (that is the reason she is portrayed as a whore).

She must be at a physical area that not just had Babylonian hones in the season of John yet the religious framework "must saint every one of the holy people" (verse 6). The Roman Empire did slaughter holy people yet all the blood of the holy people and saints can't be put on account of the political and religious forces of the old Roman Empire. The mistress was clearly conceived before Rome (in Babylon) and she likewise did not pass on in Rome in 312 AD when the Church joined with the political arrangement of the Roman Empire. After the Jewish and afterward the Roman Empire oppressions finished, just the religion that related to Christianity could be rebuked for genuine Christians being martyred (e.g. the examinations). That stayed valid until Islam assumed control over the authority part of the butcher of genuine Christians.

There is one and only area and religious element on earth that understands this prediction and its more prominent satisfaction in the most recent days. The whore lady of the most recent days must be all composed religion that at the satisfaction of this prescience will be head quartered in Rome.

It ought to be evident that I am not saying the present Roman Catholic Church can be named as the division that satisfies the end time part of the lady. All Babylonian affected world religion makes up this lady on the Beast. The world religion that will get to be head quartered at the Vatican might tackle an altogether distinctive name from Roman Catholicism in the most recent days. Be that as it may, there is little uncertainty in my brain that this lady who rides the Antichrist Beast will be an agnostic Babylonian penetrated mistress head quartered at the area that is presently called the Vatican in Rome.

On the off chance that more illumination of the lady is still vital let me further clarify. The Babylonian mistress was conceived in the season of Nimrod in Babylon and in the end defiled Judaism. The agnostic Babylonian religious practices really moved from Babylon to Pergamos. (where Satan's throne is - Rev 2:13). After the congregation converged with the state in 312 AD, the whore took living arrangement in the top positions of the Christian church. As of right now, the Babylon cleric framework had effectively joined with the Roman framework. By around 600 AD, the Christian institutional church got to be what we know today as the Roman Catholic Church.

Amid this time of Christianity blended with agnostic practices the probes occurred and killed numerous more genuine Christians than did any earlier mistreatment of God's kin. After the investigations, the lady can be seen inside of the Protestant holy places who had their own oppressions and witch-chases in which numerous joined in their own holocausts against God's kin. Today the lady's traits are found in Islam as the essential killer of God's kin.

At last time, the lady will ride a one world religious framework. The lady entirely leaves Judaism, Catholicism, Protestantism or Islam on the grounds that the lady is truth be told all mistress religion of all periods. In any case, the lady rides the Beast as the religion that has the most impact on the legislative domain that happens to control the earth.

Today the Vatican speaks to the religion that has the most impact on the earth however Protestantism likewise has world impact and Islam is quickly going to the bleeding edge. All prostitute religion will have influence and finish the satisfaction of the prediction about the lady who rides the mammoth.

At the point when the euphoria of the genuine Church of Jesus Christ happens, genuine Christians from a wide range of sections including reliable Catholics will be brought to be with Jesus. The backslider Christians deserted in all groups will unite with different religious to frame a pluralist world religion drove at the central station of the biggest Christian division.

I need to make one thing clear here: By saying the Vatican as the future base camp of the world prostitute, I am not Catholic bashing. There are numerous practices in the Catholic Church that I accept are blasphemies however there are generally the same number of or more apostasies in most mainline Protestant chapels today. For a thousand years, there was one and only church government on earth and that was the Catholic Church. The Catholic Church is still the biggest Christian division on the planet by a wide margin. Subsequently, if there will be harlotry all through history since Babylon and the harlotry is among the individuals who case to know the God of creation, it must be among the main sorted out Christian Church that exists amid this period.

The prostitute lady was among this composed body called Catholics, however so were genuine Christians as wheat among the tares. Today Islam has assumed control over the part of the boss whore religion that oppresses the holy people. Islam is established on agnosticism and in our time has effectively martyred a huge number of Christians. The end time whore religious framework that John is seeing is going in Rome in the most recent days and it was established in Babylon, however all major sorted out world religions in the most recent days that reject genuine Christianity are a piece of the mistress. Indeed, even Islam at last will join with this world religion authority in Rome despite the fact that it might take wicked misleading or an incredible religious war first.

The congregation that relates to Christianity, similar to old Israel, has genuine devotees and frauds. That is the reason Paul said that not all Israel is genuine Israel, and that is the reason not all named Christians are genuine Christians. The new agreement guarantee to Israel and the Church is to devotees yet a substantial part of the Church such as Israel is in unbelief. According to God, she has submitted harlotry with the universe of agnosticism.

The story of two countries or two ladies. The battle between the lady from the substance (whore lady) and the lady from the guarantee (the individuals who accept and trust God) can be followed in the accompanying timetable (This is just an example to offer you some assistance with understanding and it is not intended to be all convincing - the lady of the guarantee is in striking print):

- The Babylonian defiance to God by Nimrod - the secret religion and the Babylonian organization is established at Babylon.

- Abraham is taken out to be the father of all who live by confidence in the genuine Creator. He trusts God's guarantee.

- Ishmael is conceived of the tissue from Abraham's slave young lady - Ishmael blends with the agnostics of Babylon.

- Isaac is conceived of the guarantee and takes after the God of his dad (Abraham).

- Esau is the primary child of Isaac yet Esau puts no quality on the guarantee of his claim and offers it to Jacob for a feast.

- Jacob gets to be Israel and turns into a country that is to keep the prophets and guarantee of God for the advantage of the considerable number of individuals of the guarantee.

- Israel's child Joseph talks about the vision God gave him for the general population of guarantee.

- Joseph is sold into servitude to Egypt by desirous stepbrothers.

- Joseph gets to be PM of Egypt with the assistance of God and recoveries the relatives of Israel from physical starvation.

- The Egyptian world government overlooks Joseph, turns out to be completely adulterated by Babylonian agnostic practices, and oppresses and abuses the relatives of Israel.

- God raises up Moses to convey Israel from Egypt and the Law is given to Israel to lead them to the guaranteed area and Savior.

- Judaism gets to be debased by harlotry with agnostic divine beings.

- The world domain of Babylon subjugates Israel.

- The Mystical Brotherhood of the Babylonian request moves its headship to Pergamos after the fall of Babylon.

- Some of the Jews come back to Israel and revamp God's sanctuary.

- The Babylonian organization is moved to Rome by the last will of Attalus lord of Pergamos.

- Julius Caesar gets to be incomparable Pontiff (esteemed minister) of the Babylonian Order in BC 63.

- John the Baptist is destined to restore Israel so they are prepared to get their guarantee.

- Jesus "is the guarantee" and comes to spare all humanity.

- The Babylonian affected Jewish brotherhood and the Roman world framework execute Jesus. The ministers dismisses the guarantee in return for infidelity with Rome.

- Jesus becomes alive once again and the guarantee is given to all who by confidence trust in this risen Savior.

- There is a withdrawal of Pontiffs from Julius Caesar to the year when the Babylonian Order turns into the leader of the Roman Church in 378 AD (a long story).

- The wheat develops in the same field (the institutional church) as the prostitute tares and grows up with them.

- Islam is conceived and it instructs the children of Ishmael and Esau to venerate a solitary agnostic God that mistreats those conceived of the guarantee.

- The tares in the institutional church stifle to death a large portion of the general population of the guarantee in the examinations.

- The Protestant transformation is conceived by the individuals who show that salvation originates from confiding in the guarantee of Jesus alone.

- Most of Protestantism plays the prostitute with theory, brain science, new age agnosticism, humanism, practicality and realism.

- The general population of the guarantee are currently

the wheat among the tares in the Catholic and Protestant Churches.

- The printed Bible gets to be accessible to the general population. Littler fields develop so much wheat the tares discover little space to root.

- Higher basic speculation rationalities war against the individuals who trust the guarantee in God's oath.

- The general population of the guarantee are evacuated in the delight and all the wheat not entrapped with the tares (prostitute) is expelled from the earth.

- All religions of the world unite after an awesome world religious war to frame a world religion drove by the Vatican at Rome. This lady will ride the Beast into her end time part.

- The Beast eats up the lady that rode on his back (world religious organizations and pioneers). The tares are smoldered.

- Satan through the lying marvels of His Beast and False Prophet sets himself up as God, proclaims the Kingdom of God has come, and he moves the political and religious state house of the world to Babylon where he fabricates a city of gold for himself.

- The wheat bound with agnosticism is sifted amid the immense tribulation the Beast brings on the earth.

- All individuals of the guarantee that were in infidelity come back to her spouse - the genuine God of paradise - and are accumulated into His animal dwelling place.

- God retaliates for every one of the general population of guarantee by setting so as to crush the Beast and up the genuine kingdom of God on the earth ruled by Jesus.

The lady who rides the Beast has really existed subsequent to the times of Babylon yet she will assume her significant part in the most recent days. She at last will be eaten by the Beast she rides since he will claim to be God and won't endure the love of anybody or anything other that himself. Numerous who were in harlotry will come to comprehend reality in those days through the instructing and the judgments that happen in this season of trial for the entire world.

These who leave Babylon won't love the Beast and these alongside a remainder in Israel will come back to the genuine God of paradise yet it will cost a hefty portion of them their mortal lives. In those days all who look to spare their lives by worshiping the Beast will lose their spirit and the individuals who lose their life for Jesus' purpose will increase interminable life.

Mat 16:25 For whosoever will spare his life might lose it: and whosoever will lose his life for my purpose should discover it.

For a more point by point study on the history and eventual fate of the lady who rides the Beast I exceedingly prescribe the book "A Woman Rides the Beast" by Dave Hunt, Harvest House, 1994.

The mistress lady was among this sorted out body called Catholics, yet so were genuine Christians as wheat among the tares. Today Islam has assumed control over the part of the boss prostitute religion that aggrieves the holy people. Islam is established on agnosticism and in our time has effectively martyred a large number of Christians. The end time whore religious framework that John is seeing is going in Rome in the most recent days and it was established in Babylon, however all major sorted out world religions in the most recent days that reject genuine Christianity are a piece of the prostitute. Indeed, even Islam at last will join with this world religion administration in Rome despite the fact that it might take wicked misdirection's or an awesome religious war first.

The congregation that relates to Christianity, similar to antiquated Israel, has genuine devotees and imposters. That is the reason Paul said that not all Israel is genuine Israel, and that is the reason not all named Christians are genuine Christians. The new contract guarantee to Israel and the Church is to adherents however an expansive part of the Church such as Israel is in unbelief. According to God, she has submitted harlotry with the universe of agnosticism.

The story of two countries or two ladies. The battle between the lady from the substance (whore lady) and the lady from the guarantee (the individuals who accept and trust God) can be followed in the accompanying timetable (This is just a specimen to offer you some assistance with understanding and it is not intended to be all convincing - the lady of the guarantee is in intense print):

- The Babylonian defiance to God by Nimrod - the secret religion and the Babylonian organization is established at Babylon.

- Abraham is taken out to be the father of all who live by confidence in the genuine Creator. He trusts God's guarantee.

- Ishmael is conceived of the tissue from Abraham's slave young lady - Ishmael blends with the agnostics of Babylon.

- Isaac is conceived of the guarantee and takes after the God of his dad (Abraham).

- Esau is the primary child of Isaac yet Esau puts no quality on the guarantee of his claim and offers it to Jacob for a feast.

- Jacob gets to be Israel and turns into a country that is to keep the prophets and guarantee of God for the advantage of the considerable number

- Israel's child Joseph talks about the vision God gave him for the general population of guarantee.

- Joseph is sold into subjection to Egypt by envious relatives.

- Joseph gets to be PM of Egypt with the assistance of God and recoveries the relatives of Israel from physical starvation.

- The Egyptian world government overlooks Joseph, turns out to be completely defiled by Babylonian agnostic practices, and subjugates and oppress the relatives of Israel.

- God raises up Moses to convey Israel from Egypt and the Law is given to Israel to lead them to the guaranteed area and Savior.

- Judaism gets to be debased by harlotry with agnostic divine beings.

- The world domain of Babylon oppresses Israel.

- The Mystical Brotherhood of the Babylonian request moves its headship to Pergamos after the fall of Babylon.

- Some of the Jews come back to Israel and remake God's sanctuary.

- The Babylonian brotherhood is moved to Rome by the last will of Attalus lord of Pergamos.

- Julius Caesar gets to be preeminent Pontiff (esteemed minister) of the Babylonian Order in BC 63.

- John the Baptist is destined to restore Israel so they are prepared to get their guarantee.

- Jesus "is the guarantee" and comes to spare all humankind.

- The Babylonian impacted Jewish brotherhood and the Roman world framework murder Jesus. The ministers dismisses the guarantee in return for infidelity with Rome.

- Jesus becomes alive once again and the guarantee is given to all who by confidence trust in this risen Savior.

- There is a withdrawal of Pontiffs from Julius Caesar to the year when the Babylonian Order turns into the leader of the Roman Church in 378 AD (a long story).

- The wheat develops in the same field (the institutional church) as the whore tares and grows up with them.

- Islam is conceived and it instructs the children of Ishmael and Esau to venerate a solitary agnostic God that oppress those conceived of the guarantee.

- The tares in the institutional church stifle to death large portions of the general population of the guarantee in the examinations.

- The Protestant reorganization is conceived by the individuals who show that salvation originates from confiding in the guarantee of Jesus alone.

- Most of Protestantism plays the whore with theory, brain science, new age agnosticism, humanism, realism and realism.

- The general population of the guarantee are currently the wheat among the tares in the Catholic and Protestant Churches.

- The printed Bible gets to be accessible to people in general. Littler fields develop so much wheat the tares discover little space to root.

- Higher basic deduction rationalities war against the individuals who trust the guarantee in God's assertion.

- The general population of the guarantee are uprooted in the delight and all the wheat not trapped with the tares (prostitute) is expelled from the earth.

- All religions of the world unite after an extraordinary world religious war to shape a world religion drove by the Vatican at Rome. This lady will ride the Beast into her end time part.

- The Beast eats up the lady that rode on his back (world religious foundations and pioneers). The tares are smoldered.

- Satan through the lying miracles of His Beast and False Prophet sets himself up as God, proclaims the Kingdom of God has come, and he moves the political and religious state house of the world to Babylon where he fabricates a city of gold for himself.

- The wheat bound with agnosticism is sifted amid the considerable tribulation the Beast brings on the earth.

- All individuals of the guarantee that were in infidelity come back to her spouse - the genuine God of paradise - and are accumulated into His horse shelter.

- God retaliates for every one of the general population of guarantee by setting so as to obliterate the Beast and up the genuine kingdom of God on the earth ruled by Jesus.

The lady who rides the Beast has really existed subsequent to the times of Babylon yet she will assume her real part in the most recent days. She at last will be eaten by the Beast she rides since he will claim to be God and won't endure the love of anybody or anything other that himself.

Numerous who were in harlotry will come to comprehend reality in those days through the instructing and the judgments that happen in this season of trial for the entire world. These who leave Babylon won't revere the Beast and these alongside a leftover in Israel will come back to the genuine God of paradise however it will cost a large portion of them their mortal lives. In those days all who look to spare their lives by worshiping the Beast will lose their spirit and the individuals who lose their life for Jesus' purpose will increase endless life.

Mat 16:25 For whosoever will save his life shall lose it: and whosoever will lose his life for my sake shall find it.

For a more detailed study on the history and future of the woman who rides the Beast I highly recommend the book "A Woman Rides the Beast" by Dave Hunt, Harvest House, 1994.

CHAPTER 18

Babylon The Great Clarified

The center of the past part was about the judgment of the prostitute religious framework that rode the Beast. The principle center of this part will be about the judgment of the Babylonian fake kingdom of God called "Babylon the Great". Babylon speaks to all world government and religious frameworks under Satan. They have been in composed resistance to God since their origination at the tower of Babel under Nimrod. This insubordination will peak with the end time world government and religion that will have its central command situated at Babylon, Iraq. The otherworldly being behind this resistance to God is the fake divine force of this world framework (2 Co 4:4). This section lets us know about the world kingdom Satan completely builds up when he is permitted downright control over the earth for 3 ½ years. The part likewise lets us know about the judgment upon this evil kingdom and religion from the genuine God in paradise.

Babylon supplemental material:

This section in Revelation can be better comprehended by likewise knowing the other primary predictions about Babylon given in the Bible. Isaiah and Jeremiah likewise cover Babylon top to bottom. The sections in Isaiah and Jeremiah are underneath with a few remarks to clarify them:

The predictions of Isaiah against Babylon:

Isa 13:1 The weight of Babylon, which Isaiah the child of Amoz did see.

2 Lift ye up a standard upon the high mountain, commend the voice unto them, shake the hand, that they might go into the entryways of the nobles.

3 I have charged my purified ones, I have additionally called my powerful ones for mine displeasure, even them that celebrate in my Majesty.

4 The clamor of a huge number in the mountains, as starting an awesome individuals; a tumultuous commotion of the kingdoms of countries assembled: the LORD of hosts mustereth the host of the fight.

5 They originate from a far nation, from the end of paradise, even the LORD, and the weapons of his resentment, to decimate the entire area.

6 ¶ Howl ye; for the day of the LORD is close by; it should come as a decimation from the Almighty.

Notice that amid the "Day of the Lord" this armed force comes to devastate the place where there is Babylon. The "Day of the Lord" is the season of decimation on the earth in the most recent days before God's kingdom.

7 Therefore should all hands be black out, and each man's heart might dissolve:

8 And they should be perplexed: throbs and distresses might grab hold of them; they should be in agony as a lady that travaileth: they should be flabbergasted one at another; their countenances should be as blazes.

9 Behold, the day of the LORD cometh, remorseless both with fury and wild outrage, to lay the area barren: and he might crush the delinquents thereof out of it.

10 For the stars of paradise and the groups of stars thereof might not give their light: the sun should be obscured in his going forward, and the moon should not bring about her light to sparkle.

This is not history; it is discussing the future "Day of the Lord". We have the same references to the sun, moon and stars as we do in Joel and the Olivet talk. We know of no time in history when these things happened and there unquestionably was no time that all delinquents were pulverized out of the place that is known for Babylon. There have dependably been miscreants in the place where there is Iraq and on the planet's religious and political frameworks, so the prediction couldn't have been satisfied in the past is still future.

11 And I will rebuff the world for their malevolence, and the insidious for their wrongdoing; and I will bring about the arrogancy of the glad to stop, and will hide out the haughtiness of the awful.

12 I will make a man a bigger number of valuable than fine gold; even a man than the brilliant wedge of Ophir.

The world will be rebuffed for its fiendishness and there will be so couple of men left those men will be rarer than gold.

13 Therefore I will shake the sky, and the earth should uproot out of her place, in the fury of the LORD of hosts, and in the day of his savage displeasure.

In the day of the Lord's outrage, the earth will be uprooted out of her place. Numerous different predictions demonstrate that the earth in the final days will be altogether shaken and the surface of the earth will be changed. It ought to be clear that these entries are not talking about the Babylonian domain of the past.

14 And it should be as the pursued roe, and as a sheep that no man taketh up: they might each man swing to his own kin, and escape each one into his own particular area.

15 Every one that is found should be pushed through; and each one that is joined unto them might fall by the sword.

16 Their kids likewise might be dashed to pieces before their eyes; their homes should be ruined, and their wives violated.

17 Behold, I will stir up the Medes against them, which shall not regard silver; and as for gold, they shall not delight in it.

18 Their bows likewise should dash the young fellows to pieces; and they might have no compassion on the product of the womb; their eye might not save kids.

The Medes will be among the individuals who decimate Babylon. They were individuals north of Iraq. The Kurds are relatives of the Medes. At the point when the northern armed forces come against Babylon, it is sensible to accept that the Kurds will battle with them.

19 And Babylon, the heavenliness of kingdoms, the magnificence of the Chaldees' excellency, might be as when God toppled Sodom and Gomorrah.

20 It might never be occupied, neither should it be abided in from era to era: neither should the Arabian set up portable shelter there; neither might the shepherds make their fold there.

21 But wild brutes of the desert might lie there; and their homes should be brimming with doleful animals; and owls should abide there, and satyrs might move there.

22 And the wild brutes of the islands might cry in their barren houses, and winged serpents in their lovely royal residences: and her time is close to come, and her days should not be drawn out.

This section was never satisfied, subsequent to the zone of Babylon is occupied even today. The entry particularly calls it the excellence of Chaldees. The Chaldeans lived in Iraq. Arabians do contribute their tents south-east Iraq and will in the kingdom of the Beast that will develop past Iraq. The individuals who ponder Babylon are depicting the annihilation of the United States or Europe overlook numerous such entries. The Arabians don't contribute tents the United States or in Europe unless they are on an outdoors get-away. Zechariah section five makes it clear that insidiousness will have a house worked for her in the most recent days in the place where there is Shinar: "where it should be set up, and set there upon her own particular base". The plain of Shinar is in Iraq. The base it discusses is the same site as the tower of Babel. On this base, a sanctuary will be worked for the Beast.

Zechariah portrays the move of the Beast Kingdom world base camp from Europe to Babylon Iraq.

Zec 5:6 And I say, 'What is it?' And he saith, 'This—the ephah that is approaching.' And he saith, 'This is their angle in all the area.

7 And lo, a cake of lead lifted up; and this is a lady sitting amidst the ephah.'

8 And he saith, 'This is the mischievous lady.' And he casteth her unto the middle of the ephah, and casteth the heaviness of lead on its mouth.

9 And I lift up mine eyes, and see, and lo, two ladies are approaching, and twist in their wings; and they have wings like wings of the stork, and they lift up the ephah between the earth and the sky.

10 And I say unto the delivery person who is talking with me, 'Whither would they say they are bringing on the ephah to go?'

11 And he saith unto me, 'To work to it a house in the place where there is Shinar.' And it hath been readied and hath been set there on its base.

Isaiah chapter 14 additionally has much to say in regards to Babylon and we will be looking at these passages on Babylon.

Isa 14:1 For the LORD will show kindness toward Jacob, and will yet pick Israel, and set them in their own particular area: and the outsiders should be joined with them, and they might divide to the place of Jacob.

2 And the general population might take them, and convey them to their place: and the place of Israel should have them in the place that is known for the LORD for hirelings and handmaids: and they should take them prisoners, whose hostages they were; and they should principle over their oppressors.

3 And it might happen in the day that the LORD should give thee rest from thy distress, and from thy dread, and from the hard servitude wherein thou wast made to serve,

God will show benevolence toward Jacob (Israel). The Babylonians took Israel hostage in the past and it is prone to happen again to some degree in the final days. The prediction demonstrates the general population in Babylon who don't kick the bucket will get to be workers in Israel amid the kingdom age.

4 That thou shalt take up this adage against the lord of Babylon, and say, How hath the oppressor stopped! the brilliant city stopped!

At the point when the Antichrist Beast sets up his kingdom at Babylon, he will obviously manufacture a brilliant city for himself.

5 The LORD hath broken the staff of the mischievous, and the staff of the rulers.

6 He who destroyed the general population in rage with a consistent stroke, he that managed the countries in indignation, is oppressed, and none hindereth.

At the point when the Lord pulverizes Babylon, none will frustrate him. Notice this pioneer destroyed the general population in fierceness and ruled the countries in resentment. This is the man indwelt by Satan. He will administer the world for the last 3 ½ years before an end time disobedience from the north pulverizes his kingdom just before the arrival of Jesus.

7 The entire earth is very still, and is calm: they break forward into singing.

8 Yea, the fir trees cheer at thee, and the cedars of Lebanon, saying, Since thou craftsmanship set out, no feller is come up against us.

9 Hell from underneath is moved for thee to meet thee at thy coming: it stirreth up the dead for thee, even all the boss ones of the earth; it hath raised up from their thrones every one of the lords of the countries.

10 All they might talk and say unto thee, Art thou likewise get to be feeble as we? workmanship thou get to be similar to unto us?

11 Thy pageantry is conveyed down to the grave, and the clamor of thy viols: the worm is spread under thee, and the worms spread thee.

The world will have peace when Satan is thrown down to the pit. Indeed, even the lords of the earth in damnation will be blended up and ridicule him at his fall into the pit.

12 How craftsmanship thou tumbled from paradise, O Lucifer, child of the morning! how craftsmanship thou chop down to the ground, which didst debilitate the countries!

13 For thou hast said in thine heart, I will rise into paradise, I will lift up my throne over the stars of God: I will sit likewise upon the mount of the assembly, in the sides of the north:

14 I will rise over the statures of the mists; I will be similar to the most High.

Isaiah here portrays the fall of Lucifer (Satan) out of paradise. At the point when Satan is thrown out of paradise, he incarnates the body of the dead world pioneer and they rise out of the pit. He will magnify himself over the blessed messengers and play God. We are told in this book of Revelation and in Daniel that the Beast is given practically add up to control of the earth for 3 ½ years. God is going to give Satan his wish to be similar to God on the earth yet Satan as God in a man will convey the world to aggregate demolition. Jesus said unless he reduces nowadays no tissue would be spared (Mat 24:22).

15 Yet thou shalt be conveyed down to hellfire, to the sides of the pit.

16 They that see thee might barely look upon thee, and consider thee, saying, Is this the man that made the earth to tremble, that did shake kingdoms;

17 That made the world as a wild, and annihilated the urban communities thereof; that opened not the place of his detainees?

The prediction leaves probably this man will bring about awesome obliteration on the earth amid the season of his energy. All will ask why they thought this Satan incarnated man was God after they see him cast down to the pit.

18 All the rulers of the countries, even every one of them, lie in superbness, each one in his own particular house.

19 But thou workmanship cast out of thy grave like a terrible branch, and as the clothing of those that are killed, pushed

through with a sword, that go down to the stones of the pit; as a carcase trodden under feet.

20 Thou shalt not be joined with them in internment, since thou hast decimated thy land, and killed thy individuals: the seed of scalawags should never be prestigious.

The sacred writings demonstrate this man won't be covered yet he and his false prophet will be thrown into the Lake of Fire alive. There is some secret here since the past section says he will be conveyed down to damnation (Hades). Yet, here and in Revelation 19:20, it says he won't abide in Hades yet he will be thrown alive into the Lake of Fire. Our absence of comprehension does not make the entries struggle. The past entry could be discussing the soul of Satan who incarnated the man, since we know from sacred writing that Satan will be thrown into the pit for a thousand years. Satan does not go into the Lake of Fire until after the thousand years are over. Satan beguiles the countries again toward the end of the millennial rule.

Another clarification could be that this extraordinary man called the Beast will go through Hades on his way to the measurement known as the Lake of Fire. The Lake of Fire could be the last period of a descending winding for those in the measurement of the dead. More than one thousand years after the fact, Satan, demise and damnation itself are additionally thrown into the Lake of Fire and also all who are not composed in the book of life. The Beast and False Prophet will in any case be alive in the Lake of Fire around then. (Rev 20:10, Rev 20:14,15)

21 Prepare butcher for his youngsters for the wrongdoing of their fathers; that they don't rise, nor have the area, nor fill the substance of the world with urban communities.

At the time Satan and his Beast are removed, every one of the offspring of Satan will be butchered. Nobody who takes the characteristic of the Beast will go into the kingdom of God on earth. This section ought to make it copiously clear that not all people are offspring of God.

22 For I will ascend against them, saith the LORD of hosts, and cut off from Babylon the name, and remainder, and child, and nephew, saith the LORD.

23 I will likewise make it an ownership for the bittern, and pools of water: and I will clear it with the besom of annihilation, saith the LORD of hosts.

24 The LORD of hosts hath sworn, saying, Surely as I have thought, so should it happen; and as I have purposed, so might it stand:

25 That I will soften the Assyrian up my territory, and upon my mountains tread him on the ground: then might his yoke leave from off them, and his weight withdraw from off their shoulders.

26 This is the reason that is purposed upon the entire earth: and this is the hand that is extended upon every one of the countries.

27 For the LORD of hosts hath purposed, and who might disannul it? furthermore, his hand is extended, and who should turn it back?

The Assyrian will be broken when he comes against Israel. From this section some trust the Beast Antichrist is liable to be from the Assyrian tribe. This pioneer will control the Assyrian individuals that will come against Israel in the most recent days. The Assyrians stayed in north Iraq and ranges north of advanced Iraq. Regardless of the fact that the Antichrist ends up being an Assyrian that does not mean the Antichrist will be a Muslim on the grounds that not all Assyrians are Muslims furthermore in light of the fact that as of right now the Antichrist will be venerated by all through the world that reject Jesus.

The predictions of Jeremiah about Babylon:

Jer 50:1 The word that the LORD spoke against Babylon and against the place where there is the Chaldeans by Jeremiah the prophet.

The expression of the Lord comes against the place that is known for the Chaldeans. Book of scriptures researchers concur that the Chaldeans lived in the area that is today recognized as Iraq.

2 Declare ye among the countries, and distribute, and set up a standard; distribute, and disguise not: say, Babylon is taken, Bel is jumbled, Merodach is softened up pieces; her godlike objects are perplexed, her pictures are softened up pieces.

3 For out of the north there cometh up a country against her, which might make her territory barren, and none should stay in that: they might uproot, they might leave, both man and brute.

Bel and Merodach were the Satanic lords of Babylon. In the most recent days, Babylon proceeds in icon adore when a picture of the Beast is set up in Jerusalem and worshiped. Jeremiah and Isaiah show that Babylon will be wrecked by a country or countries from the north. At the point when the Babylonian Empire fell in old days to the Medes from the north it was not wrecked, so the prescience has not yet been satisfied.

4 In those days, and in that time, saith the LORD, the offspring of Israel should come, they and the offspring of Judah together, going and sobbing: they might go, and look for the LORD their God.

5 They should ask the best approach to Zion with their countenances thitherward, saying, Come, and let us join ourselves to the LORD in a never-ending pledge that might not be overlooked.

6 My kin hath been lost sheep: their shepherds have made them wander off-track, they have dismissed them on the mountains: they have gone from mountain to slope, they have overlooked their resting place.

7 All that discovered them have eaten up them: and their foes said, We affront not, on the grounds that they have trespassed against the LORD, the home of equity, even the LORD, the trust of their fathers.

8 Remove out of the middle of Babylon, and go forward out of the place that is known for the Chaldeans, and be as the he goats before the groups.

The pioneers of Israel have driven some off track. The world history of the Jews affirms what was composed. Previously, some in the Christian church guaranteed they were just doing God's will in murdering and aggrieving the Jews. Presently Islam is stating the same thing. The Jews will have a misguided feeling that all is well and good under the last world pioneer and might even stay in his kingdom for a period while it ascends among the countries as the seat of world government. God will advise His kin to escape Babylon before He crushes her and He will give the way to their break. God is advising the individuals who turn out to lead whatever remains of the Jews of the world to security.

9 For, lo, I will raise and cause to come up against Babylon a gathering of incredible countries from the north nation: and they should set themselves in cluster against her; from thereupon she should be taken: their bolts might be starting a compelling master man; none might return futile.

10 And Chaldea should be a ruin: all that ruin her might be fulfilled, saith the LORD.

This entry is predictable with Isaiah that a get together of incredible countries will originate from the north to annihilate Babylon.

11 Because ye were happy, in light of the fact that ye cheered, O ye destroyers of mine legacy, on the grounds that ye are developed fat as the yearling at grass, and cry as bulls;

12 Your mom should be sore jumbled; she that uncovered you might be embarrassed: see, the hindermost of the countries should be a wild, a dry area, and a desert.

13 Because of the rage of the LORD it should not be possessed, but rather it might be completely destroy: each one that goeth by Babylon should be amazed, and murmur at all her sicknesses.

14 Put yourselves in exhibit against Babylon indirect: all ye that curve the bow, shoot at her, extra no bolts: for she hath trespassed against the LORD.

15 Shout against her circuitous: she hath given her hand: her establishments are fallen, her dividers are tossed down: for it is the retaliation of the LORD: take retribution upon her; as she hath done, do unto her.

16 Cut off the sower from Babylon, and him that handleth the sickle in the season of harvest: inspired by a paranoid fear of the persecuting sword they should turn each one to his kin, and they might escape each one to his own territory.

17 Israel is a scattered sheep; the lions have pushed him away: first the lord of Assyria hath ate up him; and last this Nebuchadrezzar ruler of Babylon hath broken his bones.

18 Therefore in this manner saith the LORD of hosts, the God of Israel; Behold, I will rebuff the ruler of Babylon and his territory, as I have rebuffed the ruler of Assyria.

19 And I will convey Israel again to his residence, and he should eat Carmel and Bashan, and his spirit might be fulfilled upon mount Ephraim and Gilead.

20 In those days, and in that time, saith the LORD, the injustice of Israel should be looked for, and there might be none; and the transgressions of Judah, and they might not be found: for I will excuse them whom I hold.

Verse 19 and 20 are plainly saying that God will take Israel back to their territory and take away their wrongdoings. The witness Paul said that all Israel will be spared after the seasons of the Gentiles are satisfied. This can just happen when God uncovers himself to Israel in the most recent days.

21 Go up against the place where there is Merathaim, even against it, and against the occupants of Pekod: waste and completely decimate after them, saith the LORD, and do as indicated by all that I have directed thee.

22 A sound of fight is in the area, and of incredible decimation.

23 How is the mallet of the entire earth cut into pieces and broken! how is Babylon turned into a devastation among the countries!

Babylon is named the mallet of the entire earth in light of the fact that the Antichrist and his kingdom were utilized by Satan to crush the earth. The section shows Babylon will be crushed in light of the fact that she pounded the world.

24 I have laid a catch for thee, and thou craftsmanship additionally taken, O Babylon, and thou wast not mindful: thou workmanship found, furthermore got, in light of the fact that thou hast endeavored against the LORD.

25 The LORD hath opened his arsenal, and hath delivered the weapons of his irateness: for this is the work of the Lord GOD of hosts in the place where there is the Chaldeans.

Babylon will be wrecked on the grounds that she will contradict the Lord God. He will manage those renegades at last days in the place that is known for the Chaldeans (Iraq).

26 Come against her from the most extreme fringe, open her storage facilities: give her up a role as loads, and crush her totally: let nothing of her be cleared out.

27 Slay every one of her bullocks; let them go down to the butcher: misfortune unto them! for their day is come, the season of their appearance.

28 The voice of them that escape and escape out of the place that is known for Babylon, to announce in Zion the retribution of the LORD our God, the retaliation of his sanctuary.

The Antichrist Beast that sets up his kingdom from Babylon has tainted the sanctuary in Jerusalem and this occasion began this season of retribution from the Lord God Almighty. The entry shows that the Jews that escape from Babylon will advise Israel this is the retribution the prophets expounded on. It comes in light of the Beast's defilement of God's sanctuary in Jerusalem.

29 Call together the bowmen against Babylon: all ye that twist the bow, camp against it indirect; let none thereof escape: reward her as indicated by her work; as per all that she hath done, do unto her: for she hath been pleased against the LORD, against the Holy One of Israel.

30 Therefore should her young fellows fall in the boulevards, and every one of her men of war might be cut off in that day, saith the LORD.

31 Behold, I am against thee, O thou most glad, saith the Lord GOD of hosts: for thy day is come, the time that I will visit thee.

32 And the most glad should falter and fall, and none might raise him up: and I will fuel a flame in his urban communities, and it might eat up all indirect him.

The sign of Satan and his Antichrist Beast is pride. The wrongdoing of pride wins in the urban areas of his fake kingdom and God will crush every one of them. Notice God is against the proud. God is against all those who set themselves up as their own God.

33 Thus saith the LORD of hosts; The offspring of Israel and the offspring of Judah were persecuted together: and all that took them hostages held them quick; they declined to release them.

34 Their Redeemer is solid; the LORD of hosts is his name: he might throughly argue their cause, that he might offer rest to the area, and restlessness the tenants of Babylon.

35 A sword is upon the Chaldeans, saith the LORD, and upon the tenants of Babylon, and upon her rulers, and upon her savvy men.

36 A sword is upon the liars; and they should gush: a sword is upon her strong men; and they might be unnerved.

37 A sword is upon their steeds, and upon their chariots, and upon all the blended individuals that are amidst her; and they should get to be as ladies: a sword is upon her cherishes; and they might be ransacked.

38 A dry spell is upon her waters; and they might be gone away: for it is the place where there is graven pictures, and they are frantic upon their godlike objects.

39 Therefore the wild mammoths of the desert with the wild monsters of the islands should stay there, and the owls might abide in that: and it should be not any more occupied for ever; neither might it be stayed in from era to era.

40 As God ousted Sodom and Gomorrah and the neighbor urban communities thereof, saith the LORD; so should no man withstand there, neither might any child of man abide in that.

God says here and in different sections of sacred text that no man will ever dwell in this area again. At the point when in the past was Babylon ever toppled like Sodom and Gomorrah? It has never happened, however it will and next we perceive how:

41 Behold, an individuals might originate from the north, and an extraordinary country, and numerous lords should be raised up from the shores of the earth.

42 They might hold the bow and the spear: they are barbarous, and won't shew benevolence: their voice should thunder like the ocean, and they might ride upon stallions, each one put in cluster, similar to a man to the fight, against thee, O little girl of Babylon.

43 The lord of Babylon hath heard the report of them, and his hands waxed weak: anguish grabbed hold of him, and strings starting a lady in travail.

44 Behold, he should come up like a lion from the swelling of Jordan unto the home of the solid: however I will make them abruptly flee from her: and who is a picked man, that I might delegate over her? for who is similar to me? also, who will designate me the time? also, who is that shepherd that will remain before me?

45 Therefore hear ye the insight of the LORD, that he hath taken against Babylon; and his reasons, that he hath purposed against the place where there is the Chaldeans: Surely the minimum of the herd might coax them out: most likely he should make their residence ruined with them.

46 At the clamor of the taking of Babylon the earth is moved, and the cry is heard among the countries.

Here we see that the countries that come against Babylon originate from the north as well as originate from the shorelines of the earth. The shepherd that will remain before God must be Jesus; it won't be the Beast. At the point when Babylon is taken the entire earth will be moved, all urban areas will fall, and the cry will be heard among every one of the countries. This happens at the pouring out of the seventh vial judgment in Revelation.

This cry among the countries will be completely portrayed in this part of Revelation.

Jer 51:1 Thus saith the LORD; Behold, I will raise up against Babylon, and against them that stay amidst them that ascent up against me, an obliterating wind;

2 And will send unto Babylon fanners, that should fan her, and might purge her property: for stuck in an unfortunate situation they might be against her indirect.

3 Against him that bendeth let the bowman twist his bow, and against him that lifteth himself up in his brigandine: and extra ye not her young fellows; wreck ye totally all her host.

4 Thus the killed should fall in the place where there is the Chaldeans, and they that are pushed through in her lanes.

Babylon, and in addition being the religious, political and financial kingdom of a fake god, is additionally a physical area on the earth. The entry says these individuals are killed in the place that is known for the Chaldeans (Iraq).

5 For Israel hath not been neglected, nor Judah of his God, of the LORD of hosts; however their territory was loaded with sin against the Holy One of Israel.

6 Flee out of the middle of Babylon, and convey each man his spirit: be not cut off in her wrongdoing; for this is the season of the LORD'S retaliation; he will render unto her a recompence.

The individuals who think God is finished with Israel need to peruse this section; it says "Israel hath not been neglected, nor Judah". At the point when God goes to bat for His kin, they are to escape out of religious and political Babylon or they will share of her judgments.

7 Babylon hath been a brilliant glass in the LORD'S hand, that made all the earth inebriated: the countries have tipsy of her wine; consequently the countries are distraught.

8 Babylon is all of a sudden fallen and demolished: wail for her; take analgesic for her torment, if so be she might be recuperated.

9 We would have mended Babylon, yet she is not recuperated: spurn her, and let us go each one into his own particular nation: for her judgment reacheth unto paradise, and is lifted up even to the skies.

The entire world has been tricked by the untruths that originated from the kingdom of the Beast Antichrist and the False Prophet. The countries soon get to be mindful that Babylon is not the guaranteed "kingdom of God". The countries have been come clean by God's blessed messengers and they are irate. They are accompanying awesome armed forces to demolish the Kingdom of the Beast at Babylon. The section says that Babylon will fall all of a sudden and be devastated. This is presumably in light of the intrusion from the north against the kingdom and in addition direct judgment from God when a shooting star hits the city of Babylon.

10 The LORD hath delivered our nobility: come, and let us announce in Zion the work of the LORD our God.

11 Make splendid the bolts; assemble the shields: the LORD hath raised up the soul of the rulers of the Medes: for his gadget is against Babylon, to wreck it; since it is the retribution of the LORD, the retaliation of his sanctuary.

"The soul of the lords of the Medes" is undoubtedly the rulers of the north and east that come against Babylon in the most recent days to devastate it. God raised up this pulverizing armed force from numerous countries in light of the fact that the Antichrist contaminated His sanctuary and His heavenly name in Jerusalem.

12 Set up the standard upon the dividers of Babylon, make the watch solid, set up the gatekeepers, set up the ambushes: for the LORD hath both contrived and done what he spake against the occupants of Babylon.

13 O thou that dwellest upon numerous waters, plentiful in fortunes, thine end is come, and the measure of thy greed.

Verse 13 is the primary verse that leads some to the false conviction that Babylon is Rome or New York City. Babylon is said here to stay upon numerous waters and Iraq does not fit their perspective of a country sitting on numerous waters. The first Babylonian realm did sit on three oceans and the kingdom of the Beast should. Regardless, the vast majority of the world's transportation today is in close vicinity to Iraq. The Tigris and Euphrates Rivers course through her also. Babylon in the most recent days may again have admittance to the ocean through the heavenly powers of the Beast or through the earth changes that happen in earlier seismic tremors talked about in Revelation. Additionally remember that "home on numerous waters" could simply mean the kingdom called Babylon will comprise of numerous countries. As we read in Rev 17:15 "numerous waters" can truly mean numerous people groups, countries.

14 The LORD of hosts hath sworn independent from anyone else, saying, Surely I will fill thee with men, as with caterpillers; and they should lift up a yell against thee.

15 He hath made the earth by his energy, he hath set up the world by his intelligence, and hath extended the paradise by his comprehension.

16 When he uttereth his voice, there is a huge number of waters in the sky; and he causeth the vapors to climb from the finishes of the earth: he maketh lightnings with downpour, and bringeth forward the wind out of his fortunes.

17 Every man is brutish by his insight; each organizer is perplexed by the graven picture: for his liquid picture is lie, and there is no breath in them.

18 They are vanity, the work of blunders: in the season of their appearance they should die.

19 The segment of Jacob is not care for them; for he is the previous for goodness' sake: and Israel is the bar of his legacy: the LORD of hosts is his name.

20 Thou craftsmanship my fight hatchet and weapons of war: for with thee will I soften up pieces the countries, and with thee will I wreck kingdoms;

21 And with thee will I soften up pieces the steed and his rider; and with thee will I soften up pieces the chariot and his rider;

22 With thee additionally will I soften up pieces man and lady; and with thee will I soften up pieces old and youthful; and with thee will I soften up pieces the young fellow and the cleaning specialist;

23 I will likewise soften up pieces with thee the shepherd and his run; and with thee will I soften up pieces the cultivator and his yoke of bulls; and with thee will I soften up pieces skippers and rulers.

This entry is discussing how the Lord will break all countries and people groups that come against Israel.

24 And I will render unto Babylon and to every one of the tenants of Chaldea all their insidious that they have done in Zion in your sight, saith the LORD.

25 Behold, I am against thee, O obliterating mountain, saith the LORD, which destroyest all the earth: and I will extend mine hand upon thee, and roll thee down from the stones, and will make thee a blazed mountain.

26 And they might not take of thee a stone for a corner, nor a stone for establishments; yet thou shalt be destroy for ever, saith the LORD.

God says Babylon is an annihilating mountain that demolished the greater part of the earth. He says Babylon will be destroy for eternity. Today this zone is still involved.

27 Set ye up a standard in the area, blow the trumpet among the countries, set up the countries against her, assemble against her the kingdoms of Ararat, Minni, and Ashchenaz; select a skipper against her; cause the steeds to come up as the harsh caterpillers.

28 Prepare against her the countries with the rulers of the Medes, the commanders thereof, and every one of the rulers thereof, and all the place that is known for his domain.

29 And the area might tremble and distress: for each motivation behind the LORD should be performed against Babylon, to make the place where there is Babylon a destruction without an occupant.

The rulers of the north and east come without wanting to end up an area without a tenant.

30 The forceful men of Babylon have forborn to battle, they have stayed in their holds: their strength hath fizzled; they got to be as ladies: they have blazed her dwellingplaces; her bars are broken.

31 One post might raced to meet another, and one delivery person to meet another, to shew the lord of Babylon that his city is taken toward one side,

32 And that the sections are ceased, and the reeds they have smoldered with flame, and the men of war are dismayed.

33 For hence saith the LORD of hosts, the God of Israel; The girl of Babylon is similar to a threshingfloor, the time has come to sift her: yet a short time, and the season of her harvest should come.

34 Nebuchadrezzar the ruler of Babylon hath ate up me, he hath squashed me, he hath made me a void vessel, he hath gobbled me up like a winged serpent, he hath filled his paunch with my delicates, he hath cast me out.

35 The viciousness done to me and to my substance be upon Babylon, might the occupant of Zion say; and my blood upon the tenants of Chaldea, should Jerusalem say.

36 Therefore subsequently saith the LORD; Behold, I will argue thy cause, and take retribution for thee; and I will become scarce her ocean, and make her springs dry.

37 And Babylon should turn out to be loads, a dwellingplace for monsters, an amazement, and a murmuring, without an occupant.

38 They should thunder together like lions: they might holler as lions' whelps.

39 In their warmth I will make their dining experiences, and I will make them plastered, that they might celebrate, and rest an interminable rest, and not wake, saith the LORD.

40 I will cut them down like sheep to the butcher, similar to smashes with he goats.

The little girl of Babylon is similar to a sifting floor. A sifting floor is a spot where wheat is beaten to evacuate the polluting influences. The reason for God permitting Satan's fake kingdom of God to go ahead earth is to independent the good product from the debris. The section alludes to Nebuchadnezzar since he was a hint of the Beast Antichrist. The section again says Babylon will turn into a foul spot without occupant aside from some dreadful animals.

41 How is Sheshach taken! what's more, how is the applause for the entire earth astounded! how is Babylon turned into an amazement among the countries!

42 The ocean is come up upon Babylon: she is secured with the huge number of the waves thereof.

43 Her urban communities are a destruction, a dry area, and a wild, an area wherein no man dwelleth, neither doth any child of man pass along these lines.

In the event that despite everything it is not clear, God says again that no man will abide in the area or even go close it. This area will most likely turn into a radioactive no man's land after the wars.

44 And I will rebuff Bel in Babylon, and I will deliver out of his mouth what he hath gobbled up: and the countries should not stream together any more unto him: yea, the mass of Babylon might fall.

Bel is Satan. What he took for his ownership God will take back. Satan in the Beast was a fake God for 42 months. The verse demonstrates that amid the Beast's control over the countries as their god, they came to him to give their wealth,

45 My kin, go ye out of the middle of her, and convey ye each man his spirit from the furious resentment of the LORD.

46 And or your heart faint, and ye dread for the talk that should be heard in the area; gossip might both come one year, and after that in one more year might come talk, and roughness in the area, ruler against ruler.

47 Therefore, see, the days come, that I will do judgment upon the graven pictures of Babylon: and her entire area should be bewildered, and all her killed might fall amidst her.

48 Then the paradise and the earth, and all that is in that, might sing for Babylon: for the spoilers should come unto her from the north, saith the LORD.

49 As Babylon hath created the killed of Israel to fall, so at Babylon should fall the killed of all the earth.

God again cautions his kin to escape her. He says it will begin with gossipy tidbits. A year or two later, there will be roughness and afterward polite war in the area and after that the attack from the North. All the killed of the earth couldn't in any way, shape or form fall at Babylon. A superior rewording of the entry may say, "The Babylonian fake kingdom ruled by the Beast will be in charge of every one of those killed on the earth amid the period ruled by Babylon the Great".

50 Ye that have gotten away from the sword, leave, stand not in any case: recall the LORD a remote place off, and let Jerusalem come into your psyche.

51 We are frustrated, in light of the fact that we have heard censure: disgrace hath secured our appearances: for outsiders are come into the asylums of the LORD'S house.

The most blessed spot in the sanctuary is contaminated by outsiders. This is the point at which the "day of anger" starts.

52 Wherefore, observe, the days come, saith the LORD, that I will do judgment upon her graven pictures: and through all her property the injured should moan.

53 Though Babylon ought to mount up to paradise, and however she ought to strengthen the stature of her quality, yet from me should spoilers come unto her, saith the LORD.

54 A sound of a cry cometh from Babylon, and incredible pulverization from the place where there is the Chaldeans:

This could be discussing pride, or it could be discussing military space stages, or both. One thing that is apparent is that this devastation comes in the place where there is the Chaldeans from God and there will be no getaway.

55 Because the LORD hath ruined Babylon, and annihilated out of her the colossal voice; when her waves do thunder like incredible waters, a clamor of their voice is articulated:

56 Because the spoiler is happened upon her, even upon Babylon, and her forceful men are taken, each one of their bows is broken: for the LORD God of recompences should without a doubt compensate.

57 And I will make smashed her sovereigns, and her astute men, her chiefs, and her rulers, and her strong men: and they should rest a never-ending rest, and not wake, saith the King, whose name is the LORD of hosts.

58 Thus saith the LORD of hosts; The expansive dividers of Babylon should be totally broken, and her high doors might be blazed with flame; and the general population should work futile, and the society in the fire, and they should be fatigued.

59 The word which Jeremiah the prophet charged Seraiah the child of Neriah, the child of Maaseiah, when he ran with Zedekiah the ruler of Judah into Babylon in the fourth year of his rule. What's more, this Seraiah was a tranquil sovereign.

60 So Jeremiah wrote in a book all the abhorrent that ought to happen upon Babylon, even every one of these words that are composed against Babylon.

61 And Jeremiah said to Seraiah, When thou comest to Babylon, and shalt see, and shalt read every one of these words;

62 Then shalt thou say, O LORD, thou hast talked against this spot, to cut it off, that none should stay in it, neither man nor brute, however that it might be devastate for ever.

A huge number of years have gone since this prediction and the area is not yet devastate. The majority of this prescience will be satisfied at the second happening to Jesus.

63 And it should be, when thou hast made an end of perusing this book, thou shalt tie a stone to it, and cast it into the middle of Euphrates:

64 And thou shalt say, Thus should Babylon sink, and might not ascend from the detestable that I will bring upon her: and they might be exhausted. Hitherto are the expressions of Jeremiah.

In the event that there stays any uncertainty in anybody's brain where Babylon is, God denote the spot when he advises Jeremiah to cast the predictions of her judgments into the middle of the Euphrates. The Euphrates River moves through Babylon, Iraq. Any individual who still thinks Babylon is the United States or Europe has not been focusing and has biased partialities with no establishment in sacred text.

Since we have gently inspected the major prophetic sacred texts about Babylon by the Old Testament prophets, we can have a superior handle on the sacred writings in Revelation that additionally discuss the judgment of the Beast's fake kingdom of God called "Babylon the Great".

*** End of Babylon supplement material ***

Disclosure Chapter 18:

1 And after these things I saw another blessed messenger descend from paradise, having extraordinary force; and the earth was helped with his wonderfulness.

2 And he cried forcefully with a solid voice, saying, Babylon the immense is fallen, will be fallen, and is turned into the residence of fiends, and the hold of each foul soul, and a confine of each unclean and scornful fowl.

After the judgment of Mystery Babylon that John depicted in part 17, an intense blessed messenger descends from paradise with wonderfulness that is so brilliant it illuminates the earth. The heavenly attendant reports with a strong voice that the organization of Satan is fallen. Satan's fake kingdom has been judged by God and has fallen before Him. It has turned into the home of fallen angels (Satan's heavenly attendants) and each foul soul (devils) and a jail for each unclean and contemptuous winged creature (all the malicious posterity of Satan). The physical spot talked about as "Babylon the Great" is the base camp of the kingdom set up by the Beast that principles over the earth in the most recent days. It incorporates the city of Babylon, yet the zone presumably covers all of Iraq, and a great deal more land territory too. There additionally is a more extensive implying that goes past simply the physical area. This is discussing the coming judgment on the individuals who joined with this fake kingdom of God that standards over the world.

3 For all countries have tanked of the wine of the rage of her sex, and the lords of the earth have submitted sex with her, and the traders of the earth are waxed rich through the plenitude of her delights.

Every one of the countries on earth became tied up with the untruths that God was in Babylon and His kingdom had come. The administration of the Beast actualized an arrangement of world exchange that made the traders of the earth exceptionally rich.

4 And I heard another voice from paradise, saying, Come out of her, my kin, that ye be not partakers of her wrongdoings, and that ye get not of her maladies.

5 For her wrongdoings have come to unto paradise, and God hath recollected that her injustices.

We likewise found in Isaiah and Jeremiah that God advises His kin to leave her so they won't get her judgments or diseases. These infections were portrayed in Chapter 16. The sicknesses will be the vial judgments poured out on the seat of the Beast Kingdom. Precisely how God's kin turn out is not caught on. I expect the former judgments have something to do with conveying them out, as God's judgments conveyed Israel out of Egypt.

6 Reward her even as she compensated you, and twofold unto her twofold as indicated by her works: in the container which she hath filled fill to her twofold.

The organization of Satan on the earth executed the holy people of God and the glass with the blood of the holy people is presently full. At the fifth seal judgment it was obvious that the container was not full but rather now it is full. So as of right now, we are toward the end of the tribulation period for God's kin. Presently the time possesses a great deal of return to pay the individuals who have oppressed God's kin.

7 How much she hath celebrated herself, and lived scrumptiously, so much torment and distress give her: for she saith in her heart, I sit a ruler, and am no dowager, and might see no distress.

Sinister Babylon truly imagines that she is past judgment and that she will see no distress like separated Israel. This is a definitive substitution religious philosophy. This lady supposes she is a ruler. She trusts she makes up the genuine kingdom of God. There are those in substitution philosophy in Christianity who say that God is finished with Israel and they are the guaranteed kingdom on earth however those that are found in Babylon are so determined about it that they get to be prideful. A large portion of us realize that pride goes before a fall and this is precisely what this entry infers.

Those that surmise that Israel is a dowager and say that God is through with Israel and will have no further dealings with the Jews need to see some pivotal truths. God sent John the Baptist and His Son to the country of Israel even after they sold themselves into divorcement. God's calling to Israel is irreversible (Rom 11:29). At the point when Israel comes back to God and acknowledges the Messiah He decided for her, she will be restored.

Isa 50:1 Thus saith the LORD, Where is the bill of your mom's divorcement, whom I have secured? then again which of my loan bosses is it to whom I have sold you? View, for your wrongdoings have ye sold yourselves, and for your transgressions is your mom set away.

A little side study into Hosea and Roman's is with a specific end goal to illuminate that God will restore common Israel.

Hos 2:14 Therefore, view, I will appeal her, and bring her into the wild, and talk easily unto her.

15 And I will give her vineyards from thus, and the valley of Achor for an entryway of trust: and she might sing there, as in the times of her childhood, and as in the day when she came up out of the place that is known for Egypt.

The wild Hosea is discussing is the place the steadfast and devoted of Israel escape. Israel is extraordinarily shielded by God from the Beast in the mountains close Petra.

16 And it might be at that day, saith the LORD, that thou shalt call me Ishi; and shalt call me no more Baali.

Ishi signifies "he spares me". Baali signifies "my Lord" furthermore is a variety of the name Baal (Satan) who was the ruler of Israel in her harlotry.

17 For I will take away the names of Baalim out of her mouth, and they might no more be recollected by their name.

Baalim is plural for Baal (the boss agnostic god in the season of Hosea). This section is stating the icons of Baal won't be recollected in Israel any more.

18 And in that day will I make an agreement for them with the monsters of the field, and with the fowls of paradise, and with the inching things of the ground: and I will break the bow and the sword and the fight out of the earth, and will make them to rests securely.

This verse in Hosea is discussing the end of roughness on the earth. Indeed, even the way of creatures will be changed to be as their temperament was before the fall of man.

19 And I will pledge thee unto me for ever; yea, I will bind thee unto me in nobility, and in judgment, and in lovingkindness, and in leniencies.

20 I will even promise thee unto me in steadfastness: and thou shalt know the LORD.

21 And it might happen in that day, I will listen, saith the LORD, I will hear the sky, and they should hear the earth;

22 And the earth might hear the corn, and the wine, and the oil; and they should hear Jezreel.

23 And I will sow her unto me in the earth; and I will show kindness upon her that showed not got leniency; and I will say to them which were not my kin, Thou workmanship my kin; and they might say, Thou craftsmanship my God.

The section is not discussing the united in Gentiles as some say. In the setting, it is discussing the same individuals that God rejected for harlotry. The section is discussing the rebuilding of Israel. Israel sold herself into divorcement. At the point when Israel comes back to God He won't dismiss her since God abhors separate and has given a path back through the New Covenant! At the point when was the united in Church as of now in the New Covenant ever not His kin?

The book of Hosea happened as composed as well as the book is a genuine prophetic story of God managing Israel until the end. These truths devastate the falsehood that God is finished with Israel. All who surmise that God is finished with Israel don't have a clue about the prophetic sacred writings and have become tied up with an evil falsehood. Prophetic sacred text makes it clear that God picked Israel for His own particular purposes and that He will run His kingdom on earth from Jerusalem in an Israelite kingdom. The greater part of the pioneers of Israel of the past rejected Him and thus, God has postponed the kingdom of the Jews until the country recognizes its offense. This postponement gave trusting Gentiles a period of effortlessness to be joined into the New Covenant guarantee that was really given to Israel and Judah.

Hos 5:15 I will go and come back to my place, till they recognize their offense, and look for my face: in their torment they will look for me early.

It was forever God's arrangement for those slipped from Israel to satisfy the physical kingdom guarantees to Israel for his calling is unavoidable.

Rom 9:4 Who are Israelites; to whom pertaineth the selection, and the superbness, and the agreements, and the giving of the law, and the administration of God, and the guarantees;

Rom 11:25 For I would not, brethren, that ye ought to be unmindful of this secret, for fear that ye ought to be savvy in your own particular prides; that visual impairment to a limited extent is happened to Israel, until the fulness of the Gentiles be come in.

26 And so all Israel should be spared: as it is composed, There might leave Sion the Deliverer, and should dismiss corruption from Jacob:

27 For this is my agreement unto them, when I should take away their transgressions.

28 As concerning the gospel, they are foes for your sakes: yet as touching the decision, they are cherished for the fathers' sakes.

29 For the endowments and calling of God are without atonement.

(Verse 29 implies they can't be changed.)

30 For as ye in times past have not trusted God, yet have now acquired leniency through their unbelief:

31 Even so have these likewise now not trusted, that through your leniency they additionally might acquire kindness.

32 For God hath finished up all of them in unbelief, that he may show benevolence upon all.

From these sections and numerous others, it is clear that God arrangements to restore Israel in the most recent days.

*** end of Hosea and Roman's side study***

Rev 18:8 Therefore might her infections come in one day, demise, and grieving, and starvation; and she should be absolutely blazed with flame: for solid is the Lord God who judgeth her.

Babylon and the kingdom of the Beast will be smoldered with flame amid the "Day of the Lord". The "Day of the Lord" in judgment is during the last half of a seven-year period for Israel also known as the seventh week of Daniel. The plagues here do not last a literal day of 24 hours. The passage is saying when these things come; they will all come together in a very short time period.

9 And the lords of the earth, who have submitted sex and lived flavorfully with her, might bewail her, and mourn for her, when they should see the smoke of her smoldering,

10 Standing a remote place off for the apprehension of her torment, saying, Alas, oh dear, that incredible city Babylon, that relentless city! for in one hour is thy judgment come.

The lords of the earth have an awesome time with this fraud god and the world government and world exchange that he sets up. They will turn out to be genuinely disturbed when she smolders. These same rulers that now regret Babylon cheered when Mystery Babylon blazed in part 17. Subsequently, the two Babylons couldn't be the same. "Secret Babylon" of part 17 is religion that played the mistress with otherworldly agnosticism yet "Babylon the Great" depicted in this section is a world political, monetary and religious framework that incorporates constrained love of the Beast as God.

These lords won't get close to her when they see her judgment and see her blaze with flame. This infers there is literally nothing at all they can do. The "colossal city" depicted is the revamped brilliant city of the Antichrist Beast that will be worked at Babylon in Iraq. This city is the real last seat of the Beast kingdom of the final days, however the judgment represented by this judgment on a real city likewise goes ahead the urban areas of the entire world. Disclosure

16:19 lets us know that every one of the urban communities of the world will fall at the season of Babylon's pulverization. What happens as of now is the seventh vial judgment.

11 And the dealers of the earth might sob and grieve over her; for no man buyeth their stock any more:

12 The stock of gold, and silver, and valuable stones, and of pearls, and fine cloth, and purple, and silk, and red, and all thyine wood, and every way vessel of ivory, and every way vessel of most valuable wood, and of metal, and iron, and marble,

13 And cinnamon, and smells, and salves, and frankincense, and wine, and oil, and fine flour, and wheat, and mammoths, and sheep, and stallions, and chariots, and slaves, and souls of men.

14 And the natural products that thy soul craved are left from thee, and all things which were dainty and goodly are withdrawn from thee, and thou shalt discover them no more by any means.

Every one of these items lead numerous to theorize that Babylon is some city or nation other than Babylon, Iraq. In spite of the fact that Babylon, Iraq today is not close satisfying this prediction, things there could change rapidly if the divine force of this world sets up his throne and his "Kingdom of God" from that area. He will request tributes and expenses from the entire world. Babylon will then turn into a city of gold and extravagance in short request.

Isa 14:4 That thou shalt take up this precept against the lord of Babylon, and say, How hath the oppressor stopped! the brilliant city stopped!

These entries might likewise discover some satisfaction in the devastation of the world financial framework that under the organization of Satan ruined the world through the desire of the eyes.

15 The shippers of these things, which were made rich by her, might stand a remote place off for the apprehension of her torment, sobbing and wailing,

16 And saying, Alas, tsk-tsk, that awesome city, that was dressed in fine cloth, and purple, and red, and decked with gold, and valuable stones, and pearls!

17 For in one hour so incredible wealth is come to nothing. Furthermore, every shipmaster, and all the organization in boats, and mariners, and the same number of as exchange via ocean, stood a far distance off,

18 And cried when they saw the smoke of her blazing, saying, What city is similar to unto this incredible city!

19 And they cast dust on their heads, and cried, sobbing and wailing, saying, Alas, oh, that incredible city, wherein were made rich all that had ships in the ocean by reason of her excessiveness! for in one hour is she made barren.

The shippers of the world and the shipmasters stand far from her sobbing over the wealth they will lose. The city is dressed in the articles of clothing and gems of religion and eminence (Purple and Scarlet). It is essentially not possible that any current awesome city on the planet could qualify to satisfy these sections. This is a city not yet constructed.

20 Rejoice over her, thou paradise, and ye sacred missionaries and prophets; for God hath vindicated you on her.

Paradise and the messengers and prophets celebrate over her pulverization, in light of the fact that the world religious and political frameworks that started at Babylon and that debased all legislature and religion to mistreat the general population of the guarantee have now been retaliated for. World government and world religion that achieves its zenith with constrained love of the sinister Beast (counting Judaism and Christianity in its whore structure) is in charge of murdering every one of the missionaries and every one of the prophets of God.

21 And a powerful heavenly attendant took up a stone such as an extraordinary grindstone, and cast it into the ocean, saying, Thus with savagery might that awesome city Babylon be tossed down, and should be found no more by any means.

22 And the voice of harpers, and artists, and of flute players, and trumpeters, should be heard no more at all in thee; and no skilled worker, of at all art he be, might be found any more in thee; and the sound of a grinder might be heard no more at all in thee;

23 And the light of a flame might sparkle no more at all in thee; and the voice of the groom and of the spouse should be heard no more at all in thee: for thy dealers were the considerable men of the earth; for by thy divinations were all countries misdirected.

Reliable with the predictions of Isaiah and Jeremiah nobody will ever live around there again. This unmistakably is future since it has never happened. After this pulverization from God on the seat of the Beast, nobody will ever live in that land again, nor will there be a different universe kingdom controlled by Satan on the earth.

Those in this world framework are the considerable world pioneers of the earth however the force behind these pioneers is Satan. The colossal men of the earth swindle the whole world and show them to take after the lord of realism and childishness. They lead the world to trust the god they take after is the maker when actually the god they take after is a fallen blessed messenger known as Satan and the Devil.

24 And in her was found the blood of prophets, and of holy people, and of all that were killed upon the earth.

No city or nation on earth could qualify to satisfy this verse. This verse is not saying all holy people ever murdered were executed in a city or a spot on earth called "Babylon the Great". What it is stating is that the religious and political frameworks that ruined the earth under the whole regulatory standard of Satan is named "Babylon the Great". In God's eyes, the entire organization of Satan is called Babylon and not only the zenith of his kingdom in the last days.

Satan has been in charge of every one of those killed on the earth. The evil organization started at the fall of Adam. In any case, it initially showed up as a sorted out political and religious element on the earth after the surge, at Babylon under Nimrod. "Babylon the Great" is the evil political and religious substitute for the genuine kingdom of God on earth that God guaranteed through His prophets. This genuine kingdom is to be administered from Jerusalem by His Son Jesus.

The prediction about "Babylon the Great" goes past simply the area of its introduction to the world and demise as a real city. It likewise uncovers the profound war on earth that has been pursued for six thousand years against the offspring of light and God's guarantees to them. At the natural climax of "Babylon the Great" under the false Messiah incarnated by Satan there will be an overall uncivilized fake kingdom of god loaded with everything evil. This agnostic Babylonian world framework will then be judged by God and will be thrown down all of a sudden and will be found no more. God will then acquire the guaranteed Jewish kingdom of God on earth ruled by Jesus and those that trust in Him.

CHAPTER 19

Jesus Starts His Rule On Earth

After John is demonstrated an extended clarification of the judgment of Babylon he is presently going to see the crowning ordinance and marriage of the Lamb of God in paradise.

1 And after these things I heard an awesome voice of much individuals in paradise, saying, Alleluia; Salvation, and superbness, and respect, and power, unto the Lord our God:

2 For genuine and exemplary are his judgments: for he hath judged the considerable prostitute, which did degenerate the earth with her sex, and hath retaliated for the blood of his hirelings at her hand.

3 And again they said, Alleluia. What's more, her smoke ascended for ever and ever.

God judged the considerable prostitute named "Babylon the Great". She is known as a prostitute on the grounds that the earth was debased by her association with Satan set up of God. The judgments of God on Babylon retaliated for the blood of the individuals who were killed by her in every past time and also amid this end time tribulation.

The smoke of her smoldering ascents on the earth truly until the new paradise and earth over a thousand years after the fact. It may appear to be difficult to trust this area in Iraq would seethe for over a thousand years yet this sacred text and the one in Isaiah demonstrate that it will and that just animals of the night will ever involve this area.

Evidently the nuclear wars in the territory of Iraq or the falling shooting stars touch off the colossal oil tar pits in that land that give the fuel to the smoldering. We know of coal mines that keep on blazing underground for scores of years so this is not out the domain of common potential outcomes. The smoke of the considerable prostitute keeps on rising forever even after the thousand years, when all that are related to her are judged at the colossal white throne judgment and cast into the Lake of Fire (Rev 20:11 – Rev 20:15).

4 And the four and twenty seniors and the four mammoths tumbled down and adored God that sat on the throne, saying, Amen; Alleluia.

5 And a voice left the throne, saying, Praise our God, all ye his workers, and ye that trepidation him, both little and extraordinary.

6 And I heard so to speak the voice of an incredible large number, and as the voice of numerous waters, and as the voice of powerful thunderings, saying, Alleluia: for the Lord God supreme reigneth.

At the end of the day, we see the twenty-four seniors and the four mammoths that encompass the throne of God venerating Him, saying "So be it; Alleluia". (On the off chance that the word so be it is utilized before any talk - for this situation the word alleluia - the word so be it signifies "really" or "unquestionably".

In the event that the word were utilized after any talk, the word so be it would signify "so be it" or "even so". The word alleluia signifies "acclaim the Lord". Hence, the words "So be it; Alleluia" in the connection of verse 4 show that the twenty-four older folks say, "genuinely, we applaud you Lord".)

Some surmise that everybody will be equivalent in paradise yet sacred text is clear this is not the situation. Verse 5 demonstrates that there will be little and incredible in paradise thus do different entries. God certainly dependably had a progressive system in paradise and dependably will. Jesus even had an internal circle when he was incarnated on earth.

The large number of billions will thunder like Niagara Falls saying "acclaim ye the Lord for the Lord God Almighty rules." This verse denote the crowning ordinance function of Jesus Christ. Next, we will see that the Lamb takes a wife.

7 Let us be happy and cheer, and offer honor to him: for the marriage of the Lamb is come, and his wife hath made herself prepared.

This verse lets us know the marriage of the Lamb has come to fruition. The spouse of Christ is presently a wife and she is prepared to run with Jesus to earth. The wife is prepared on the grounds that she was enhanced with endowments at the judgment of prizes that occurred in paradise only before this time. It was a period when prizes were given to devotees for how they permitted the Holy Spirit to work in their physical bodies after they were conceived from above.

The blessings are authority positions in the millennial rule - probably they will likewise be administration positions for all endlessness they are discussed in Luke. This section in Luke additionally discusses Jesus' dismissal, His second coming, His judgment of prizes or taking ceaselessly of prizes and His judgment on his foes.

Luke 19:3 And he called his ten workers, and conveyed them ten pounds, and said unto them, Occupy till I come.

14 But his nationals despised him, and communicated something specific after him, saying, We won't have this man to rule over us.

15 And it happened, that when he was returned, having gotten the kingdom, then he charged these workers to be called

unto him, to whom he had given the cash, that he may know how much every man had picked up by exchanging.

16 Then came the primary, saying, Lord, thy pound hath increased ten pounds.

17 And he said unto him, Well, thou great worker: since thou hast been dedicated in a practically nothing, have thou power more than ten urban areas.

18 And the second came, saying, Lord, thy pound hath increased five pounds.

19 And he said in like manner to him, Be thou additionally more than five urban communities.

20 And another came, saying, Lord, observe, here is thy pound, which I have kept laid up in a napkin:

21 For I dreaded thee, on the grounds that thou craftsmanship a somber man: thou takest up that thou layedst not down, and reapest that thou didst not sow.

22 And he saith unto him, Out of thine own mouth will I judge thee, thou insidious hireling. Thou knewest that I was a grave man, taking up that I laid not down, and harvesting that I didn't sow:

23 Wherefore then gavest not thou my cash into the bank, that at my coming I may have required mine own particular with usury?

24 And he said unto them that remained by, Take from him the pound, and offer it to him that hath ten pounds.

25 (And they said unto him, Lord, he hath ten pounds.)

26 For I say unto you, That unto each one which hath should be given; and from him that hath not, even that he hath might be detracted from him.

27 But those mine foes, which would not that I ought to rule over them, bring here, and kill them before me.

All were advised to involve until He comes. Notice the fiendish worker lost his prize to a reliable hireling however those killed were not His shrewd workers. Those killed were His adversaries who might not have Him guideline over them. These are the children of Satan.

8 And to her was allowed that she ought to be exhibited in fine cloth, spotless and white: for the fine material is the nobility of holy people.

Researchers contrast on the significance of the fine material. It could mean the "uprightness of the holy people" (that gets through the blood of Jesus) or the "equitable demonstrations of the holy people" (that gets through the Holy Spirit working in adherents). Both perspectives are right; there was an inward and an external piece of clothing. The white inward article of clothing that is worn was given by Christ when a man was spared however the white external piece of clothing is the equitable deeds that were done through the work of the Holy Spirit. This external piece of clothing in Roman times could be woven with gold and silver string and studded with valuable stones.

Everybody that is a piece of the spouse will have fine cloth underpants given uninhibitedly by Jesus yet not everybody will have the gold silver and valuable stones to show in their external article of clothing. These enhancements will be recompensed at the judgment of prizes and will be founded on how every individual based upon the place of God. The judgment will be about positions of power and administration.

1 Co 3: 12 Now if any man expand upon this establishment gold, silver, valuable stones, wood, roughage, stubble;

13 Every man's work might be made show: for the day should pronounce it, since it might be uncovered by flame; and the fire should attempt each man's work of what sort it is.

14 If any man's work withstand which he hath fabricated immediately, he might get a prize.

15 If any man's work might be blazed, he should endure misfortune: yet he himself should be spared; yet so as by flame.

9 And he saith unto me, Write, Blessed are they which are called unto the marriage dinner of the Lamb. What's more, he saith unto me, These are the genuine idioms of God.

This verse says favored or upbeat are the individuals who are called to the marriage dinner of the Lamb this additionally could be known as the marriage dining experience of Jesus. This is not the marriage; the marriage has officially occurred in paradise before the Father in paradise (preceding verse 7). The marriage dining experience is on earth and has welcomed visitors. These visitors will be the individuals who fled to the mountains at Petra and were ensured by God. It will likewise incorporate every one of the individuals who survived the immense tribulation who did not take the characteristic of the Beast and who did not obstruct God's 144,000 Israelite first natural product brethren that now take after Jesus wherever He goes (Rev 14:4).

10 And I fell at his feet to love him. Also, he said unto me, See thou do it not: I am thy fellow servant, and of thy brethren that have the confirmation of Jesus: love God: for the affirmation of Jesus is the soul of prediction.

John was so awed by the holy messenger that demonstrated to him these things that he tumbled down to love him. Rather than Satan who requests love, the holy messengers of God won't permit anybody to love them. All love is to be coordinated to God. The blessed messenger told John that Jesus is the satisfaction of all God given prediction; revere only him.

11 And I saw paradise opened, and view a white stallion; and he that sat upon him was called Faithful and True, and in uprightness he doth judge and make war.

12 His eyes were as a fire of flame, and on his head were numerous crowns; and he had a name composed, that no man knew, however he himself.

13 And he was dressed with a vesture plunged in blood: and his name is known as The Word of God.

John saw the second happening to Jesus and what will happen to the armed forces that assemble against the Lord at Megiddo. Section 16 let us know every one of the armed forces of the world will be collected at Megiddo against the Lord. At that point part 17 gave us the riddle of the lady that rides the Beast and her obliteration by the Beast. After that section 18 gave us the insights about the demolition of the Beast kingdom called "Babylon the Great". Presently we get again where part 16 left off.

The seventh vial was at that point poured out and obliteration went ahead all urban communities of the world and Babylon was totally devastated. In any case, the Beast and False Prophet were not in Babylon when it was pulverized. They likely escaped town in the maladie of dimness at the fifth vial. The armed forces of the world that obliterated Babylon are cheated by the unclean spirits (evil presences) that leave the mouth of the Dragon, the Beast and the False Prophet (Rev 16:13).

The armed forces from the north and the east move to Megiddo in northern Israel where the Beast and False Prophet have migrated. These unclean sinister spirits persuade the rulers of the considerable number of countries and multitudes of the world to restrict Jesus when He comes.

There ought to be probably about the character of the individual on this white stallion. As opposed to the rider on the white stallion in part six that just wears a solitary victors reef brought in the Greek "stephanos", Jesus comes wearing "numerous" brilliant crowns of sovereignty. The Greek word for crowns utilized here is "diadems".

The Son of God is known by numerous names in the sacred writings yet the name the celebrated Son of God gives Himself when He comes to crush the armed forces of the Beast no man knows. The name of God given to Moses (Jehovah) signifies "the self-existing one" or "I am who I am". The name Jesus Christ essentially signifies "YHWH is the Savior anointed". At the point when the Son of God comes in force, He will have a name composed that He will be called by for endlessness.

His "vesture" is the article of clothing He wore. These garments are presumably "sprinkled in blood", not plunged like this is deciphered. This verse is alluding to Isaiah 63:3 were He treads the winepress alone. This entry likewise gives us another name we do know Him by. He is known as The Word of God. John additionally gives this name for the Son of God in first John 2:14 and in John 1:1 he lets us know the word was God. The individuals who think Jesus is not God ought to rethink their conviction; they are incorrect! Jesus is the living expression of God. Jesus is the main sired picture of God that communicates everything about God that can be appreciated by any being in His own creation.

Joh 1:1 In the starting was the Word, and the Word was with God, and the Word was God.

Joh 1:14 And the Word was made tissue, and abided among us, (and we observed his radiance, the wonderfulness as of the main sired of the Father,) loaded with beauty and truth

Isa 63:1 Who is this that cometh from Edom, with colored pieces of clothing from Bozrah? this that is heavenly in his clothing, going in the enormity of his quality? I that talk in uprightness, compelling to spare.

2 Wherefore workmanship thou red in thine clothing, and thy articles of clothing such as him that treadeth in the winefat?

3 I have trodden the winepress alone; and of the general population there was none with me: for I will tread them in

mine resentment, and trample them in my wrath; and their blood might be sprinkled upon my pieces of clothing, and I will recolor all my attire.

4 For the day of retribution is in mine heart, and the year of my reclaimed is come.

5 And I looked, and there was none to help; and I pondered that there was none to maintain: along these lines mine own particular arm brought salvation unto me; and my fierceness, it maintained me.

6 And I will tread down the general population in mine indignation, and make them plastered in my anger, and I will cut down their quality to the earth.

14 And the armed forces which were in paradise tailed him upon white stallions, dressed in fine material, white and clean.

These armed forces (plural) incorporate every one of the hosts of paradise, the heavenly attendants and all who make up the assemblage of Christ. They all come wearing fine material, white and clean. This demonstrates the greater part of their wrongdoings have been uprooted and they have on the exemplary nature of Christ. All who came rode on white steeds so doubtlessly there are a few indications of creatures in paradise?

Jud 1:14 And Enoch likewise, the seventh from Adam, forecasted of these, saying, Behold, the Lord cometh with ten a great many his holy people,

15 To execute judgment upon all, and to persuade all that are wicked among them of all their profane deeds which they have indecent submitted, and of all their hard addresses which corrupt heathens have talked against him.

15 And out of his mouth goeth a sharp sword, that with it he ought to destroy the countries: and he should principle them

with a bar of iron: and he treadeth the winepress of the wildness and rage of Almighty God.

16 And he hath on his vesture and on his thigh a name composed, KING OF KINGS, AND LORD OF LORDS.

Jesus swore under vow to the devout minister of Israel that He would come in this way however the cleric blamed Him for irreverence.

Mat 26:63 But Jesus held his peace. Also, the devout minister addressed and said unto him, I implore thee by the living God, that thou let us know whether thou be the Christ, the Son of God.

64 Jesus saith unto him, Thou hast said: in any case I say unto you, Hereafter might ye see the Son of man sitting on the right hand of force, and coming in the billows of paradise.

65 Then the esteemed minister lease his garments, saying, He hath talked lewdness; what further need have we of witnesses? view, now ye have heard his sacrilege.

Jesus will destroy the countries by the words that leave His mouth. This is the same being who talked and the universe appeared. When He accompanies His holy people, He will come in anger against every one of the individuals who are against Him, for He is the KINGS OF KINGS, AND LORD OF LORDS. Jesus is coming to earth to overcome His foes and to set up His kingdom on earth. He is coming to satisfy how he instructed us to implore "thy the afterlife thy will be done on earth as it is in paradise" (Mat 6:10).

He is not coming, as some instruct, to take His adherents to some indistinct paradise where all will be one. He is coming to earth to overcome His foes and to build up the Kingdom of God on earth. He will govern amid the seventh thousand years with a bar of iron. The world in that allotment will live under the principle of the Messiah. God's everlasting law will be trailed by their own particular choice on the grounds that the law will be composed in their souls. Jesus came to satisfy the prerequisites of the law for all who broke it yet He didn't come to get rid of the law. The law is interminable and it will be a joy to the spirit when Jesus comes to run the show. One reason the Antichrist and the general population of the world battle against God is that they cherish wilderness.

Psa 2:1 Why do the rapscallion rage, and the general population envision a vain thing?

2 The rulers of the earth set themselves, and the rulers take guide together, against the LORD, and against his anointed, saying,

3 Let us break their groups in two, and cast away their lines from us.

4 He that sitteth in the sky should chuckle: the Lord might have them in ridicule.

5 Then should he talk unto them in his fierceness and vex them in his sore disappointment.

6 Yet have I set my lord upon my heavenly slope of Zion.

7 I will announce the pronouncement: the LORD hath said unto me, Thou craftsmanship my Son; this day have I conceived thee.

8 Ask of me, and I might give thee the rapscallion for thine legacy, and the furthest parts of the earth for thy ownership.

9 Thou shalt break them with a bar of iron; thou shalt dash them in pieces such as a potter's vessel.

10 Be insightful now hence, O ye lords: be told, ye judges of the earth.

11 Serve the LORD with apprehension, and celebrate with trembling.

12 Kiss the Son, keeping in mind that he be furious, and ye die from the way, when his fierceness is encouraged however a bit. Favored are all they that put their trust in him.

17 And I saw a blessed messenger remaining in the sun; and he cried with an uproarious voice, saying to every one of the fowls that fly amidst paradise, Come and accumulate yourselves together unto the dinner of the immense God;

18 That ye might eat the substance of rulers, and the tissue of commanders, and the tissue of compelling men, and the tissue of steeds, and of them that sit on them, and the tissue of all men, both free and bond, both little and incredible.

19 And I saw the monster, and the rulers of the earth, and their armed forces, assembled to make war against him that sat on the steed, and against his armed force.

This is the great skirmish of Armageddon. It happens after the obliteration of "Babylon the Great" that occurred at the overflowing of the seventh vial. This truly is not a fight by any means. It is a butcher of the greater part of the adversaries of God on earth.

Every one of the armed forces of the world are assembled against Jesus and His holy people by Satan and by his lying spirits. The armed forces accumulated by Satan will all end up being nourishment for the vultures. Lying spirits leave the mouths of the Dragon, the Beast and the False Prophet to bamboozle the entire world and the armed forces that crush Babylon. These lying spirits by one means or another persuade the rulers of the earth to move every one of their armed forces against Jerusalem. The genuine inquiry is the reason would the world set out to battle against the God of paradise?

The answer may be that the lying spirits by one means or another figure out how to persuade the rulers of the earth that the God of Heaven is not God-like and can likewise be ceased from setting up His kingdom on earth by enough military power (such as the fake kingdom of god at Babylon was at any rate halfway toppled by common military power). At the point when these armed forces battle against the Kingdom of the genuine God of creation they will all go to their annihilation.

This persuades when Satan is thrown out of paradise he truly means to wreck the whole human race so Jesus will have nobody alive for His Kingdom. Disclosure 12:12 says he "descends in incredible fierceness knowing his time is short". Why then does Satan much try to play God and to set up the kingdom of the Beast? Clearly in the event that he knows his time is short he additionally knows he will be vanquished.

The fake kingdom of god called "Babylon the Great" evidently is just a façade utilized by Satan to realize the annihilation of humankind. Indeed, even after the decimation of the fake kingdom that Satan set up and realized that God would crush, Satan misleads every one of the armed forces of the world to move against Jerusalem where he additionally realizes that they unquestionably will be wrecked.

Jesus implied this arrangement by Satan to devastate humanity when he said unless He abbreviated the times of annihilation brought about by Satan no tissue would be saved money on earth.

Mat 24:22 And with the exception of those days ought to be abbreviated, there ought to no substance be spared: however for the chose's purpose those days should be abbreviated.

The accompanying section in Joel portrays the invitation to battle for this war against God:

Jol 3:9 Proclaim ye this among the Gentiles; Prepare war, wake up the powerful men, let every one of the men of war draw close; let them come up:

10 Beat your plowshares into swords, and your pruninghooks into lances: let the feeble say, I am solid.

11 Assemble yourselves, and come, all ye pagan, and accumulate yourselves together circuitous: thither cause thy relentless ones to descend, O LORD.

12 Let the pagan be wakened, and come up to the valley of Jehoshaphat: for there will I sit to judge all the rapscallion indirect.

13 Put ye in the sickle, for the harvest is ready: come, get you down; for the press is full, the fats flood; for their underhandedness is awesome.

14 Multitudes, hoards in the valley of choice: for the day of the LORD is close in the valley of choice.

15 The sun and the moon might be obscured, and the stars should pull back their sparkling.

16 The LORD likewise might thunder out of Zion, and utter his voice from Jerusalem; and the sky and the earth should shake: yet the LORD will be the trust of his kin, and the quality of the offspring of Israel.

17 So might ye realize that I am the LORD your God abiding in Zion, my blessed mountain: then should Jerusalem be sacred, and there might no outsiders go through her anymore.

20 And the brute was taken, and with him the false prophet that created marvels before him, with which he swindled them that had gotten the sign of the mammoth, and them that loved his picture. These both were thrown alive into a pool of flame blazing with brimstone.

21 And the leftover were killed with the sword of him that sat upon the steed, which sword continued out of his mouth: and every one of the fowls were loaded with their tissue.

The Antichrist Beast and his False Prophet, who worked supernatural occurrences by the force of Satan and betrayed all who took the sign of the Beast and those that loved his picture, are taken hostage. Pretty much as Satan misled and took 33% of the holy messengers in his disobedience to God, Satan in the Beast and False Prophet will hoodwink and take an extensive number of people in this defiance to God. Those that tail him don't need the Son of God to manage over them. Notice, there is no genuine resistance against the genuine God of creation. The armed forces are assembled for butcher since every one of the powers of Satan and man are no match against the God of creation. I am certain Satan knows this yet he detests humankind and God so much that he plans to convey mankind to aggregate decimation.

The Beast and False Prophet are judged by Jesus and they are thrown alive into the Lake of Fire. In the following part we will discover that they are still alive in the Lake of Fire over a thousand years after the fact. There is no non-presence of souls taught in the Bible. Either one goes into the new creation for forever or the Lake of Fire for time everlasting. This truth ought to wind up evident when we read the following part (which happens after the thousand-year rule of Christ). After the judgment there we will see that the Beast and False Prophet are still "alive" in the Lake of Fire when Satan, Satan's blessed messengers and every one of those that are not composed in the Lamb's book of life are additionally thrown into the Lake of Fire. The Lake of Fire is the place all will go that reject the God who made them.

Every one of the armed forces that took after the Beast and False prophet will be slaughtered and their substance will encourage the flying creatures. Flying creatures of prey today are secured in Israel and they are even given nourishment to build their numbers. Awesome quantities of these feathered creatures can be seen flying in the mountains of Israel. They have turned into a vacation destination and obviously that is the principle motivation behind why they are ensured and nourished however God has an incredible dinner gotten ready for these winged creatures sooner rather than later. They will satisfy the end time prediction of verse 17.

Around then the accompanying Old Testament prescience of Isaiah will be satisfied:

Isa 13: 1 The weight of Babylon, which Isaiah the child of Amoz did see.

2 Lift ye up a standard upon the high mountain, magnify the voice unto them, shake the hand, that they might go into the entryways of the nobles.

3 I have charged my blessed ones, I have additionally called my compelling ones for mine resentment, even them that cheer in my Excellency.

4 The clamor of a huge number in the mountains, as starting an incredible individual; a tumultuous commotion of the kingdoms of countries assembled: the LORD of hosts mustereth the host of the fight.

5 They originate from a far nation, from the end of paradise, even the LORD, and the weapons of his ire, to devastate the entire area.

6 Howl ye; for the day of the LORD is close by; it might come as an obliteration from the Almighty.

7 Therefore might all hands be black out, and each man's heart should melt:

8 And they should be anxious: strings and distresses might grab hold of them; they might be in agony as a lady that travaileth: they might be stunned one at another; their appearances should be as blazes.

9 Behold, the day of the LORD cometh, barbarous both with fury and wild outrage, to lay the area forsaken: and he might obliterate the miscreants thereof out of it.

10 For the stars of paradise and the heavenly bodies thereof might not give their light: the sun should be obscured in his going forward, and the moon should not bring about her light to sparkle.

11 And I will rebuff the world for their malevolence, and the underhanded for their evildoing; and I will bring about the arrogancy of the glad to stop, and will hide out the haughtiness of the repulsive.

12 I will make a man a bigger number of valuable than fine gold; even a man than the brilliant wedge of Ophir.

13 Therefore I will shake the sky, and the earth might uproot out of her place, in the rage of the LORD of hosts, and in the day of his savage annoyance.

14 And it might be as the pursued roe, and as a sheep that no man taketh up: they should each man swing to his own kin, and escape each one into his own particular area.

15 Every one that is found might be pushed through; and each one that is joined unto them should fall by the sword.

16 Their youngsters likewise might be dashed to pieces before their eyes; their homes should be ruined, and their wives violated.

17 Behold, I will blend up the Medes against them, which might not respect silver; and concerning gold, they should not savor the experience of it.

18 Their bows additionally should dash the young fellows to pieces; and they might have no compassion on the product of the womb; their eye should not save kids.

19 And Babylon, the wonderfulness of kingdoms, the magnificence of the Chaldees' excellency, might be as when God toppled Sodom and Gomorrah.

20 It should never be occupied, neither might it be abided in from era to era: neither should the Arabian set up portable shelter there; neither should the shepherds make their fold there.

21 But wild brutes of the desert should lie there; and their homes might be loaded with doleful animals; and owls should stay there, and satyrs should move there.

22 And the wild brutes of the islands should cry in their ruined houses, and mythical serpents in their charming castles: and her time is close to come, and her days might not be delayed.

Isa 14: 1 For the LORD will show leniency toward Jacob, and will yet pick Israel, and set them in their own particular area: and the outsiders might be joined with them, and they should sever to the place of Jacob.

2 And the general population should take them, and convey them to their place: and the place of Israel might have them in the place where there is the LORD for workers and handmaids: and they should take them hostages, whose prisoners they were; and they should standard over their oppressors.

3 And it might happen in the day that the LORD should give thee rest from thy distress, and from thy dread, and from the hard subjugation wherein thou wast made to serve,

4 That thou shalt take up this precept against the ruler of Babylon, and say, How hath the oppressor stopped! the brilliant city stopped!

5 The LORD hath broken the staff of the underhanded, and the staff of the rulers.

6 He who destroyed the general population in fierceness with a ceaseless stroke, he that led the countries in annoyance, is oppressed, and none hindereth.

7 The entire earth is very still, and is tranquil: they break forward into singing.

8 Yea, the fir trees celebrate at thee, and the cedars of Lebanon, saying, Since thou craftsman up against us.

9 Hell from underneath is moved for thee to meet thee at thy coming: it stirreth up the dead for thee, even all the boss ones of the earth; it hath raised up from their thrones every one of the rulers of the countries.

10 All they should talk and say unto thee, Art thou additionally get to be feeble as we? craftsmanship thou get to be similar to unto us?

11 Thy pageantry is conveyed down to the grave, and the commotion of thy viols: the worm is spread under thee, and the worms spread thee.

12 How craftsmanship thou tumbled from paradise, O Lucifer, child of the morning! how craftsmanship thou chop down to the ground, which didst debilitate the countries!

13 For thou hast said in thine heart, I will rise into paradise, I will lift up my throne over the stars of God: I will sit additionally upon the mount of the assemblage, in the sides of the north:

14 I will climb over the statures of the mists; I will be similar to the most High.

15 Yet thou shalt be conveyed down to hellfire, to the sides of the pit.

16 They that see thee might barely look upon thee, and consider thee, saying, Is this the man that made the earth to tremble, that did shake kingdoms;

17 That made the world as a wild, and decimated the urban areas thereof; that opened not the place of his detainees?

18 All the rulers of the countries, even every one of them, lie in wonderfulness, each one in his own home.

19 But thou craftsmanship cast out of thy grave like a loathsome branch, and as the clothing of those that are killed, pushed through with a sword, that go down to the stones of the pit; as a carcase trodden under feet.

20 Thou shalt not be joined with them in internment, since thou hast devastated thy land, and killed thy individuals: the seed of scoundrels might never be famous.

21 Prepare butcher for his youngsters for the wrongdoing of their fathers; that they don't rise, nor have the area, nor fill the substance of the world with urban communities.

22 For I will ascend against them, saith the LORD of hosts, and cut off from Babylon the name, and remainder, and child, and nephew, saith the LORD.

23 I will likewise make it an ownership for the bittern, and pools of water: and I will clear it with the besom of devastation, saith the LORD of hosts.

24 The LORD of hosts hath sworn, saying, Surely as I have thought, so might it happen; and as I have purposed, so should it stand:

25 That I will soften the Assyrian up my property, and upon my mountains tread him on the ground: then might his yoke withdraw from off them, and his weight leave from off their shoulders.

26 This is the reason that is purposed upon the entire earth: and this is the hand that is extended upon every one of the countries.

27 For the LORD of hosts hath purposed, and who might disannul it? furthermore, his hand is extended, and who should turn it back?

This entry in Isaiah is a rundown of the occasions that will happen in the day of the Lord. It will happen as He forecasted. Give all you who a chance to allegorize and who put profound implications on prophetic sacred writing in Revelation attempt to do that with what Isaiah said. It isn't possible; your Eschatology is all off-base. All some of you can say is that every one of these things as of now happened in the past and that is much more ludicrous.

The powers of Satan talked about here, that convey obliteration to the entire earth, will be managed by Jesus. The Beast and the False Prophet that keep out Satan's arrangement won't run a secret forever with their predecessors however will be thrown alive into the Lake of Fire.

Rev 19:20 And the brute was taken, and with him the false prophet that created supernatural occurrences before him, with which he cheated them that had gotten the characteristic of the monster, and them that adored his picture. These both were thrown alive into a pool of flame, a lake of fire burning with brimstone.

CHAPTER 20

The Dead Ascent, Satan Is Judged

1 And I saw a holy messenger descend from paradise, having the key of the no-limit pit and an extraordinary chain in his grasp.

2 And he laid hang on the mythical beast, that old serpent, which is the Devil, and Satan, and bound him a thousand years,

Satan is binded by a heavenly attendant and is bound in the no-limit pit for a thousand years. The unlimited pit is the spot where the Beast Antichrist rose from at some point after the holy messenger with the key opened it. The unlimited pit is by all accounts a measurement where abhorrent spirits are briefly detained. As of now, Satan is thrown into the endless pit and fastened so he can't rise out of it and delude the countries amid the thousand-year rule of Christ on earth are finished.

Those in the philosophy of a millennialism say that Satan has been bound amid the whole Church age. They are not appropriately perceiving numerous sacred writings that show that Satan has not been bound on earth or even in the lives of the individuals who relate to Christianity. Truth be told, the sacred writing calls Satan the divine force of this age and the ruler of the force of the air. Beyond any doubt Satan does not have control over any genuine adherent, but rather just if that individual is strolling in the Spirit. The pitiful story we see on earth through the regulation of beauty to the Gentiles since the cross makes it clear that the Devil is not yet bound and does not get to be bound until this time.

The sacred writings demonstrate that Satan has the ability to pulverize fragile living creature and to prevent and cheat devotees. Dwindle urges Christians to oppose him. Moreover, sacred text says that one is originating from Satan who will have all force and signs and lying ponders. This book lets us know that Satan has a throne and a synagogue on earth. By the investigation of sacred text and by taking a gander at world conditions it ought to be clear to anybody that Satan is not bound in the Church age and is going about as a thundering lion looking for whom he might eat up.

1Pe 5:8 Be calm, be cautious; in light of the fact that your foe the fallen angel, as a thundering lion, walketh about, looking for whom he might eat up:

3. Also, cast him into the endless pit, and quiets him down, and set a seal upon him, that he ought to betray the countries no more, till the thousand years ought to be satisfied: and after that he should be loosed a little season.

After the thousand-year rule of Jesus on earth, Satan will be permitted to come up out of the unlimited pit. He by and by will bamboozle the countries. We may ask why? The answer is to test every one of the billions who were conceived amid the thousand years.

In each of the former agreements, man was tried and those living either were spared "by confidence" or they kicked the bucket in unbelief. In all regulations of time, man must be spared "by confidence" in the Savior God alone. In this last administration, man will be living under perfect conditions on earth and even passing will be vanquished yet when Satan is discharged, a lot of humankind will be swindled in much the same conditions as when Adam and Eve were beguiled. This last misleading will isolate those that are living "by confidence" from those living in dismay.

The last adversary to be crushed by Jesus will be passing. My guess is that when man sees he will no more beyond words, will be totally open to the same trickiness that Adam and Eve fell for in the greenery enclosure. Satan will leave the no-limit pit and as he did with our guardians before us, he will delude the countries by saying "you should not kick the bucket you have ended up like God knowing great and malice".

At the end of the day, since we know great and wickedness everybody ought to have the capacity to make the wisest decision in his own particular eyes. Despite the fact that Adam and Eve were made everlasting creatures, they did bite the dust thus will those that partake in this last defiance. Humankind's first resistance prompted passing of the body. Humankind's last resistance will bring about death of his spirit when man by his defiance, unbelief and absence of trust in the Creator, is isolated from the Creator for endlessness.

4 And I saw thrones, and they sat upon them, and judgment was given unto them: and I saw the souls of them that were decapitated for the witness of Jesus, and for the expression of God, and which had not adored the brute, neither one of the hises picture, neither had gotten his imprint upon their brows, or in their grasp; and they lived and ruled with Christ a thousand years.

5 But whatever remains of the dead lived not again until the thousand years were done. This is the principal restoration.

This section is discussing the restoration of the tribulation holy people. It says that all who participate in this first restoration will live and lead with Christ through the thousand-year period. The section demonstrates that the individuals who pass on and who are not brought up in the primary restoration won't live again until after the thousand years are done. This section says six times that the time of the Lord's Kingdom on earth is a thousand years. The amillennial religious philosophy that says this period is an obscure timeframe is past basic reason. The principle of the holy people for this thousand-year period begins toward the end of the immense tribulation.

6 Blessed and sacred is he that hath part in the primary revival: on such the second demise hath no force, yet they might be ministers of God and of Christ, and should rule with him a thousand years.

The second demise will have no force on those that participate in the principal revival since they make up the assortment of Christ and they have as of now been raised to unceasing existence with Jesus. Once more, this verse says they will control with Him as ministers to God and the rule will be a thousand years.

7 And when the thousand years are lapsed, Satan should be loosed out of his jail,

8 And might go out to swindle the countries which are in the four quarters of the earth, Gog and Magog, to assemble them together to fight: the quantity of whom is as the sand of the ocean.

At the point when the thousand years are over, Satan will be loosed out of the jail to bamboozle the countries (ethnic gatherings) to accumulate them together to fight. Some think this is the war of Ezekiel parts 38 and 39 due to Gog and Magog being said. It can't be for some reasons. One reason is that after the war of Ezekiel 38 and 39 individuals are covered and weapons are smoldered. Be that as it may, when these come against the camp of the holy people they are devoured by flame. Quickly thereafter, the white throne judgment happens in paradise.

Relatives of the tribes of Gog and Magog might be the most unmistakable on the earth around then or God might simply name areas on the earth after these conspicuous tribes. Gog and

Magog might simply be another method for saying close and far, or north and south or something comparable.

Notice the number is as the sand of the ocean. Obviously, under the close impeccable conditions on earth amid the thousand-year rule, a bigger number of billions will be conceived than in all times of the earth set up together. The former six thousand years on earth were essentially to set up an administration of rulers and clerics for this holiday millennial age. The rulers and ministers will control over the colossal harvest of souls that God proposed when He advised Adam to be productive and increase and quell the earth.

9 And they went up on the broadness of the earth, and compassed the camp of the holy people about, and the darling city: and flame descended from God out of paradise, and ate up them.

The Kingdom of Jesus will keep going forever as indicated by sacred writing yet Satan clearly has beguiled these into imagining that since the millennial rule is finished, that God is finished with standard from Jerusalem by the holy people. It is a wrong presumption.

A few researchers feel that most in the assortment of Christ amid this thousand-year period won't live on earth yet will very in the Holy City that is in paradise. Like the blessed messengers of Jacob's stepping stool, they might be rising and diving from the Holy City to do their assignments (Gen 28:12). I surmise that is right since every single spared people couldn't fit in the territory of Israel allocated.

After death is vanquished and the thousand years, it is my guess that Christ will present the kingdom to the Father (1Co 15:24) and pull back to the Holy City where His lady is. Thusly, Jesus will leave the issues of the kingdom on earth to the common holy people that govern on earth in Israel. Satan will see this as a chance to again betray the world as he did Adam and Eve. Satan couldn't climb out of the pit and beguile the world the length of Jesus was administering on the earth in any case. God will give Satan enough rope to hang himself and this he will do.

The evacuation of the organization over the earth by those in the profound assortment of Christ will permit Satan to rise out of the pit and to betray the world with the same falsehood he hinted in the Garden of Eden that man would get to be similar to God. Presently he will say that they have accomplished it. The earth amid the thousand years gets to be similar to the Garden of Eden and normal passing will even be won.

The arrival of this lying soul on the earth will persuade numerous that since death has been vanquished, they no more need to submit to God's holy people administering from Jerusalem and they will come against them. Numerous on the planet will defy this administration in Israel and try to live as divine forces of their own spirit. At the point when the world is tricked to come against the camps of Israel to oust the holy person's guideline on earth, flame will descend from paradise from God and eat up every one of them.

10 and the fiend that betrayed them was thrown into the pool of flame and brimstone, where the mammoth and the false prophet are, and might be tormented day and night for ever and ever.

Not just are those that oppose Israel ate up yet this occasion denote the judgment of the Devil. He for the last time has betrayed the world. This time the world is hoodwinked specifically by him and not by men controlled by his soul. The Devil is thrown into the pool of flame where the Beast and False Prophet still are after over a thousand years. They will all be tormented day and night in the Lake of Fire forever and ever. By the way, the scripture says the Lake of Fire was actually created for the Devil and his angels (Mat 25:41).

11 And I saw an incredible white throne, and him that sat on it, from whose face the earth and the paradise fled away; and there was found no spot for them.

The white throne is the last judgment seat of God. While the judgment is continuous, the section would appear to demonstrate that the earth and paradise escape away. The earth won't not be obvious in this neutron bomb like brilliance originating from the substance of God. This might be something like a supernova yet it will start from the substance of God and the light will uncover all obscurity in the whole universe. Different entries demonstrate the earth will exist everlastingly, so I don't think the earth really is wrecked. Notwithstanding, it might be moved to a more ideal area or circle around the sun.

The announcement that no spot was found for them can likewise be clarified. For instance, if the sun itself had a nova there could be such a development of the sun and its splendor that one watching would not see the earth circling around the sun. In any case, novas don't keep going long. After the sun settled down the onlooker would see another paradise and another earth recharged by flame.

This occasion might be more noteworthy than a nova; it might be the substance of God. I don't expect anything characteristic will be noticeable while the splendor of God's face sparkles and His judgment happens with all creation being inspected in His own particular awesome light. All that can remain in the light will remain in a cleaned reestablished creation that will be as it was before the fall of heavenly attendants and man. The environment and the earth as of now will be reestablished by flame (2Pe 3:10). John tells about the new paradise and earth reestablished by this flame in the following section.

12 And I saw the dead, little and extraordinary, stand before God; and the books were opened: and another book was opened, which is the book of life: and the dead were judged out of those things which were composed in the books, as per their works.

The Bible does not show demolition or non-presence. Those ate up by flame from paradise and all who passed on in the past and whom did not ascend in the principal restoration will ascend in this second revival. Those in the main revival won't need to face this dreadful judgment since they put on the exemplary nature of Christ. In the second restoration, all who did not participate in the first will remain before God at what is ordinarily called the "Incomparable White Throne Judgment". Every concealed thing will be inspected in the genuine light. There was a judgment of prizes at the judgment seat of Christ on every one of the individuals who ascended in the main revival. In this second restoration, there will be diverse degrees of discipline for all that are judged in the light of His ideal law as indicated by their works.

13 And the ocean surrendered the dead which were in it; and demise and hellfire conveyed up the dead which were in them: and they were judged each man as indicated by their works.

14 And demise and hellfire were thrown into the pool of flame. This is the second passing.

15 And whosoever was not discovered written in the book of life was thrown into the pool of flame.

Everybody is judged and whoever is not discovered written in the book of life is thrown into the pool of flame, and demise and damnation were additionally thrown into the Lake of Fire. The Lake of Fire is the second demise. After the judgment, passing and hellfire (the makeshift home the dead) are themselves thrown into the Lake of Fire.

These things will never again be found in God's new creation. Verse 15 makes it clear that all who are not discovered written in the book of life will be thrown into the Lake of Fire until the end of time. Similarly as those in His new creation are concerned, those in the Lake of Fire will no more exist or even ring a bell however for those home in the Lake of Fire will exist for time everlasting in their fallen condition with no trust of partnership with God. This is the thing that Jesus cautioned individuals about when He cautioned:

Mat 10:28 And trepidation not them which execute the body, but rather are not ready to slaughter the spirit: yet rather fear him which can crush both soul and body in damnation.

Mat 16:26 For what is a man benefitted, on the off chance that he should pick up the entire world, and lose his own spirit? on the other hand what might a man give in return for his spirit?

CHAPTER 21

Another Paradise and Earth

1 And I saw another paradise and another earth: for the principal paradise and the main earth were passed away; and there was no more ocean.

At the time revival and the judgment, John likewise sees another paradise and another earth. This is still the same planet since sacred text says in a few sections that the earth is without end. The Greek word utilized for "passed away" can likewise be utilized for changing starting with one condition then onto the next. The earth and all creation were totally redesigned by flame.

Eph 3:21 Unto him be greatness in the Church by Christ Jesus all through all ages, world without end. So be it.

Psa 78:69 And he manufactured his haven like high castles, similar to the earth which he hath built up for ever.

Ecc 1:4 One era passeth away, and another era cometh: yet the earth abideth for ever

As the earth and its air were changed by water amid the season of Noah, the earth and air will be remodeled by flame before its unceasing state. The verse says there was no more ocean. This might simply mean no more Mediterranean ocean, or it could imply that there will again be stand out mainland on the earth and the seas will be outside of the landmass such as they were before the earth was partitioned in the times of Peleg

(1Ch 1:19). The sacred writings say the earth will dependably have seedtime and harvest and for this to happen seas are liable to be required (Gen 8:22). Obviously I could not be right.

2Pe 3:12 Looking for and scurrying unto the happening to the day of God, wherein the sky being ablaze should be broken down, and the components might liquefy with intense warmth?

13 Nevertheless we, as indicated by his guarantee, search for new sky and another earth, wherein dwelleth exemplary nature.

2 And I John saw the blessed city, new Jerusalem, descending from God out of paradise, readied as a spouse enhanced for her spouse.

Numerous individuals get befuddled on this entry since they translate the section by the figurative philosophy they have been taught. They assume that in light of the fact that New Jerusalem is readied as a lady for her spouse that New Jerusalem is the Church. No place in sacred text does it say that the city of New Jerusalem is the Church or the lady. Notwithstanding, the spouse of Christ will be residents that possess New Jerusalem in light of the fact that New Jerusalem is the unceasing residence of the Lamb's wife.

Jon 14:2 In my Father's home are numerous manors: in the event that it were not really, I would have let you know. I go to set up a spot for you.

3 And on the off chance that I go and set up a spot for you, I will come back once more, and get you unto myself; that where I am, there ye might be too.

The Passage says the Holy City descends from paradise as a lady embellished for her spouse. The spouse is not Jesus. In the event that there really is a spouse, it is the general population on the new earth however the entry is likely only a metaphor for what John saw drawing nearer the earth.

To comprehend the entry one should seriously think about some guess that is not specifically taught in sacred writing. It is not physically feasible for the billions in the Body of Christ to stay in Israel. The holy people will live in the Holy City circling over the earth or in the third paradise and they will rise and slide from it on task. Jacob had a fantasy vision where he saw blessed messengers climbing and dropping upon the earth from paradise. In the time of the thousand-year rule, the eternal spared individuals will be climbing and sliding to and from the Holy City.

Gen 28:12 And he imagined, and observe a stepping stool set up on the earth, and the highest point of it came to paradise: and see the holy messengers of God rising and descending on it.

After the new paradise and earth are made, the Holy City takes circle over the earth in seeing the individuals who harp on the earth. The city is so wonderful it is said to come in appearance as a spouse decorated for her spouse. She will be a lovely perfect city made by God. The city presumably won't really lay on the earth as a result of her tremendous size. The laws of material science make that amazingly impossible.

3. And I heard an extraordinary voice out of paradise saying, Behold, the sanctuary of God is with men, and he will abide with them, and they should be his kin, and God himself might be with them, and be their God.

Up until this point God had his own particular sanctuary in the third paradise yet now it says the sanctuary of God is with men. All humankind in the new creation will be indwelt by the Holy Spirit of God and His city will be noticeable in His creation.

4 And God might wipe away all tears from their eyes; and there should be no more demise, neither distress, nor crying, neither might there be any more torment: for the previous things are passed away.

There will be no more demise or distress on the new earth in light of the fact that the previous things have passed away. The previous things were the old creation and every one of the individuals who defiled it by transgressing God's heavenly law. All creation will be recovered back to the way God made it before Satan, his heavenly attendants and fallen man debased it.

5 And he that sat upon the throne said, Behold, I make all things new. Furthermore, he said unto me, Write: for these words are genuine and dedicated.

The individual that sits upon the throne and that makes all things new is Jesus. He is the maker. He didn't commit an error with His unique creation. He will recover creation back to the way He made it with the expansion of the enhancement of the Holy City and the lady who possesses it.

6 And he said unto me, It is finished. I am Alpha and Omega, the starting and the end. I will give unto him that is athirst of the wellspring of the water of life unreservedly.

From former entries in this book, we see that Jesus utilizes the title Alpha and Omega for Himself. Jesus makes it clear that the water of life He gives is a free present for any individual who is anxious for it.

7 He that overcometh should acquire all things; and I will be his God, and he might be my child.

The sacred texts make it clear that we overcome by being washed in the blood of the Lamb. All who acknowledge the making up penance of Jesus on the cross for absolution of their wrongdoings and beverage the living water that originates from Jesus will turn into the children of God and acquire every one of the things of God. In the event that one acquires all things, it would prohibit nothing given.

8 But the frightful, and unbelieving, and the odious, and killers, and whoremongers, and magicians, and worshipers of

another god, and all liars, should have their part in the lake which burneth with flame and brimstone: which is the second demise.

At the end of the day, the individuals who don't come to Jesus for pardoning will hold their wrongdoings. Subsequently, they will have their part in the Lake of Fire. Being thrown in the Lake of Fire is the second demise. (The principal passing is demise of the assortment of tissue.) I asked why it said the dreadful would get this destiny with whatever is left of these characters, until I comprehended that it is discussing those that dreaded the demise of the body more than the demise of the spirit such as those that got the characteristic of the Beast to spare their physical lives.

9 And there came unto me one of the seven heavenly attendants which had the seven vials brimming with the seven last torment, and chatted with me, saying, Come here, I will shew thee the lady, the Lamb's wife.

One of the seven holy messengers is going to take John to see the lady of Christ. Some are befuddled by this in light of the fact that after the heavenly attendant advises John he will take him to see the spouse we see the structures of the Holy City depicted. They then hop to the conclusion that the Holy City is some magical similitude portraying the group of Christ. Trusting that John saw the Church as a structure by this announcement, is equivalent to me saying I will take you to see the French and when we land in Paris you see the structures of Paris and after that trust the structures are French.

John can really see the spouse inside of the structure of the city in light of the fact that the dividers of the city are totally obvious. Indeed, the entire city is straightforward. There is nothing to stow away. It ought not astonish to anybody that the Holy City would be made to mirror the excellence of the spouse of Christ. The city was made to be an interminable remembrance of God's work in His kin.

This city really was made before the establishments of the world however Jesus is the person who set it up for the entry of His lady. The real lady is the general population that are unified with Jesus inside of the city. There dependably has been one habitation God in paradise and one Holy City. God has possessed it following the time when He made it. This is the Father's home that Jesus discussed; it is the place Jesus originated from and it is the place He followed He became alive once again. Jesus said in His Father's home are numerous residences and that He will go and set up a spot for adherents with the goal that they can be the place He is.

Joh 14:2 In my Father's home are numerous houses: in the event that it were not really, I would have let you know. I go to set up a spot for you.

3 And in the event that I go and set up a spot for you, I will come back once more, and get you unto myself; that where I am, there ye might be too.

This is the city that Jesus arranged for His lady. New Jerusalem is the city of God enhanced for the Lamb's wife, the general population of confidence and the guarantee. This is the same city that Abraham the father surprisingly of confidence anticipated that would discover (Heb 11:10). Jesus set it up by composing names of the messengers on the establishments and the tribes of Israel on the entryways and by enhancing it with each sort of magnificence, which reflects God in her. The names composed on her foundational dividers and on her doors are names of twenty-four Israelites, so it ought to be clear that the whole district of Israel stays in the Holy City and not only the Church since Pentecost.

10 And he diverted me in the soul to an extraordinary and high mountain, and shewed me that incredible city, the sacred Jerusalem, sliding out of paradise from God, John is conveyed in the soul to an extraordinary and high mountain he could have even been taken to the moon. He was presumably some place

in space so he could get an unhindered perspective of this city leaving the second or third paradise toward the earth. The Holy City will be a great thing to see. It doesn't say the heavenly city will really touch the earth. It may very well stay in circle. From the earth, it might resemble a jeweled moon in the sky. It might cast diverse hues and light shows on the earth from the light inside of her and from the light reflected or refracted from the sun and moon through her twelve foundational hues that are studded with a wide range of valuable stones.

11 Having the magnificence of God: and her light was similar to unto a stone most valuable, even like a jasper stone, totally obvious;

12 And had a divider awesome and high, and had twelve entryways, and at the doors twelve blessed messengers, and names composed subsequently, which are the names of the twelve tribes of the offspring of Israel:

13 On the east three doors; on the north three entryways; on the south three entryways; and on the west three doors.

14 And the mass of the city had twelve establishments, and in them the names of the twelve missionaries of the Lamb.

Some like to make this structure the spouse of Christ yet what is being portrayed is a city of awesome magnificence that mirrors the excellence of the recovered of the district of Israel inside of her. John was taking a gander at this city and depicting what he saw. The city is of heavenly outline. The names of the twelve tribes of Israel are composed on the entryways and the names of the twelve messengers are composed on the twelve establishments. No place does it say that the entryways and establishments are really those twenty-four men. The entryways of the city will be a confirmation always that salvation is through the Jews. This is the thing that Jesus told the lady at the well.

Joh 4:22 Ye venerate ye know not what: we realize what we love: for salvation is of the Jews.

23 But the hour cometh, and now is, the point at which the genuine admirers should revere the Father in soul and in truth: for the Father seeketh such to love him.

24 God is a Spirit: and they that love him must love him in soul and in truth.

The entrance to the city is just through the entryways of Israel; holy messengers secure the doors (not St. Diminish). The names on the establishments let us know that the spared in the city live on the teachings laid by the messengers. The city has three doors on every side and is four square in configuration.

The foursquare plan talks about God's incarnation on earth as Messiah, Servant, Man, and Son of God. We additionally see this in the four animals that encompass His throne that have a face of a Lion, Ox, Man and Eagle. Indeed, even the four accounts of his stay on earth are composed to mirror this truth. Matthew's accentuation is that Jesus is the Messiah, the Lion from the tribe of Judah (Lion); Mark's accentuation is that Jesus came as a misery worker (bull); Luke's accentuation talks about Jesus coming as the child of (man); and John's accentuation recounts Jesus' magnificent source (falcon).

15 And he that conversed with me had a brilliant reed to quantify the city, and the doors thereof, and the divider thereof.

16 And the city lieth foursquare, and the length is as expansive as the expansiveness: and he quantified the city with the reed, twelve thousand furlongs. The length and the broadness and the tallness of it are equivalent.

The Holy City is enormous! It is 12,000 furlongs or roughly 1,500 miles long, width and stature. With this portrayal, the Holy City either must be a block or a pyramid. I incline toward it being pyramid fit as a fiddle and I would not rebate the likelihood that the Great Pyramid of Egypt was a scale model of what was once found in paradise or portrayed as being in paradise. The first Great Pyramid had an external covering that reflected light. This covering has been looted so the pyramid does not look as superb as it once did. In the event that this pyramid is a scale model of the Holy City, it was a model of the city before it was embellished for the Lamb's wife.

The physical measurements of the city itself decides out any thought that what is being portrayed is the magical assortment of Christ. Those that hold the religious philosophy that the Holy City itself is the assemblage of Christ appear to be stating that the individuals who live in this city have turned out to be a piece of a spatial structure – something like the Borg did in the Star Trek arrangement. The part these scholars appear to show that we have in paradise is to be stuck in a structure for forever playing our harps while consistently commending God for staying us in the dividers. Some paradise! No big surprise those stuck in the seats of such houses of worship have little inspiration to accept and trust God for salvation so they can go to the wonderful city.

17 And he gauged the divider thereof, a hundred and forty and four cubits, as indicated by the measure of a man, that is, of the blessed messenger.

18 And the working of the mass of it was of jasper: and the city was unadulterated gold, as unto clear glass.

19 And the establishments of the mass of the city were embellished with all way of valuable stones. The principal establishment was jasper; the second, sapphire; the third, a chalcedony; the fourth, an emerald;

20 The fifth, sardonyx; the 6th, sardius; the seventh, chrysolite; the eighth, beryl; the ninth, a topaz; the tenth, a chrysoprasus; the eleventh, a jacinth; the twelfth, an amethyst.

21 And the twelve entryways were twelve pearls; each few door was of one pearl: and the road of the city was immaculate gold, so to speak straightforward glass.

John gives further portrayal of the blessed city. It is amazing in magnificence. There are twelve establishment shades of gems and the establishments themselves are embellished with a wide range of valuable stones. The city itself is made of clear gold glass precious stone as are the boulevards. Every door is made out of a solitary pearl. Some of these hues said have changed in significance throughout the years so we can't be sure about all the real hues.

22 And I saw no sanctuary in that: for the Lord God Almighty and the Lamb are the sanctuary of it.

There will be no spot of love in the Holy City since God and the Lamb are noticeable to all and worshiped by all. The Spirit of God will indwell all who live there. All in the city will have direct access to the Holy of Holies. God will be worshiped there in soul and in truth (Joh 4: 23, 24).

Notice, the Lamb in this city is equivalent in status to the Lord God Almighty yet they are particularly distinctive persons.

23 And the city had no need of the sun, neither of the moon, to sparkle in it: for the magnificence of God did help it, and the Lamb is the light thereof.

The city itself is not the new earth. Sacred writing demonstrates that there will be daylight, moonshine, and seasons on the earth perpetually (Psa 72:5). The Holy City won't require the light of the sun or moon since it will be lit by the heavenliness of God.

24 And the countries of them which are spared should stroll in the light of it: and the rulers of the earth do bring their greatness and honor into it.

The countries truly mean the distinctive tribes of gentiles. All the spared will stroll in the light of the Holy City. Notice that it says the rulers of the earth will keep on bringing their wonderfulness and honor into the Holy City so the city is not every one of that exists. They in all likelihood will bring endowments into the city on uncommon dining experience days. These sections appear to demonstrate that there is a qualification between the individuals who live in the Holy City and the spared that harp on the new earth.

25 And the doors of it should not be closed at all by day: for there might be no night there.

26 And they should bring the wonderfulness and honor of the countries into it.

The entryways would not by any means exist if all spared make up the Holy City and the spouse as a few scholars educate. Somebody other than simply the Lamb's wife is going all through the doors.

27 And there might in no insightful go into it anything that defileth, neither at all worketh plague, or maketh an untruth: however they which are composed in the Lamb's book of life.

Just those written in the Lamb's book of life will be permitted to enter the doors to the Holy City. Those in the Lake of Fire will never have admittance to the Holy City. In the event that those in the Lamb's book of life enter the Holy City, it infers that some likewise go out the doors and leave, so not all in the new creation abide in the Holy City. In the event that all that have endless life abided in the Holy City there would be no requirement for these entries about doors to be composed by any means. I can't help thinking that most in the Lamb's book of life are living on the earth (or conceivably somewhere else in the universe see section 22). Be that as it may, they will be permitted to enter the Holy City. Why even have another earth if nobody spared is living on it? The thought most Christians hold that all individuals will be living in either paradise or damnation in forever bodes well from the sacred texts.

CHAPTER 22

Water Giving Power

22:1 And he shewed me an unadulterated waterway of water of life, quite obvious, continuing out of the throne of God and of the Lamb.

"Unadulterated River of Water of life." Water of Life In one last look into the future, John sees this waterway spilling out of the throne of God. It is the wellspring of endless life that radiates from God. Indeed, even in paradise, we will drink water and eat sustenance, most likely not out of need for our wellbeing, but rather in view of the delight and association it will give us. This is typical of unceasing life.

Jesus told the lady at the well in the event that she drank of the water He gave her, she would never thirst again, John 4:14. This is the "water" He was discussing here. This "water" had nurturing powers. The Source is the Father and the Lamb. This "water" springs up into continually enduring life. In our day of contaminations, it is difficult to imagine water this unmistakable. At the point when the officer penetrated Jesus' side, water and blood spouted forward, John 19:34. This is the water of life.

Much the same as everything else in the New Jerusalem, the stream was totally obvious so it could mirror the brilliance of God as it falls down from the throne of God and of the Lamb in a stunning, shining endless stream of everlasting life from God's throne to His kin.

22:2 amidst the road of it, and on either side of the stream, [was there] the tree of life, which uncovered twelve [manner of] natural products, [and] yielded her organic product consistently: and the leaves of the tree [were] for the recuperating of the countries.

Here at the end of the Bible we are reintroduced to the tree of life, which has not been said in the Bible since Genesis 3, where Adam and Eve trespassed in the Garden of Eden. Heaven is restored in the everlasting state. Every one of that was lost in the fall is reclaimed by the sheep. The leaves of this tree will be utilized to mend the connections of the countries toward one another with the goal that we may live evenhandedly and reasonably in forever. Tree of Life

The tree bears twelve sorts of organic product that yields its natural product consistently recommending the boundless assortment that will fill paradise.

Month to month, since time exists no more, stresses the outflow of the happy procurement of forever utilizing well known terms of time.

Countries: which means the general population that are in paradise. Infection will never again be, so the mending doesn't suggest sickness. The leaves along these lines will be to advance general wellbeing or another method for expressing that would be: life in paradise will be completely empowered, rich and energizing ceaselessly.

The sacred text likewise doesn't let us know whether we will eat the leaves or the natural product. Blessed messengers ate sustenance on earth with Abraham and Sarah as did Jesus after the restoration with his supporters. Maybe the holy people in paradise will eat for happiness and not out of need.

22:3 And there should be no more revile: however the throne of God and of the Lamb might be in it; and his workers might serve him:

The impacts of the post-Edenic curse (Gen. 3:14-19) will be completely gone for eternity. There will be no more revile. No More Curse God's holy people will serve him (Rev. 7: v.15) and rule with Him forever (Dan 7: verses 18 and 27).

The photo of unceasing life in these verses demonstrates that we will be occupied with serving God for all forever. We will both serve Him (v. 3) and rule with Him (v.5). Since He is an unbounded God, we can make certain He will have limitless things for us to do as we rule there for eternity. The expression, "they might see his face," implies that, as devotees, we will be conceded a crowd of people with the King all the time.

Here we see "throne of God" and on his right hand is "the Lamb" These "hirelings" that should serve him are us. We Christians have been purchased and paid for with the blood of the Lamb. We will be with the Lamb and the Father, however we won't be their equivalent. We will be their workers.

22:4 And they might see his face; and his name [shall be] in their brows.

The best gift of endlessness is that they should see his face (Matt. 5: v.8; Heb. 12: v.14). In spite of the fact that this is currently outlandish for an unknown individual (Exodus 33: v.20), it will happen in the interminable state. The name of God in their temples demonstrates possession and sanctification (Rev. 3: v.12; 13: v.16; Exodus 28: verses 36 to38).

All through the Bible, we have been taught that you couldn't look upon the substance of God and live. Indeed, even Moses, who was so near God, needed to see God, and God let him know no. He put His hand over Moses and went by him, and Moses saw his rear, Exodus 33:22. There we will be in his vicinity all the time and can look in his face at whatever time we need to. We are fixed with the Lamb's seal. They Shall See His Face

The holy people in New Jerusalem will see God's face. Being splendidly blessed and equitable, they'll have the capacity to persevere through the bursting, great light from God's vicinity without being expended. That was unimaginable for mortal men.

22:5 And there should be no night there; and they require no flame, neither light of the sun; for the Lord God giveth them light: and they might rule for ever and ever.

Subsequent to in the New Jerusalem God is constantly present, His eminence makes every single other wellspring of light superfluous (Rev. 21:23; Isaiah 60:19, 20; Zech. 14:7). There Shall Be No Night

We have spoken such a great amount about our Lord Jesus being the Light. He is the wellspring of all Light. At the point when the Light is on full power, you absolutely needn't bother with a flame. The sun has no more reason any all the more either. This vicinity of this Light is everything they need. This Kingdom has no end. It is for all of time everlasting.

As a last word depicting the holy person's brilliant experience, they are let it know by and by that it will never end. They might rule always and until the end of time.

22:6 And he said unto me, These idioms [are] dependable and genuine: and the Lord God of the sacred prophets sent his holy messenger to shew unto his hirelings the things which should in no time be finished.

Verses 6-21 shape a conclusion or synopsis to the book. They underline two topics: (1) the realness of the book as a divine revelation; and

(2) the approach of the arrival of Christ.

These adages allude to the whole Book of Revelation. They are confirmed as certified by the heavenly attendant whom God sent to give them through John to His workers, that is, the individuals from the houses of worship (Rev. 1: verses 3 and 11).

Here is only a consolation that the greater part of this is not to be taken softly. This is the outright truth. The prophets, for example, Daniel, Ezekiel, and Isaiah (to give some examples), have all talked about this unique time ever. We even read this in the 24th part of Matthew and in the 21st and 22nd section of Luke. It is the same data, paying little heed to who pens it, in light of the fact that the creator is God.

The blessed messenger's words fortify a vital truth: Everything John found in Revelation will happen. John's words are not enchanted and the Apocalypse is not a record of his strange dreams or the aftereffect of an over dynamic creative ability. Further it is not a purposeful anecdote (a type of interpretation) from which perusers can discover shrouded implications of their own creation. It is a precise portrayal of occasions and persons that are yet to come.

Verses 6 to 9 takes us back to the early part of this book, when the dedicated and genuine witness let us know that He would send His heavenly attendant to pass on His message concerning the things that should happen.

22:7Behold, I come immediately: honored [is] he that keepeth the expressions of the prediction of this book.

This is Jesus talking when He says, "View, I am coming soon".

Three times we discover this expression in the last verses of this book. Some have been confounded about the exacting significance of the expression since it was articulated right around 2000 years prior. It is all the more precisely deciphered, "View, I come all of a sudden." This platitude does not allude to a named time soon to come however implies that His coming will occur all of a sudden and abruptly. Huge points of interest are given in relationship with each of these three guarantees of our Lord.

1. Verse 7 contains the guarantee, "Favored is he who keeps the expressions of the prediction in this book." This might be a reference to the Rapture of the Church. "Upbeat are those" who are adequately mindful of the prescience of this book to be prepared when that Day arrives.

2. "Observe, I am coming soon! My prize is with me, and I will provide for everybody as indicated by what he has done". (Rev. 22 v.12) Added to Christ's guarantee of his second coming, this verse declares a prize by method for judgment, a standard part of the condition of adherents after the Resurrection.

3. On the premise of this prize we will rule with Christ for eternity.

There is a sacred writing that talks about feeling worn out on holding up and backtracking in sin, Hebrews 12: verses 3 and 4. We should not do this. We should watch and sit tight for we know not at what hour He cometh. Matt. 24:

v.36. "Favored is he that keepeth the adage of the prescience of this book". Rev. 1 v.3: This is alluding to the Book of Revelation.

Be that as it may, how on the planet would you be able to keep the idioms, in the event that you don't know what these expressions are? A great many people keep away from Revelation at all costs, however in the event that we should keep the idioms, then we should read and comprehend what they are.

Adherents are called to monitor or secure the book of Revelation. To shield against spoilers who deny its significance, against those commentators who deny its veracity and power and in addition against befuddled translators who darken its importance. They are called to watch Scripture, as well as to obey it.

You may ask, what does it intend to comply with the book of Revelation? Consider it a general order to ache for Christ's arrival and our unceasing partnership with Him. It calls adherents to craving paradise, to longing blessedness, to yearning to see Christ vindicated and for Him to triumph over His adversaries, to want the end of the condemnation and to fancy the glories of Christ's natural kingdom and the new paradise and the new earth.

To see God's face, to see an end of the Babylonian Harlot and the degenerate business and political framework, to anticipate an existence of peace and satisfaction.

Therefore the motivation behind Revelation is not to give diversion and to just fulfill the interest of adherents about the future however to uncover the wonderfulness of God's Son and call devotees to live genuine, dutiful lives in light of His soon return.

22:8 And I John saw these things, and heard [them]. Furthermore, when I had heard and seen, I tumbled down to revere before the feet of the heavenly attendant which shewed me these things.

A few times in Revelation, we see John overpowered by the vicinity and the force this heavenly attendant demonstrates to him. He, being overcome by the size of everything, begins to love this blessed messenger. A few individuals have false regulation fixated on holy messenger love. We should not adore holy messengers. They are made creatures. We should love the Creator. We are cautioned again and again not to love blessed messengers. John is told a few times here in Revelation not to love this blessed messenger.

22:9 Then saith he unto me, See [thou do it] not: for I am thy fellow servant, and of thy brethren the prophets, and of them which keep the expressions of this book: adore God.

The heavenly attendant rapidly reminds the messenger that he as well, was a made being by his affirmation. His as well as of John's brethren the prophets, and of all adherents that are characterized here as "Them which keep the truisms of this book."

At that point the blessed messenger summons John to love God as God alone is the main adequate Person to revere. The book of scriptures disallows the love of any other individual including heavenly attendants, holy people, the Virgin Mary or some other made being.

22:10 And he saith unto me, Seal not the adages of the prescience of this book: for the time is close by.

The summon not to seal this prophetic message is entirely not quite the same as what the Lord told Daniel, "Yet thou, O Daniel, quiets down the words, and seal the book, even to the season of the end" (Dan 12:4). The explanation behind the distinction in the guidelines is essentially expressed, "the time is within reach." Until the demise and restoration of Christ, the ideal opportunity for this prescience had not come. Since Jesus officially opened the seven seals prophetically (Rev. 5 and 6) to uncover the future, it is just fitting that the whole book stay open for us to peruse too.

Interestingly with Daniel, why should told "seal" up his book of prediction (since the end was still in the far off future, however here John is advised to leave his book open (Seal not). The Messiah had come, His second coming is inescapable, and in this way now the time is close by.

The purpose behind the distinction in the guidelines is that one lived after the season of Christ's torturous killing, the other sometime recently. In John's Day it was conceivable to see the developing of the occasions forecasted; in Daniel's day they were far off.

22:11 He that is vile, given him a chance to be low still: and he which is foul, given him a chance to be smudged still: and he that is upright, given him a chance to be equitable still: and he that is sacred, given him a chance to be blessed still.

Verse 11 is not an order, but instead an announcement of truth and a notice. Character has a tendency to end up altered and unchangeable, dictated by a lifetime of continual activity. The landing of the end will keep any change of predetermination.

The individuals who hear reality yet keep on doing incorrectly will by that solidified reaction settle their interminable fate in damnation. Alternately, the individuals who keep on rehearsing exemplary nature and keep himself blessed give confirmation of honest to goodness sparing confidence.

At the point when Christ gives back, the planned decision of every individual will have settled his interminable destiny.

We can't conceal from God. God sees into the heart. On the off chance that you are a delinquent, He definitely knows it. You don't need to let him know. In the event that you fit in with Jesus, He realizes that, as well. Whatever you are down profound, Jesus definitely knows.

22:12 And, observe, I come rapidly; and my prize [is] with me, to give each man to the extent that his work might be.

Again Christ announces the approach of His arrival. This is in red in the Bible, so this is Jesus talking straightforwardly here. All Christians ought to be viewing the eastern sky for in a minute when you think not, the eastern sky will open, the trumpet will blow, and Jesus might yell. Around then, we will be called to paradise to be with Him until the end of time.

Our prizes will be for the things (treasures) we have put away in paradise. Rewards are constantly in view of works done by devotees in light of their unwaveringness in serving Christ in this life. Their works will be tried and just those with unceasing worth "will be uncovered by flame; and the fire should attempt each man's work of what sort it is." (1 Cor. 3 v.13)

The prizes devotees will appreciate in paradise will be limits for serving God. The more noteworthy their steadfastness is in this life, the more prominent will be their chance to serve in paradise, also the crowns adherents will get.

Having information that Jesus could return at any minute shouldn't lead Christians to an existence of unmoving sitting tight for His coming. Rather it ought to deliver industrious, submissive, reverential administration to God, and dire announcement of the gospel to unbelievers.

Have a go at taking a gander at it along these lines. By educating everybody you meet now regarding the uplifting news of Jesus yet they don't hear you out, then all of a sudden the Rapture happens, those individuals will then recall each word you said to them. That is the reason I for one trust that directly after the Rapture, more individuals will start instantly look for reality about Jesus and that will start the biggest soul reap the world has each known.

22:13 I am Alpha and Omega, the starting and the end, the first and the last.

The three assignments of verse 13 are basically equal in importance.

1. Alpha and Omega

2. The starting and the end

3. The first and the last

By applying them to Himself, Christ claims boundless, endless fairness with God (Rev. 1: v.8 and 17; 2: v.8; 21: v.6).

These three assignments express Christ's unendingness, time everlasting and vast life rising above all confinement. These depictions portray the culmination, immortality and sovereign power of the Lord Jesus Christ.

22:14 Blessed [are] they that do his edicts, that they might have right to the tree of life, and might enter in through the entryways into the city.

These end verses of the Bible make it consummately clear that salvation is a matter of the will - whoever wishes might come. This obviously infers whoever wills not to come is lost. This educating flourishes all through the Scriptures.

As opposed to the individuals who reject Christ, we experience the condition of the favored portrayed here in verse 14. The individuals who have washed their robes in the honorability of Christ have a privilege to the Tree of Life and in this manner are qualified for live until the end of time. Tree of Life He portrays their state as "favored," signifying "cheerful". Each individual needs bliss. The best approach to everlasting satisfaction is to get Christ as Lord and Savior, which qualifies you for passage into the Holy City, access to the Tree of Life furthermore, the glorious gifts of a cherishing God. On the off chance that there is any inquiry in your brain regarding regardless of whether you have gotten the living Christ, I ask you, on the premise of His test, to change your will and get Him as your Lord and Savior today.

They that do his precepts are adherents John 14:15: If ye adore me, keep my edicts. See (Rev. 12: v.17; Rev. 14: v.12; Matthew 7: verses 13 to 21; 1 John 3: verses 6 to10).

The tree of life demonstrates everlasting life and awesome gift (Rev. 2: v.7 and 22: v.2). To have the capacity to enter in through the doors into the city is to have glorious citizenship in the unceasing abode of God and reclaimed humanity.

All unbelievers are without (outside) the city, i.e., in the pool of flame. See Rev. 21: v.8 for a rundown of the sort of sins that bar individuals from paradise that was given to John. Additionally read Rev. 21 verse 27.

In James 1:22 we read, "However be ye practitioners of the Word, and not listeners just, beguiling your own particular selves."

We are to be about the Father's business. On the off chance that we really are sold out to God and have made Jesus the Lord of our lives, the longing of our souls will be to do His Commandments. The Jews were the characteristic branches of the tree. We Christians (when we are conceived once more), are joined into the Tree of Life, who is Jesus Christ our Lord.

22:15For without [are] mutts, and alchemists, and whoremongers, and killers, and misguided worshipers, and whosoever loveth and maketh an untruth.

The mutts are debased and noxious individuals or somebody with a low character. The first run through obtrusively sullied miscreants were called puppies is in Deut. 23: verse 18. This is the place male gay person whores were in perspective.

Alchemists are the individuals who hone mysterious or witchcraft. Greek Pharmakos is the foundation of the English word drug store which frequently goes with those practices.

Whoremongers are the individuals who hone a wide range of sexual perversion. Greek pornos is the base of the English word explicit entertainment.

Killers: implies pre-reflected homicide. This has nothing to do with incidental executing or murdering in war. They are incorporated into the rundown given in Rev. 21 v.8: "However the dreadful, and unbelieving, and the odious, and killers, and whoremongers, and magicians, and barbarians, and all liars, might have their part in the lake which burneth with flame and brimstone: which is the second demise."

Misguided worshipers are only the individuals who put anything in front of God which incorporates mammon (cash) or the adoration for everything which takes one's consideration off serving God. Somebody once said: Show me somebody's datebook and checkbook and I'll let you know where their heart lies. Consider that. Barbarians are additionally the individuals who venerate false divine beings or love the genuine God in an unsatisfactory matter.

Maketh at Lie: Everyone in some cases amid their life has lied as It's human instinct. Some tell harmless untruths, even some Christians. However, all untruths are demonstrations of deluding and can be exceptionally hurtful to others. Just withholding a percentage of reality when posed a question is in itself lying.

Consider painstakingly how you answer and rather than a white lie or withholding a part of reality, find another way. I would rather be come clean no way how awful it is as opposed to discover later I had been beguiled. The individuals who "loveth and maketh an untruth" needs to do with harming another person. At whatever time we hurt another person, it is sin.

It is not all who have ever dedicated any of these wrongdoings recorded over that will be prohibited from paradise. However, it is the individuals who love and periodically hone these transgressions and unyieldingly stick to them and decline Christ's welcome to salvation who will be the ones cast into the pool of flame.

22:16 I Jesus have sent mine holy messenger to affirm unto you these things in the places of worship. I am the root and the posterity of David, [and] the splendid and morning star.

"I Jesus have sent mine holy messenger to affirm." This is the first occasion when that the words "I Jesus" show up in the book of scriptures. It sets up that this last welcome in Scripture is not a human welcome, but rather a heavenly call issued by and by to delinquents by the Lord Jesus Christ Himself.

This verse is Jesus' seal of endorsement overall book of Revelation. It denote the principal utilization of "chapel" since section three. Why would that be no reference of the Church amid the season of tribulation on earth depicted in sections 6 through 18? Since the congregation, having been raptured to paradise, won't be on earth.

By what method can Jesus be "the root and the posterity of David" both? In the Flesh this is unimaginable. David, in the tissue, was the predecessor of Jesus. In the Spirit, Jesus was David's predecessor. Jesus was David's God.

We read in II Peter 1:19 "We have additionally an all the more beyond any doubt expression of prescience; whereunto ye do well that ye take regard, as unto a light that shineth in a dim spot, until the daybreak, and the day star emerge in your souls:"

It is not uncommon symbolically to talk about Jesus as a star. Here is our Bright Star. Until we get this Star into our life, we are brimming with murkiness.

22:17 And the Spirit and the lady say, Come. What's more, let him that heareth say, Come.

Furthermore, let him that is athirst come. What's more, whosoever will, let him take the water of life unreservedly.

The Lord's Last Invitation to Humankind - The Lord Jesus Christ, ever worried for the souls of the lost, shuts His extraordinary disclosure with a test for distinct individuals to approach His name. He shows that there are two who welcome us to come to Him: the "Soul" and the "lady". What's more, He will even utilize "him who listens."

God the Holy Spirit will utilize the printed page and also the individuals who are simply rehashing what they have heard yet may not accept what they are stating. He additionally utilizes the "spouse", which demonstrated that the essential service of the Church of Christ amid the whole Church Age is to educate others concerning the Savior. All Christians all over the place ought to be occupied with saying to their kindred people: "Whoever is parched, let him come; and whoever wishes, let him take the free endowment of the water of life." Jesus Christ, obviously, is the water of life. How Do I Become a Christian

The Holy Spirit, subsequent to the starting, has been stating "Come". Unless the Holy Spirit of God charms you, you can overlook being spared. It is God's wish that all ought to be spared. I truly accept what this is stating, in this specific example, is that the Spirit and the devotees are stating, "Come rapidly Lord Jesus". Salvation is interested in whosoever will.

Everybody has a craving and yearning for God. Some don't comprehend what they are yearning for. It is so basic just to give in and let Jesus bring you salvation, peace, satisfaction, and life that keeps going forever. When we take of this Water of Jesus, it brings Eternal Life. The water, Spirit, and blood affirm for us and guarantee us of a grand home, John 5:8.

22:18-19 "For I affirm unto each man that heareth the expressions of the prediction of this book, If any man should include unto these things, God might include unto him the infections that are composed in this book:" "And if any man should detract from the expressions of the book of this prescience, God should take away his part out of the book of life, and out of the sacred city, and [from] the things which are composed in this book."

The speaker who vouches for the power and certainty of the expressions of the prediction of this book is the Lord Jesus Christ.

A Severe Warning to the Detractors From This Prophecy - I (Jesus) cautions everybody who hears the expressions of the prescience of this book: If anybody adds anything to them, God will add to him the infections portrayed in this book. What's more, in the event that anybody removes words from this book of prediction, God will detract from him his offer in the tree of life and in the blessed city, which are depicted in this book.

This is a standout amongst the most great difficulties in the Word of God against messing with Holy Writ. Unreasonably numerous today loquaciously criticize, diminish, and cast vilifying comments on Holy Scripture. This is their day of chance, however their judgment will happen upon them quickly.

God's great time. It is a frightful thing to question God, and it is unbelief that makes somebody take away from His Holy Word.

In spite of the fact that this is not a reference to Bible trusting pundits of the Word who erroneously interpret some entry and coincidentally minimize it. The Lord's notice here is tended to the individuals who participate in conscious adulteration or confusion of Scripture, the individuals who Paul decries as merchants of the Word of God, (2 Cor. 2 v.17.

Still it serves as a spirit blending test to the individuals who have taken close by to compose and lecture on this brilliant book.

22:20 He which testifieth these things saith, Surely I come rapidly. So be it. Indeed, even thus, come, Lord Jesus.

As already expressed, the interpretation is "clearly I come all of a sudden", when slightest anticipated. The cry of each Christian ought to be "come rapidly Lord Jesus", as I said some time recently. My cry, as I experience the area telling individuals of my Savior and Lord, is "JESUS IS COMING".

John represents every genuine devotee when he composes, "Come Lord Jesus", since Christians are those "who have cherished His showing up" (2 Tim. 4 verse 8). Scoffers might mockingly solicit, "Where is the guarantee from His coming?

For following the time when the fathers nodded off, all proceeds pretty much as it was from the earliest starting point of creation" (2 Peter 3 verse 4).

Be that as it may, things won't proceed everlastingly as they seem to be. Jesus will return, generally as Revelation predicts. In the event that the assurance of Christ's arrival to judge heathens does not inspire individuals to apologize, then nothing will.

"So be it" implies so be it.

22:21 The finesse of our Lord Jesus Christ [be] with all of you. So be it.

This sacred writing is a declaration of God's elegance toward fallen humankind. The Lord of grandness, as He guaranteed in Scripture, offers paradise only to the individuals who acknowledge His benevolent welcome. Without the "beauty of our Lord Jesus" none of us would be spared.

BIBLIOGRAPHY

Henry, M, (date unk.) Matthew Henry's Commentary On The Whole Bible, Vol. 6: Acts-Revelation, Old Tappan, New Jersey: Fleming H. Revell Company

Koerig, D. (2016) The Grapes Of Wrath Are Crushed. Revelation Chapter 14, retrieved January 11, 2016 from **www. thepropheticyears.com**

Miller, J.L. & Miller, M.S. (1961) Harper's Bible Dictionary. New York, New York: Harper Row Publishers

Revelation Chapter 1 retrieved January 10, 2016 from **www. discoverrevelation.com**

Stewart, T. (2016) A Commentary On The Book of Revelation: The Antichrist and False Prophet- retrieved January 10, 2016 from **www.whatsaiththescriptures.com**

The Holy Bible (1965) Authorized King James Version and Scriptural Directory. Chicago, Illinois: J.G. Ferguson Publishing Company

The Wycliff Bible Commentary (1962). Chicago, Illinois: The Moody Bible Institute

ABOUT THE AUTHOR

The Reverend Dr. John Thomas Wylie is one who has dedicated his life to the work of God's service. Shortly after his calling in 1979 into the Gospel ministry he entered the American Baptist College, Nashville, Tennessee. As a young Seminarian, he read every religious book available to him that would help him better understand his calling and purpose into the ministry.

Dr. Wylie possessed a fascination with the book of Revelation apart from his other religious studies. He was preparing a research paper on Revelation. It is then that it occurred to him to make his findings available to others in the world in the hopes they have a better understanding of this often-misunderstood book. Dr. Wylie carried out his commitment to God and for years developed a concise, easy to read commentary on the Book of Revelation. Dr. Wylie states that he is led by the Holy Spirit to undertake such a project to encourage the reading and studying of the Book of Revelation in easy-to-understand terms.

It is a book which deals with the disclosures of the end times in which we live from a spiritual perspective.

Dr. Wylie has also completed two master's degrees from Emmanuel Bible College, Nashville, Tennessee, Rossville, Georgia. Still further to be the best he pursued his studies in Theology and earned his Ph.d and Th.d as an educational specialist and Doctor of Theology from Jones International University, Centennial, Colorado and Holy Trinity College, Saint Petersburg, Florida. Dr. Wylie was nominated by *Who's Who* in January 2022.